100 MARKETING SECRETS

The Very Best Methods You Can Use to Get More People to Give You More of Their Money... More Often... for More Profit!

By T.J. Rohleder

America's "Blue Jeans Millionaire"

TABLE OF CONTENTS

INTRODUCTION

Hello, and thanks for purchasing this book! If you haven't purchased it yet—if you're standing there skimming through it in a bookstore or library—then I recommend that you do, as soon as possible. I'll admit I'm a tad biased, but I believe that you're holding in your hands a true ticket to riches. I've collected between these covers the 100 Greatest Marketing Secrets I know, secrets that could potentially make you a millionaire.

Who am I to make such wild claims? I'm T.J. Rohleder—and I'm a millionaire more than a hundred times over, so I might just know what I'm talking about. I started my company, M.O.R.E. Inc., with a budget of $300 in 1988—and now, just 25 years later, I've earned well over $120 million. I'm not telling you this to brag (though I do have to admit that I'm very proud of the fact), but to point out that if I can do it, anyone can. I'm just an average joe from the Great Plains, maybe a little more stubborn than most.

I know these methods work, because I use them every day.

Business success is mostly a matter of tenacity, inventiveness, hard work, and the continuous application of common sense to the day-to-day challenges you face as an entrepreneur. Yet oddly enough, what most of us see as common sense from a big-picture perspective often doesn't come through that way when you're right up against it. Sometimes you need someone to remind you. There's a saying you've probably heard, attributed to both Mark Twain and Will Rogers, that common sense ain't so common—and nowhere is that truer than in the

5

business of serving other people.

When you start any business, that's exactly what you're doing: serving others. Of course, you want to make a fortune while you're at it; and when you first jump into the fray, that may be your primary intention. But if you can't attract and retain customers, you'll fail miserably. As the late Zig Ziglar pointed out, the best way to get people to give you what you want is to give what they want. So if you want to make big money, you have to serve your customers and clients in the highest possible sense.

I've discovered all this the hard way—by spending more than 25 years in the trenches, learning by trial and error how to build M.O.R.E. Inc. from almost nothing to a business opportunity powerhouse. Our company has become the most successful my hometown has ever seen. Sure, along the way I've made a lot of mistakes, and I've taken some chances that caused me to fall flat on my face. But I've also succeeded a decent percentage of the time, and batted in a few grand-slam home runs that earned me millions of dollars on the basis of a single, well-executed idea. Sometimes that's all it takes to become wealthy.

I've learned some strategies that build the groundwork for success, and some that will almost inevitably earn you money if you just keep your eyes open and play your cards right. And you know something? There's nothing wrong with learning these secrets without having to go through all the wear and tear of trial and error. The learning curve can be steep, but there are simple ways, simple shortcuts, that can help you level it out.

That's the entire purpose of this book: to put you on the path of success ahead of where you'd normally start, without that whole huge hill to climb, so you can begin banking profits and reinvesting them into your business a lot faster than your competition. Some people jealously guard their success secrets. Not me. I've always believed in sharing with other entrepreneurs, because competition helps me maintain my edge—and there's plenty of room at the top. Plus, I can profit even more by sharing! Furthermore, I'm well aware of the fact that no matter how many times I repeat these strategies, no matter how many people pick up this book and start reading with the very best of intentions, only a small percentage will actually put these secrets into play in their own businesses. I'm not trying to insult anyone with that statement; it's just how it is. My hope is that I can reach a few of you and change your lives for the better.

In this book, I'll reveal 100 great but little-known methods that you can use to tempt more people to give you more of their money, more often, for more profit per transaction. That's the ultimate secret of succeeding in business: finding those rare and unusual leverage strategies that bring in more money from the same people. Keep them happy in doing that, and they'll become your best advertisements, telling all their friends, family, and others about you, attracting more people just like them. Nearly all businesses require repeat business to stay afloat and build profits. This, in turn, requires aggressive marketers determined to dominate their marketplaces.

I started my first business, a small carpet cleaning company, in December 1985 with my good friend Gary. It was a tough life, and we proceeded to make every mistake in the book. Within nine months, he and I were no longer friends and had gone our separate ways; it really is true that pre-existing friendships and business don't mix, not with all the pressures any business has to face. I kept the company name and kept moving forward; I'd been a salesman for a couple of years before I started my business, so I knew how to pick up the telephone and smile and dial. I knew had to beat on doors and talk to people all day long, and that's exactly what I did. I was out there hustling, talking to hundreds of people every month to grab a few dozen small cleaning jobs.

The only real advertising I could afford at the time was little flyers that we printed up for next to nothing and put on thousands of parked cars. That was it—it was a never-ending hustle, hustle, hustle, And then I stumbled upon an advanced marketing technique by accident—something I'd never heard about in any of the many marketing schemes and opportunities I'd subscribed to for years.

I'll tell you the whole story about this technique in a later chapter. The point is that with that simple method, I gained a huge amount of leverage just by pre-qualifying my prospects. In other words, I could work less and make more money. Instead of talking to hundreds of people every month, and wasting my time on most of them, I talked to dozens instead—and because they were precisely the kind of prospects I was looking for, I skyrocketed my closing rate. Suddenly, I was booked solid for weeks at a time.

That was the very first marketing secret I ever used, and I've tried hundreds since. I'm going to share that secret in this book, along with many more. The title's a bit misleading, actually; by the time I'm done, I'll cover well over 100 effective marketing secrets and their variations.

I've already told you that I started my first profitable business for $300, this time with my wife Eileen. We really clicked, both with each other and the marketplace: within five years, we earned over $10 million in total revenue. I'd always dreamed of being a millionaire, but that exceeded my wildest expectations. We've never looked back since, only forward, and I've been obsessed with discovering and developing the greatest marketing strategies possible. I've had a lot of help along the way from a lot of people. I've been a good student, and now I'm proud to teach you some of these things.

Becoming a great marketer gives you an almost unfair advantage over your competitors. As long as you keep offering new products and services that appeal to your prospects and customers, you'll continue to attract and re-attract the very best buyers in your marketplace, taking market share away from your competitors. This offers you a tremendous edge, and these are the secrets that can do it for you.

During the development of this book, especially the audio product it's based on, I enjoyed the assistance and input of two of my favorite co-conspirators. The first gentleman helped Eileen and I become millionaires in just a few short years. We'd been operating our direct-response marketing business for about six months when we met Russ von Hoelscher, generating about $16,000 a month in total revenue at the time. We thought that was pretty good; but within nine months of meeting Russ, we were making almost $100,000 a week. He helped us generate that first $10 million, and millions more since then. He's a true marketing genius, with 35 years of experience in the business. Russ started out as a writer; by the time he was 10 he was writing little mystery stories on the butcher paper that his father, who was a butcher, would bring home for him. Eventually he branched out into science fiction, and was even published in professional science fiction and mystery magazines. But they don't pay very well, so Russ decided to become an information marketer, writer, and publisher instead.

Since then he's written over 50 books and manuals, including Stay Home and Make Money, How to Make a Fortune Selling Information, How to Achieve Total Success, Real Estate Wealth Building, and more. He's also served as a direct marketing coach for me and plenty of others. First and foremost, he considers himself a direct-response marketer. Why? Because there's no better way to make money quickly, with the right product or service, than with direct response marketing, or DRM.

I think this book will be a real revelation for many people already in business, especially those who have no foundation in DRM. They're used to people offering traditional marketing services, which are based mostly on image advertising. That's all well and good, but the real money is in direct marketing strategies. Whether you only want to influence people who live in your city or want to expand to the state or nation, these techniques work wonders for small businesses.

Although Russ has worked with many direct response and mail-order marketers, he's also worked with many local business people over the years: jewelers, chiropractors, dentists, alternative health providers, precious metal dealers, etc. It doesn't matter what kind of business you're in, you can use these techniques. If you have a candy store on Main Street, you might say to yourself, "For God's sake, how am I going to use DRM?" Actually it would be pretty easy, given all of the holidays and special occasions when people gift each other with chocolate. You'd just have to learn a few DRM techniques to turn that little candy store into a tremendous money-maker.

This is just one example. No matter what you're doing, no

matter what service you're offering, no matter what type of store you have, you can use these techniques.

The methods I offer in this book will yield tremendous positive results if you'll just put them into play. The most exciting thing about doing so is that you won't have much competition, because few local businesses do DRM. Most do very little marketing at all, other than putting an ad in the PennySaver, newspaper, or Yellow Pages. There's a great deal of money to be made, well beyond those few places to advertise. I think this book will be a blessing to you, if you pay attention and learn what I'm about to teach you.

Aside from Russ, I've also received a great deal of help from Chris Lakey, my company's Marketing Director. He's been working in our business in one capacity or another for half his life, and brings a wide range of direct marketing experience to the table. With his help and Russ's, I've put together a book of marketing strategies that give you a leg up on starting a new business, revitalizing an existing business, or taking a thriving business to the next level of profitability.

I promise you that this book will change the way you think about marketing your business, especially in terms of attracting new customers and doing more business with those you have. I have no doubt that you'll walk away with at least several key strategies you can implement immediately, and remember: while I'll be directly discussing 100 specific actions you can take to transform your business, there are probably thousands of sub-strategies within those core principles that you can also take advantage of.

Hopefully, by the time you finish reading, you'll think a

little bit differently about your business. This may even renew your passion for your business, getting you excited all over again about the reasons you went into business in the first place. No matter what your business is, no matter who you sell to, this will give you a fresh perspective on things, including some that you may not have thought about before. Some of the things I'll discuss will be specific strategies, some more general. Many are simple actions, a few more cerebral in nature. Either way, they can help you reconsider your position on your business, customers, and marketplace, fostering the proper mindset as you go about reoffering to existing customers and attracting new ones.

I'll run the gamut here, covering a lot of ground. It'll take a while to unpack them all. But I think you'll enjoy it, and learn a lot in the process—as long as you keep your eyes open. Grab a highlighter. Underline important passages. Write in the margins. Use sticky notes. One of the great things about having this information in book form is that you can revisit it again and again as you explore these.

The first step is to be where you are today: you found this book. Whether you purchased it, received it as a gift, or borrowed it from a friend, here you are. Step two is just to get started. Read it straight through once, let the ideas start to take hold, then go back and start finding the strategies you can begin using now. Go back to your bookmarks and margin notes. Think about ways to incorporate these specific strategies into what you're doing.

I love to teach small business owners how to make more money, and I think you'll find that this isn't going to be classroom boring, one of those things you just dread reading. I'll strive to keep it fun, to keep it real, and to keep it exciting, so you're more likely to absorb strategies that will transform your business.

Remember: it all comes back to getting the most people to consistently give you more of their money, more often, for more profit per transaction. These tips, tricks, and strategies will help you attract customers, build quality relationships that allow you to retain those customers in the long-term, and extract from them the maximum amount of discretionary income along the way. Just by reading this book, you'll significantly increase your likelihood of success.

Does that sound cocky? I sure hope so. Because I do know what I'm talking about, and I know these secrets can work for you—because they worked for me, and like I mentioned earlier, I'm Joe Average in every way.

So, again: once you have your copy, don't just read it once, say "Hmmmm," and then put it away and forget it like most of your peers will. Read and reread it. Study it like a student studies a textbook—because that's exactly what this book is, and a businessperson must be a student for life if he or she expects to remain consistently successful. Make this book your marketing bible, and the 100 Secrets your scripture. These don't have to be secrets to you anymore. The more often you consult this book and put these secrets into play, the more you'll earn.

I wish you the very best of luck. See you at the top!

T.J. Rohleder, President and Co-Founder
M.O.R.E. Incorporated • Goessel, Kansas

CHAPTER ONE

SECRETS 1-10

This first chapter establishes the pattern I'll use for the structure of this book. In each, I'll introduce you to 5-6 important strategies that I and my close colleagues in the business have used to build our fortunes. The irony here is that while these strategies are hardly secrets to us, and most just seem to represent common sense, they appear to be secrets to *most* business people. Certainly, few are using them to their full potential, if they're using them at all.

Maybe it's because they don't like taking chances; maybe they're too lazy to make the changes; maybe they don't understand these secrets; maybe they've heard about these secrets and have rejected them; or (and this seems more likely) maybe they really are just secrets to most people. I'm sure the reasons for their rare use vary from person to person depending on the secret.

In any case, in each chapter I'm not going to waste any time: I'm going to dive right in, and cover each secret in detail with a minimum of fuss. So with that in mind, here we go!

Marketing Secret #1: Start Thinking

It's important to begin with this secret, because it offers an intensely powerful way for developing the most effective marketing possible. It's simply stated, too, and not at all hard to implement—but you're never going to benefit from it if you don't start doing it. You've got to get damned serious about thinking about your business, asking yourself certain questions repeatedly and then going all out to provide better and better answers. That'll put you ahead of most of the competition right there.

The fact is, most business owners are reactive rather than reflective. They scramble to respond to change as it occurs, rather than proactively planning for change in advance, by setting up systems and processes that can handle anything the world can throw at them. Businesses that do that are agile and resilient, able to get up and keep going when life knocks them flat. They're the ones that survive the unexpected, and expand to fill the vacuum left by the guys who go bust.

Thinking is a critical business process. Never forget that. Don't be afraid to engage in it on a regular basis. Sure, it may look like you're goofing off to people on the outside looking in, but you'll have the last laugh. You're asking yourself the questions that will keep your business forging ahead when others are wondering what to do next... because, ironically, you're *always* wondering what to do next. The difference is that your "next" is further ahead than theirs, so you've already got something running while they're shrugging their shoulders in confusion.

I treasure my thinking time, because it enriches me in so many ways—not least financially. I get up every morning at 5 AM so I can have some alone time while I drink my coffee. Without the sound of the phone ringing or people bustling around, I can get myself into a good meditative state and start thinking about the big questions, the vital ones at the core of any business: "Where do we go from here? What can we do for our customers next? How can we serve them better? What can give them that they can't get anywhere else? How can I beat the competition? What else can I do to make my business bigger, better, and more profitable?"

Ultimately, all these questions are interrelated, and when properly handled, result in A.) making you more profits while B.) serving your customers better. There's no point in aiming at just one or the other; that's a recipe for eventual failure. You've got to go for broke on both.

You can't allow yourself be overwhelmed by the competition—and especially not by your fear of them. Don't let emotions rule you here! I've seen small business owners just give up and close their stores when Wal-Mart came to town. Well, think of that as self-chlorination of the business gene pool. They've put themselves out of business without even trying to compete—and it's competition that makes you stronger and more fit and, ultimately, more profitable.

You can't give a damn how big they are, how powerful they are. You have to study what your competition is doing to learn from their good ideas and their errors alike. That's the only way to find the place where you can drive in the thin edge of the wedge and leverage enough space for you to succeed—and, in the long run, to try to put them out of business. It takes ruthlessness against the competition, combined with service to the customer, to maximize your profit.

You're not in business to help the competition succeed. Keep reminding yourself of that. Do all the things they're not doing for your shared marketplace, along with things that are just the opposite of what they're doing wrong. That gives you one edge.

Also: think deeply about your customers. Never forget

that they're emotional beings. They're not just looking for facts and figures to make them happy, and it's likewise a mistake to assume they're only after things they need. The things they *want* matter more often. As marketers, we have no choice but to appeal to the emotions of our customers, to provide for their wants. So you've got to think about their hopes and fears, their desires and fantasies. You have to consider what thrills them—and what chills them. When you understand your customers fully, then you'll know how to communicate the types of messages they'll respond to.

Also, ponder the question of how you can give your customers a high level of perceived value. People don't necessarily respond to the specific product or service you're trying to sell them; they just want the benefits you promise. Realize that they don't care much about who you are or what you've done in the past (at least at first), so it's foolish to spend a lot of time talking about the history of your company. Your customers are selfish, as we all are. Let's face it: you're more likely to care about the fact that you stubbed your toe this morning than about the possibility that a hurricane might hit Bangladesh, doing millions of dollars in damage and killing hundreds of people.

It might shock you to realize that, but it's just reality—and if you're wise, you'll take advantage of it in the marketplace. Mother Nature has shaped humans to be incredibly self-centered. Therefore, you have to use everything you can, every marketing tool in the arsenal, to create the best-perceived value and the best emotional messages for your customers. At the same time, of course, you must make those messages believable—while offering something your prospects really, truly want. They've got to think, "I've gotta have that, and I've gotta have it right now!"

Developing these strategies all boils down to spending a significant amount of time every day on good, quality thinking. If you're a morning person, get up early and think while you sip your coffee. If you're a night person, think things through in the evening. Whenever you're undisturbed and at a peak energy level, think how you can improve your business, get more customers, beat the crap out of the competition, offer greater value, and otherwise do everything you can to build your business. Think about what you can do to make it into something you're proud of, something that's profitable, long lasting, and inheritable. Just sitting and thinking is crucial, because it helps you establish the necessary insight on what you have to do to make your business better.

Most small business owners get so stuck in the rut of performing their business tasks that they don't spend much time thinking. But again, it's imperative to do so, whether you're an electrician, bookseller, plumber, or roofer. No matter what business you're in, you can't let yourself get so busy working *in* the business that you forget to work *on* it, thinking about your customers and the ways you can serve them best.

I suspect you're reading this book because you want more customers, and you want to make more profits with the customers you already have. This may be the edge you need, which is why it's the starting point of this book. If you're not actively thinking about all the ways you can serve your customers, and not thinking about what they want the most, then you're never going to be able to do the best possible job for them.

All this thinking sounds logical enough, right? But if you

weren't doing it before, do you think your competitors were? I suspect not; and unlike you, they're still asleep at the wheel. Pick a time when there are no distractions—no fax machines, no phones ringing, no one demanding your time—and think. That way, you'll be able to clearly focus on your customers, and how you can serve it up better than all your competitors. Just a handful of well-thought-out ideas could mean thousands of extra dollars every month, or even thousands extra every week. This really *must* be a secret (somehow!), because I guarantee you that most of your competitors aren't asking themselves these very simple questions.

Marketing Secret #2: Marketing Mistakes to Avoid

Next, let's take a quick look at nine interrelated marketing mistakes that many people make, and how you can avoid them.

The first mistake is not developing and maintaining a marketing focus. You need to home in on your best prospects: that core group most likely to become long-term customers. Sure, your market consists of a much larger group; but who do you really want to appeal to? What group do you focus your marketing efforts on? Clearly, you should focus on the people you're more likely to sell to. These are the people you asked yourself about in Marketing Secret #1.

Mistake #2 is the lack of a compelling offer. You need something that stimulates people to take action *now*. Most business owners have been misled by image-based marketing, which is designed only to keep your name out there. Brand awareness is too vague to work for small businesses. You need to be specific: "Here's my deal today and only today, and here's what you'll get if you order right now." One of the worst mistakes you can make is to *not* give people a specific call to action, something you want them to do immediately. Why should they respond without a compelling reason to do so?

Mistake #3 is not having deadlines. You have to include urgency in your offers. Do so and you'll increase your response rate, especially in direct mail based marketing, though this can be true of Internet and other types of marketing as well. As long as you sick to your fixed deadlines, you'll get higher response and conversion rates.

Mistake #4 is not using testimonials. In many cases, what other people say about you is much more convincing to a prospect than what you say about yourself; they expect you to toot your own horn, but they stand up and pay attention when someone does it for you. That's why social media is such a huge influence these days. Word of mouth is very valuable, if you can harness it for your benefit.

Mistake #5 is failing to measure the results of your marketing. Every single dollar should be accountable, so you know what works and what doesn't. Don't just throw a bunch of things out there without some way to track the results. When you know one type of promotion is working like gangbusters and another is going over like a lead balloon, you can cut the latter and focus on the former. Have identifiers for each kind of result that comes in. Track everything.

Mistake #6 is failing to following-up—or at least not following up enough. Most people give up on their prospects way too soon. In order to follow up, you have to know exactly who your customers are (there's that theme again), so you've got to build a mailing list containing every type of contact information you can think of. This should consist of people who have either opted in or already raised their hand to show interest in the type of products or services you offer. Once they've done that, follow up with a vengeance, reminding them that they haven't yet done business with you or that you have another interesting offer for them. Keep your name in front of them.

Mistake #7: Trying to be cute and funny. Forget the clever ads Coke and Geico do. These are image ads that work only for huge businesses; they generally lack any kind of direct response message. They're just meant to get people to remember your name so that when they think about a specific type of product, they think of you first. You're better served by direct-response marketing that's specific and to the point.

Mistake #8: Using bad copy. The right words are important, so you have to develop (or buy) good copywriting skills. I've written whole books and hosted entire three-day events in which I've talked about nothing but the right way to craft sales copy. You *must* have a basic understanding of copywriting in order to be able to write advertisements that compel people to take the actions you want them to take.

Mistake #9: Too much reliance on one advertising medium. You have to diversify, just as a table or chair has multiple legs. Putting all your eggs in one marketing basket is a bad idea. Multiple streams of income help you survive if one or more dries up. So do different things to generate leads and traffic to your website, or get people to your store; the more of those things you can do, the less reliant you'll be on any one method. Just make sure it's all trackable.

Those are the nine major marketing mistakes I've

identified. It all starts with focus—because when you truly focus on something with your mind's eye, that's when exciting things start to happen. When you have a project that you know will help your business, and you refuse to be distracted, you'll enjoy great results. Focus is even a metaphysical thing; as the saying goes, as you think about something, so shall it come into your life. If you focus on the right things, you'll have a happier life—and enjoy the power necessary to do the things you want and deserve.

I encourage you to take a look at all nine of these mistakes again before you move on to the next Marketing Secret. Most of your competitors are doing a terrible job with all these things; that's just reality. Remember this too: "In the land of the blind, the one-eyed man is king." By the time you're done reading this book, I guarantee you'll know so much more than 99% of your competitors that you'll be going *two*-eyed in the land of the blind—and they'll never know what hit them.

Marketing Secret #3:
The Key to Maximum Profitability

Most of your profits must come from one simple strategy: reselling to your existing customers. Why? First of all, the easiest person to sell to is someone with whom you already have an existing relationship. They know you, they like you, they trust you. A customer who buys from you twice is twice as likely to buy from you again.

Another reason you should focus on existing customers is the fact that most other entrepreneurs and companies are forever chasing new customers, putting all their energy, money, and resources into the effort. At best, they're spending 80% on attraction, 20% on retention. You can easily get ahead of them if you'll just reverse that ration. Spend 80% of your time focused on reselling to existing customers, and 20% on acquiring new customers. You're losing money if you don't do it this way.

Third, you have to realize that even when people *want* to do more business with you, you just can't wait for them to approach you. You have to be proactive, using all the ideas I'll share in this book to go after them aggressively. Make them those irresistible offers. Invite them to purchase new, related products and services from you. Look for gaps in your market, problems or needs that are not being addressed, to exploit.

What are your competitors doing right that you could be doing too? What kinds of products or services can you create? What kind of joint venture relationships can you work out with direct or indirect competitors to sell your existing customers a product or service they've developed, and vice versa? These are all good questions to ask yourself.

You're not in business to lose money, and selling to existing customers really is one key to maximum profitability. The customers you have already are absolutely golden. Some businesses just don't seem to get this. They'll make wonderful offers to new customers, but leave their existing customers high and dry. My mentor and friend, Russ von Hoelscher, was in a variety store once when someone brought in a coupon and the clerk said, "Sorry, that's for new customers only." The customer said, "I've been a customer here for years." And the clerk said, "Yes ma'am, and we appreciate that, but this special offer is for new customers only."

Russ thought to himself, "How stupid is this? You won't

cut her a deal—but someone just coming in off the street for the first time gets five or ten dollars off?" It just shows you how dumb so many businesspeople are. *You have to treat your best customers the best.* Period. Sure, you have to treat new customers well too, but save the extra-special treatment for your existing customers. Admittedly, it's harder to make a sale to a first-time customer than it is a repeat customer, which is why a lot of businesses make those killer offers to new customers. But they offend their old customers by doing so—and risk losing them in the process!

One of the reasons we love direct mail here at M.O.R.E. Inc. is that you can make good offers to both new and existing customers, and neither group has to know what you're offering the other. For example, if you're a local business, you can run a promotion where you're mailing to people in your community with a very special first-time customer offer, and at the same time you can mail your existing customers another great offer. That way, you take care of your existing customers and attract new ones to either widen your customer base, or recover your shortfall as existing customers leave the market, move, pass away, or otherwise stop spending money with you.

My point here is that there's a tremendous amount of revenue to be made by reselling your existing customers on products, and services similar to what they bought the first time. It's easier to resell to your existing customers, and in most cases, it's just not possible to overdo it with the offers. They'll always be hungry for more things related to what they bought the first time.

You have a gold mine sitting right there in your lap. Don't

forget it exists while you're angling for new customers. Given the chance, people *will* spend more money with you. Even if they don't, it's probably because you're not innovating enough—you're not developing new products or services, or finding additional related offers you can make to them. It's your fault, not theirs. Once you accept that responsibility and know you're losing money if you don't try to resell to your existing customer base, let the pain of that knowledge drive you forward.

Marketing Secret #4: Two-Step Marketing

This is the safest and most profitable way to make money with self-marketing strategies, and it works for both new and existing customers. I've successfully used two-step marketing for over 25 years now, and my mentor, Russ von Hoelscher, has used it for about 40 years. It's the easiest way I know to get people to self-qualify themselves before you spend money trying to acquire their business.

You start out by advertising something, using whatever methods work best for your business. Make a low or no-price offer to the marketplace to draw in a pack of new prospects. Once someone responds to your "front end" offer, make them a bigger offer on the "back end." That's why it's called two-step marketing. If possible, try to break even, but don't kill yourself doing it. Don't expect to make money at this point. In many cases, you'll even lose money—but in the end, it's worth it.

I realize a lot of you will respond negatively to that statement: "Oh my God, you're telling me to lose money?! That's not what I bought this book to learn!" But calm down! You've heard the saying, "You've got to spend money to make money." Nowhere is that more true than in two-step marketing.

So yes, be willing to lose a little money on the front end, so you can make a fortune on the back-end. For those of us in direct-response marketing, this has been the secret to most of our success for over a century. It can be used for local businesses just as easily. Make an offer, telling people you're going to give them something at a big discount. If you own a restaurant, you might offer two meals for one. Once they see how nice your restaurant is and how good the food tastes, then they'll return again and again—which is where your true profit margin lies.

By the way, here's a tip for you restaurant owners out there: don't be too strict about interpreting these 2-for-1 deals. Realize, as Russ did a long time ago and shared with a restaurant he was working with in San Diego, that a lot of single people eat at restaurants. Make a half-price offer to them. This idea that only couples can get your discount is hurting your business. If you don't run a restaurant, then offer a low price widget to get them in the door, or some special service if you're a service company.

If you're a doctor, dentist, or chiropractor, offer a free exam. Many in these fields balk at that idea, because such exams can be expensive—especially if they include X-rays. But so what? It's an incredible deal for the customer, which works very well for growing a business. One of Russ's clients, a chiropractor in Pacific Beach, California, initially fought him on this idea—but once she tried it, she told him it was the best business decision she'd ever made. Yes, she did spend some time and money on the exams and X-rays, but 60% of the people who came in for the free exam became customers. Some of them ended up spending thousands of dollars. Consider this if you own a real estate company: offer a booklet that tells people how to sell their homes for the maximum profit. That's a smart thing to do, because many people are thinking about selling their homes at any given time—and they'll welcome a booklet like this with open arms. In fact, they may hire you on the spot.

Realize that this works for *all* types of businesses, because you make customers feel good when you give them something for free—whether it's a profitable little booklet, a useful widget, a nice discount, a brief membership, or whatever. This makes you stand out from the pack; people think, "These people really care. They really seem to want my business, and they're doing their best to make me happy. Guess what? I'm going to give them my business." You can turn that into huge profits on the back-end.

To reiterate: the best way to find your best customers is to get them to raise their own hands and say that they want what you have to offer. Of all the people in your broader marketplace who might do business with you, only a small percentage is capable of becoming your best customers. Draw them in, using a method that weeds out the tire-kickers and the merely interested.

Once you've got those prospects, follow up with them and keep narrowing the field. With a two-step marketing system, follow-up is automatic once you've attracted that smaller subset of your marketplace that responded to the first cast of the net. Always expect that number to be relatively small; you can't appeal to everyone. Follow-up with them as long as it's profitable to do so, reminding them that they still need to do business with you. Often people ask us here at M.O.R.E. Inc., "How long should I follow up with prospects?" There's no set answer: you just do it until you stop breaking even on the follow-ups. That might mean you follow up with them just 3-5 times. In some cases, you can follow up with them 15-20 times.

Once you're no longer profiting from the prospect list, you can stop. Sadly, most people never get that far—they give up way too fast. Don't. Do all of the follow-up necessary to convert the largest percentage of responders from prospects into customers that you can add to your customer list and continue doing business with later on.

My entire life changed when I learned to do two-step marketing. I'm sure that sounds rather dramatic, but it's the absolute truth. Back in 1985 I had a tiny carpet cleaning business, and I figured that anyone who had carpets or upholstery was a potential client. I was constantly knocking on doors and making thousands of phone calls, handing out tons of free bids and basically killing myself marketing... and I was barely getting enough work to get by. That went on until I learned two-step marketing, using an amazingly simple approach to get people who were actually interested in carpet cleaning to raise their hands and come to me at least slightly presold.

My business was never the same after that. Suddenly, I was making about a third of my sales, instead of fewer than one in 10. All it took was getting people to prequalify themselves, which is the key to the two-step marketing process.

Marketing Secret #5:
Roll Your Earnings Back into Your Business

In this section, I'll let you in on the secret that P.T. Barnum used clear back in 1877 to dominate his market. This secret can help you rise to the top of your market even today. It's simple, yet probably less than one in 1,000 businesses understands or is even aware of this principle, and fewer have figured out how to cash in with it.

Now: I have to tell you, just as a lead-in here, that when I was growing up, P.T. Barnum was just a circus man to me. About all I knew was that the Ringling Brothers Barnum and Bailey Circus came to town once a year. The truth is, Barnum was an amazing entrepreneur well before he got into the circus business. The other thing you hear about Barnum is that he once said, "There's a sucker born every minute." That's not true, so how he got credited with it is beyond me. History sometimes paints him as an unscrupulous con artist, but nothing could be further from the truth. Barnum was a great marketer, a great salesman who had nothing but respect for his customers.

One of the principles he lived by and practiced in his business was this: he made sure he invested plenty of money into the areas that were already making him money. In 1877 he spent over $100,000 for advertising and publicity for his circus—almost a third of his total expenses.

Reinvesting at this level can be a difficult thing for new entrepreneurs to accomplish. People who are just starting out in business get the urge to blow that money when it starts rolling in. You might want to spend it on elaborate vacations, buy a fancy new car, buy a second home, or purchase some gadget you've always wanted. You get a few thousand dollars in, and it goes right out the door.

Young professional athletes sometimes end up with multimillion-dollar signing bonuses fresh out of college—and the first thing they do is go blow it. Sometimes just a few years into their careers, they don't have any money at all. Often they're out of work before long, without anything much to show for it. Business is a little different, but the principle is the same. You have to learn to take some of the money that comes in and invest it in the practices that made you that money in the first place.

I call this "pyramiding your profits." You simply figure out how much of your income you need to build that profitable pyramid—whether it's 10%, 20%, 30%, even up to 50%—and you put it immediately into a separate advertising account. That way, you can do more of the marketing that earned you that cash in the first place: running magazine ads, sending out direct mail, paying for more TV or radio spots—whatever's working. From the very beginning, my wife Eileen and I put 30% of our net income in a special account that we only used for advertising.

So think about P.T. Barnum, who spent $100,000 on publicity back in 1877. Even today, $100,000 is a lot of money; but in 1877, it was an *amazing* amount of money. He knew that he had to do everything he could to bring people in so they'd spend their money—and he was willing to spend *his* money on that. That meant putting money back into the business to bring in more business and make it even more successful. That was Barnum's guiding principle, and it should be one of yours as well. It really can help you dominate your market if you use it wisely.

Let me repeat: Barnum wasn't a huckster or a joke; he was an aggressive, intelligent businessman. But a large part of our society, including many in the government, chooses not respect people like Barnum, just because they *are* so successful. I say we need a National Entrepreneur's Day—because without the entrepreneurial spirit, we wouldn't have a great country like the United States of America to enjoy. When you become an entrepreneur or a small businessman, you're continuing a tradition that made this country great. When marketing is done correctly, it makes you money—it doesn't cost you. You need to realize that right from the word go.

Marketing Secret #6: The PAS Formula

This secret consists of a simple copywriting formula that will *always* make you money. In fact, not only is this a copywriting formula, it's a sales formula. Good direct response marketing is salesmanship in print.

This simple method is called the PAS formula. It's easy to remember; think "pass" with one S. The letters stands for Problem, Agitation, and Solution. The reason why this is such an effective formula is because you start by setting up the sale. To get people to understand the solutions you're offering, and what those solutions mean to them, you first have to address the Problem. Then you have to make it real to them—which is where Agitation comes in. You're showing them how that problem affects them personally, making it real. Then you offer the Solution that causes them to buy.

Why go through this process? Because sometimes, people only care about the solution after they fully understand the problem. That's why you have to set up the sale. Personalize the problem and make it real to them, which is the agitation process. Tell some stories about how annoying or painful the problem is; get them to put themselves in the picture and see that the problem is real to them. Rub salt in the wound if you have to. Then and only then are they ready to consider your solution.

When you're just starting to put together a campaign, create a master list of all the big problems your best prospective buyers are suffering from. Write them down and think about them; internalize them. You've spent months or even years trying to get inside the heads and hearts of whoever it is you're trying to reach, so you ought to know what their biggest problems are instinctively. Then think about how you can personalize those problems, making them real to the prospect, reminding them about those problems in a painful way and then offering them the solution. The more you do this, the more you'll be able to develop unique new products and services that help address those problems. *Never* try to sell the solution until you've sold the problem first.

This is also a great formula for any time you have to make any kind of sales presentation. Focus on the problem, agitate them a little, and then sell them the solution.

Make the solution as simple as possible. We live in a society where everyone wants instant gratification; we expect things to be done quickly, partly because high-tech has spoiled us, and partly because we have many demands on our time. That's why a lot of people don't have the patience it takes to lose weight. If you write copy that says, "Do this and in the next year or two, you're going to lose 25 pounds!", a lot of people will say, "To hell with that! Here's another offer that says I can start losing 4 pounds a week," and they'll go for that—even if it's an outright lie.

While you have to tell the truth—that's crucial—always try to formulate the quickest possible solution. People desperately want to solve their problems, and they want to do it *right now*. If you can come up with a quick solution to one of their biggest problems, one that really works, you can make millions of dollars.

And again, start with the problem, *not* the solution. Many business owners and entrepreneurs start with a solution and then try to fit it to existing problems. Sometimes that works, but often they don't end up with the volume of business they hoped for. The solution doesn't matter unless there's a problem. So what if you've invented a cure for green skin? Most people don't have green skin (at least on this planet), so the solution doesn't matter, and very few people will be willing to pay you anything for it. Either find a problem your solution cures—a reason why people should worry about having green skin—or start from an existing problem and create a solution that people will want. Creating a skin cream for acne would be a much more logical place to start.

PAS is a great formula—but it *does* have to start with the problem. So study your marketplace closely. Figure out what pain they're in, and that will suggest your solution. And realize this, too: often, people don't actively think about the problems they're suffering from. Actually, the term "suffering" may be a little harsh; sometimes they're just experiencing an irritation or an annoyance, but nonetheless, it's one they'd prefer not to deal with. If so, point it out to them bluntly and really talk it up so you can make it real for them. If you've done a good job of that, they'll be glad to pay what you're asking for the solution you're promising.

People are overwhelmed these days. They have so much they're trying to do, so much going on in their heads... so it's up to you to remind them of certain problems they're affected by, but may not be actively thinking about. Make those problems personal to them. Then and only then will they fully appreciate what you're offering them. Then and only then will they be willing to pay you a premium for the solution.

With that in mind, let's go on to Chapter 2, where I'll

discuss even more marketing secrets you can use to get more people to give you more money.

In our busy world, your offers have to be special to rise above all the others. You've got to pierce through the shield of apathy and skepticism most people have built up around themselves just to cope with everything thrown at them. In a sense, the people in your marketplace are conflicted: on one level they could care less about you, but at another, they want to deal with real people they can identify with. In this chapter, we'll look at secrets dealing with both issues—often individually, sometimes in combination.

Marketing Secret #7:
Build Tremendous Value into Your Offers

In order to (figuratively) grab your prospects and make them listen to what you have to say, it's critical for you to understand and remember what they want the most: value and benefits. That's basically it, at least at first. They don't give a damn about your company or you, much less your products or services—except insofar as those things give them what they want, what they hunger for. If the benefits of what you offer make it worthwhile to them, they'll happily give you their money in exchange.

Remember that it's always about the customer wants. I'll repeat that over and over throughout this book. *It's all about what the customer wants.* Not what you want or think they should want, but what they really want; and not necessarily what they need, either, because what we truly need as human beings comprises a very short list: food, water, shelter, companionship, and a little medical care.

100 MARKETING SECRETS

Our desires are what truly drive us. Most humans are selfish people, even when we're trying to do good things. I've often felt that when you give gifts you're supposed to be doing a wonderful thing and you're *not* selfish, but the truth is, it's even selfish to give people gifts sometimes, because you feel so good when you do it. I'm not a big believer in true altruism; I think we mostly do good things because they make us feel good. Fortunately a lot of people, including some super-rich individuals, feel good supporting charities; and God bless them for that. Even if they do it so someone will name a hospital after them, it's all to the good.

We serve our customers, and so we're constantly looking for ways to qualify them and get them interested in what we have to sell. We don't do it by talking about our products and services in a mundane way. We try to make them exciting, to give the prospects a reason to buy. For example, professional dentists (the smart ones!) will sometimes include something like this in their advertising copy: "Win friends and influence people with your new smile!" They'll tell you why your smile is an important part of you; and as a result, some people will start thinking about their twisted or missing teeth and say, "I really *should* do something about those, because I'd like to be able to smile more and have more friends."

I've mentioned in another Secret that Russ von Hoelscher works with a chiropractor in Pacific Beach, California. He once wrote an ad for her that began, "I'll make your pain go away." He then went on to talk about different kinds of pain: leg pain, back pain, arm pain, arthritic pain, and pain from old injuries. He went into depth about these pains, with the idea of agitating the reader (as I outlined in the last chapter). They're *already* in pain, and now they're reconsidering all their different pains and saying, "I'd better go see this chiropractor. She wants to make my pain go away." That's a powerful message.

Or take the flower shop advertisement Russ also did, which I thought was quite good. The central message was, "Wives and girlfriends love roses. Happy wives and happy girlfriends make your life so much better." Now, that really hits a guy over the head. There's a picture of a woman kissing a man on the cheek, looking sensual, and it gives him the impression of, "Hey, all you have to do is stop at our flower shop, get a dozen roses—and experience great things as a result."

Regardless of what products or services you offer, you have to deeply consider how you're going to get people excited about them, and give them good reasons why they should. People know they need this and that, but you need to hit them with their *wants*; and when you do that well, great things happen. So remember: build tremendous value into your offer, but never forget that part of that value is based on a prospect's deepest wants—and out of those wants comes his purchase.

To reiterate: at least at the beginning, your customers and prospects only care about themselves; people tend to be very self-focused. Even as an entrepreneur or small business owner, you're often thinking of yourself, about what you're trying to do for your own benefit. Channel that tendency. Think deeply about what you're trying to do as you put together your next offer to increase your online or direct mail sales or get people into your store. Look at your goals in light of what your customers want, and do your best to bring those together—but *always* make sure the prospect's wants and needs come out on top. Deliver them the benefits or the solutions they're seeking.

The only power you have in your marketplace is what you can do for the people you serve. That's it; there *is* nothing else. By and large, people only care about what's in it for them—what they can get out of the situation. A benefit is the end emotional result of whatever it is you're offering. So ask yourself: what are they really searching for? Why do they buy what you sell? In a general sense, what people are looking for is tremendous value—enormous benefit for whatever price you may be asking, the most they can possibly get for the least amount of money. That's why you have to build tremendous value into everything that you're offering. You have to spend a lot of time thinking about who your customers are and what they're searching for, getting inside their heads and hearts in almost the same way a psychiatrist would learn his patients.

Get to know your target market at an intimate, emotional level. In some ways, you have to understand them more than they understand themselves. That requires constant thinking and an awareness of why they want the kind of things you sell, which requires you to go beyond and beneath the superficial.

Marketing Secret #8: Takeaway Selling

If you want to make incredible profits, you have to arrange things so your very best prospects chase after *you* instead of you chasing after *them*. This secret helps you take control of the balance of power between you and your marketplace, while seeming to arrange things so that everything is in the prospect's favor. Use it well, and you'll never have to worry about hustling up business again.

Think about selling as you might think about a dating relationship: you want to be the one being chased. If you're the one doing the chasing, the other person may be playing you a little, but they have all the power in the relationship (whether they realize it or not). In that situation, the chaser is likely to lose in the end. The same goes for business relationships: stop chasing prospects and get them to chase you instead.

It's a subtle shift in power, but it's very important.

Most business people only chase prospects. They're out there hustling business. Car dealerships are among the worst at this kind of advertising, because they're always out there yelling and screaming at you, trying to get you to come into their locations. It seems they're always chasing you, and when you finally go to the dealership, it feels like you've been caught. It's back-and-forth after that, and sometimes you end up with a car and sometimes you just end up frustrated. No one really enjoys that experience. Occasionally you'll see a car dealer who handles things a bit differently, and it's refreshing to deal with them—but they're rare.

The truth is, most business people just don't understand any other way of doing business. They can't see how they can possibly get customers to chase them. That's why this secret is so important. If you can use it to your advantage, you can steal business from your competitors—and they won't even understand how you're doing it.

The best way to get prospects to chase you is to use takeaway selling. Now, I could spend a whole book discussing this one principle; but the basis of takeaway selling is simply that the more you say "no" to prospects about something, the more they'll want it. Your offer could be something that's available for a limited time only, or in a limited quantity. If it's readily available and anybody can get it at any time, it's less desirable—so there's no reason for them to chase you, because they know where you are and what you have. Create a reason for them to chase you.

I realize this concept is somewhat counterintuitive, since most of us are taught (by experience if nothing else) that we have to hustle for business, to track down and claim every customer we can. But takeaway selling is a smarter way of attracting prospects, by making what you have seem special. Suppose you're trying to hire someone to do some consulting work. If you contact them and that person says eagerly, "Sure! When would you like me to start? My schedule is open for the next month!" then what do you do?

Most of us start wondering, "Oh no, why is his schedule wide open?" which leads naturally to the thought, "He must not be very good!" On the other hand, how do you feel if the expert says, "Hmmm. My schedule is pretty full... It looks like I can give you 15 minutes next Thursday. Or would the following Tuesday work?" In that case, the expert looks like he's in more demand. His schedule is full and his time is valuable; so if you want to work with him, you need to get with the program and work on *his* schedule—because he doesn't have all the time in the world.

That's the position you want to be in. Ask yourself: have your customers been chasing you—or have you been doing the chasing? If the latter, arrange a shift in the balance power. The best strategy I know of to accomplish this is to use two-step marketing, as described in Marketing Secret #4. I won't describe it again here, except to point out that once you've arranged to have people raise their hands to qualify themselves, you've shifted the balance of power. Now when they come to you, they're doing so on their own volition; most forget you invited them to raise their hands in the first place. It's a subtle thing, yet it's very powerful.

This works especially well if you combine it with exclusivity—making a product scarce, often artificially. People love exclusivity. Russ von Hoelscher once had an office two doors down from an antique shop, and he got to know the owner quite well, so he'd go in and look around often. She had some very unusual objects that were 100-150 years old, including lamps, furniture, and first edition books by famous authors. He noticed that she used a certain technique with people. Someone might be looking at a century-old French lamp with a beautiful decorative lampshade, and note the price of $500 or more. The person might say, "Oh, that's nice. I just don't know, though."

Then the lady would immediately say, "Yes, it *is* nice—and you'll probably never see another one like it in your life." That technique made people buy. Of course, this method doesn't apply to all types of businesses; a sandwich shop is a good example. In a case like that, you'll have to use other marketing techniques. But if you do have a business where you offer unique items, always act as though they're limited in supply, which they probably are even if they're not antiques. Always tell people, "This is special, and if you want it, you should get it now—because you may never see another one."

People don't want things that just anybody can have. That's a universal appeal you can build into almost any business, because even if you're not selling completely unique items, you can make them seem unique. One thing you can do along these lines is to establish yourself as an expert in your field, which you probably are anyway. Some medical specialists you have to wait months to see, for example, because their expertise is so specialized, and they do such a good job.

Marketing Secret #9: Three Simple Things

Getting rich in your business requires just three simple things. Forget all that complicated MBA crap; if those business profs really know what they're doing, why aren't they doing it instead of teaching? Ditto for all those specialized business books crowding the shelves of the chain bookstores. It just breaks my heart whenever I go to the bookstore and see all that complicated BS. I've browsed thousands of these books, it seems, and they're nothing but one frustration after another—because the people who write them tend to be either business professors who have never been in business for themselves, former CEOs of gigantic Fortune 1000 companies who don't have the first clue about running a small business, or accountants who love to try to make business seem as complicated and confusing as possible.

It breaks my heart to see this, because I love being self-employed—and I see so many people being scared away from the possibility by these complicated business books. So forget about 'em. In the real-life business world, you can make massive profits with these three simple things:

1.   Get a large enough number of people...

2.   To consistently give you a large enough amount of their money on a regular basis...

3.   At a large enough profit per transaction.

Now, you have to do a few other things, like managing your customers correctly. People aren't going to do more business with you unless you treat them right, provide great service, and really understand them at an intimate level. Otherwise, these steps are all you have to worry about. They intertwine with excellent customer service anyway, so if you practice them well and consistently, you're going to make all the money you want.

It's simple when you get down to it, but don't assume it's *easy*. Business can be very frustrating, challenging, and confusing. But at the end of the day, you'll figure it out if you just keep going back to the basics. Just sell enough stuff to enough people enough times for enough profit, with maximum efficiency. Keep it simple.

Again, there are plenty of intricacies involved within those three steps. You definitely have to work hard to attract as many prospects as possible in the first place, and then winnow them down to a solid core of customers. When you get right down to it, business is all about having exciting products or services to offer—whether it's the best hamburger in town, or the best plumbing in the county, or any of hundreds of other things. You just want your products or services to be top-quality and unique, so you can be the one business in your industry who really stands out.

If you have a restaurant, include something special on the menu, something outrageous that people will talk about: a two-foot hoagie or a five pound burger, for example. Do something that draws attention to you, because again, the key here is to get enough people to come in consistently, giving you their money at a nice profit.

You don't need 300 pages' worth of abstract theory to figure that out. Let's be blunt here: most of those writers couldn't care less about the business market anyway, especially small businesses. They're trying to appeal to the general public. Most of the ideas they present aren't easy to apply on a practical level, so oftentimes when you seek out information, you end up more frustrated than ever before. Stop bothering. Boil it down to basics. Find or develop a simple formula that gets enough people to give you enough money during each transaction to make a nice profit. The same ideas that work on a small scale can be expanded to million-dollar industries if you play your cards right.

I've got the cover of a book called *The 12 Secrets to Success in Business* hanging on my wall. It's by a famous author who's written a number of other business books—and there's not one thing in there about marketing. Nothing. I've got the cover up as a reminder of just how misleading these so-called "experts" are. Marketing is *everything*. Your business *is* marketing: the process of constantly trying to attract and retain more of the very best clients or customers in your market. That's it.

It makes me sad that so many people are being seriously misled this way—that so many businesses are dying because they just don't realize that *marketing* should be their #1 focus. Whenever business gets complicated, go back to that one basic reality and stay there until you get your head straight.

Marketing Secret #10: Think Yourself Rich

How do you think yourself rich? First of all, you have to have a sincere passion for what you're doing. Here at M.O.R.E. Inc., we love our products and services. There *are* some businesses that are hard to love—or so you'd think. About 10 years back, Russ von Hoelscher worked with a businessman who had a plant in Tijuana, Mexico that made nuts, bolts, nails, and screws. Russ said to him, "I know you're successful, and you have about 80-90 Mexican workers at your plant—but are you excited about it?"

The owner said, "*Excited* about it? When I see a new screw, I jump for joy." So here's a guy making fasteners—an industry I just don't see how anyone could love. But he's excited about it, constantly looking for new innovations in that very specialized business. That's the key to thinking yourself rich: you have to get really passionate about your business, and believe in both it and yourself.

What you think about on a regular basis will materialize in your life. This can be positive or negative, so you have to watch your thoughts. Stay away from negative thinking, or negative things will happen to you. Thinking positive thoughts isn't just a bunch of New Age silliness; it's absolutely essential for success.

Now, some people will tell you, "I'm from Missouri. I'll believe it when I see it!" I think the better motto is, "If I believe it, I know I'll see it." Think about success. Think about happy business relationships. Whatever it takes to be successful according to your definition of successful, focus in on it, and get excited about your business.

I've been in direct-response marketing for almost 25 years now, and people sometimes ask, "Can you still get excited about it?" Of course I can! I'm always excited about it. The same thing's true for Russ von Hoelscher, who's been in the business more than 35 years now. That excitement keeps you going; and I think as you get older, it keeps you young. I often tell people who are getting well up there in age, "Keep working your business with a passion, and you'll live longer." My advice is to stay positive, stay focused, work hard, but work *smart* above all else—and don't forget, what you think about will become reality in your life.

You know, it never ceases to amaze me how people will say they want a certain outcome, but refuse to think heavily on those goals and determine what it's going to take to achieve them. Chris Lakey has a 13-year-old son who's very interested in sports. He plays soccer on the eighth grade soccer team, and Chris says he's finally coming around—he's starting to put serious effort into the sport that he wasn't putting into it before. Chris keeps telling him, "You need to condition. You need to train. You need to lift weights. You need to be doing sit-ups and push-ups. You need to be running a mile or two a day. You need to get into shape for when soccer season hits here. You need to be ready to go."

Well, Austin put it off and put it off... and of course soccer season arrived and he wasn't in the shape he needed to be in. Chris kept telling him, "If you want to be committed to success, you have to do what it takes to be successful." I think that's true in all walks of life.

It doesn't matter whether you're trying to make an Olympic team or earn your first million dollars: what you focus on and what you become determined to accomplish is what you'll set out to do. You have to be honest with yourself. You can hope and wish that things were a certain way all you want, but unless you're willing to expend the necessary effort and dedication, don't expect success to just come to you. Despite some famous claims to the contrary, it's not enough to wish that things were different; you have to decide you're going to do everything it takes to get there.

The reality is that no matter what you're trying to accomplish in your life, without hard work, focus, and dedication to making that happen, there are too many forces at play that will make it *not* happen. The physical law of inertia says that an object in motion tends to stay in motion, while an object at rest tends to stay at rest. It's certainly easier to keep yourself fit than to get fit in the first place. In business, it's easier to be successful once you've experienced success.

Here's a personal example: I've been a member of what I call "The 5 AM Club" since the late 1980s. As I mentioned in Chapter 1, I get up every morning at five, sometimes sooner, and try to go to work right away. Some mornings I do a better job of it than others; sometimes it takes me an hour just to get my head straight before I can start cranking out my best work. But having that time every day that's totally focused on my business—when no phones are ringing, no fax machines buzzing—that's magic.

Marketing is one of two things in your business, along with innovation, that you shouldn't delegate or abdicate to anybody else. Devote a significant part of your day to thinking about and strategizing on how you can attract and retain more of the very best buyers in your marketplace. This is what you should put your passion into, what you must fall in love with. It's the hunt, it's the chase... and remember, it's the ideas that start the money. Some people tell themselves, "I don't have enough money to do this. I don't have enough money to do that." Well, it's the ideas, the strategies, the methods that you're going to try to put into effect that cause the money to flow in in the first place.

So catch a bigger vision for your company. Work on your business daily, thinking it through—thinking yourself rich. Get passionate about marketing. Once you see some of your ideas actually materialize, and start producing a tremendous cashflow, it gets even more exciting—and you'll end up putting even more time and energy into it.

CHAPTER TWO

SECRETS 11-20

Marketing Secret #11:
The Wizard of Oz's Powerful Secret

Like the Wizard of Oz, you can dominate your marketplace without letting anyone see behind the curtain. In the movie, the main characters originally see the Wizard as a sort of freakish hologram head with a booming, ominous voice that scares people into doing what he says... until all of a sudden, Toto pulls a curtain back and they see a little man controlling the computer that creates the illusion. He's not big and powerful at all... just a man with a powerful secret.

Individually, most people aren't that powerful. What matters is the persona you create that gives you power. The way you do that is to convince or show your prospects that you know something they don't—that you're an expert in your field, which you definitely are compared to them. Proving that probably won't be too complicated. Even if you know just a little about your subject (and I'm sure you know much more than just a little), there are plenty of people who don't know even that much.

Many entrepreneurs and business owners have this false perception that they have to be extreme experts in whatever it is they're offering—that you have to know everything there is to know about your specialty. But you don't, because most people don't know *anything* about what you're offering.

The Wizard of Oz was all-powerful until people knew

who he really was—but this isn't one of those things where you have to hide who you are. You just have to know how to give people what they want, convince them that you know something they don't, and offer them good value. That's easy to do when it's true. Having that information at your fingertips puts you on a position of power so you can serve that marketplace and make big profits doing so. Using that to provide a basis for your products and services.

Recently, Russ von Hoelscher told me about a TV biography he saw about Colonel Harlan Sanders, the man who started KFC (originally Kentucky Fried Chicken). He was the first one to say in his marketing, "I'm not too smart, but I know how to fry chicken—and I've got some special herbs and spices that people love." He took that method to restaurants all over the country and told them, "I can show you how to serve the best-tasting chicken in the world, and all I'm asking from you is a little piece of every sale you make."

Some people rejected him, of course— and he'd counter with a little bag of his secret spice mix, saying, "If you start using my formula, things will change. Customers will come here in droves." Some people said yes, and he got his 5% or 10% of each chicken dinner sale. They supplied the chicken, and he supplied the herbs, spices, and his super-fast frying technique.

I think the Colonel's message epitomizes this secret. You don't have to be smarter than everyone else to be an expert; you just have to have something you do better than anyone else. That alone gives you the power to make a lot of money. The more you have something that others want, the more power you have. And keep in mind that people respond to total confidence, which is why you've heard so much about con men in the past. The "con" in "con men" is short for "confidence." In order to deceive others, they first gain their confidence.

But you can and should always use that power positively. Confidence boosts salesmanship. The more confident you are about what you're offering, the more you believe it yourself, the more power you have—just like the Wizard in *The Wizard of Oz*.

Most people are silently begging to be led. Step up and lead them. Even if you think you're Joe Average, be confident in what you're offering and convince people you have what they want. That gives you tremendous power. You may in fact be average, but you've turned up the volume, expressing yourself in the fullest possible way.

Marketing Secret #12:
Why Direct Mail is the Ultimate Form of Marketing

Direct mail—what non-marketers sometimes call "junk mail"—can make you rich beyond your wildest dreams. For some of us, it means making $100,000 a year; for others, it means making $100,000 a month... or even a day. But whatever amount of money you want to make, direct mail is the best way to do it. I'm living proof, because that's how I've built my companies and made most of my fortune.

When my wife Eileen and I first met Russ von Hoelscher, we had been in the business for six months and were generating an average of $16,000 a month—not bad for a couple of kids who didn't know what the hell they were doing. We started out by running little display ads in moneymaking magazines, and Russ happened to see one. He liked what we were doing, so he sent us his brochure and offered to help us. We took him up on it—and within nine months, we went from making $16,000 a month to almost $100,000 a *week*. That's total revenue, not profit... but still, think about it! From an average of $500 a day to over *$14,000* a day. That's quite a rise. Russ taught us so much, and we were like thirsty sponges that just soaked it all up.

The one thing Russ did that helped us more than anything else was getting us involved in direct mail marketing. It's the ultimate form of salesmanship. It's expensive, so you're spending more money up front; but you're doing a much more effective job of reaching and selling to people. Let's look at just a few of the reasons why direct mail is so exciting. First of all, it's targeted. You can customize your sales message to reach the people who are most likely to do business with you. That gives you a greater degree of control than just about any other kind of marketing.

Direct mail marketing isn't advertising in a traditional sense. A good direct mail sales letter talks to the prospect in a personal way that gives you total selling power. It lets you do a complete job of selling, replacing all the steps that a truly great salesperson would go through in order to make the sale. You can consider a direct sales letter a little master salesman in an envelope.

Think about that. A great salesperson will first go out there and somehow attract the very best prospects with whatever he's offering. Usually he does it through cold calling or knocking on doors. A good direct mail package does that for you, attracting the best people to you. Those who aren't interested in what you offer never even respond—so you never have to hear the word "no."

When it gets into the right hands, your letter answers and overcomes the prospect's biggest objections, just like the best human salesmen. Then it goes for the close. Like a good salesman, that letter convinces the prospect that what it's offering is worth more to the prospect than the money it's asking in exchange, making the prospect a great offer they just can't refuse. And your little salesmen never call in sick or have a bad day or get tired of having doors slammed in their faces.

Of course, in this high-tech era, some people say, "Why should we even bother with direct mail? We can use e-mail and the Internet." And sure, you can. But you know what I've noticed over the past few years? More and more Internet marketers are coming to us direct mail marketers and asking, "Um, will you show me how to use direct mail?"

What they're finding is that a lot of their e-mail never reaches its target, no matter how well targeted it is, mostly due to spam blockers. When 80-90% of your e-mails get filtered out, that really throws your marketing campaign off-kilter, so the return on your investment is very small. Sure, it's cheap to send... but you don't make any money. Online marketers have told us, "You know, if we can get one out of every 3,000 pieces to place a $25 order, we think that's great." Maybe so, if you're e-mailing a lot and not paying very much for the e-mailing. Those sales represent pretty much pure profit, or close to it.

But that doesn't change the fact that direct mail is still the best way to target your audience—and it has a much higher success rate than e-mail. It's easier to zero in on your prospects, because you're using a rifle approach, not a shotgun approach. More and more people are starting to wake up to the fact that the results can be amazing... which is ironic, because there for a while, it looked like everyone in direct mail and mail-order was leaving to go to the Internet. Little by little, though, they're coming back. They say, "We're still going to do some Internet marketing, but we're getting back into direct mail, because it's been profitable in the past and it can be profitable in the future."

I think that's a bit amusing, especially since some people sneered at us because we were so dedicated to direct mail when everyone was fleeing the scene for the ease and cheapness of online marketing. Well, you get what you pay for... and some of the people who were down on us before are suddenly "discovering" how useful direct mail is. C'mon, now—direct mail has been successful for well over 100 years, for many, many companies. So yes, it can be successful for all kinds of companies these days, too.

You can and should maintain an Internet presence, but don't forsake direct mail.

Traditional salesmanship—with a salesperson going out, cultivating leads, and converting them into customers—is effective, but very expensive. You can imagine how much it would cost to reach 1,000 people using that method, and how long it would take. A direct mail letter can go out to thousands for a tiny fraction of the cost; you can have millions of them working for you if you have the right offer and you're working in the right marketplace. It's especially effective if you're using the Two-Step Marketing to turn those prospects into customers after they raise their hands on their own, and works even better when you automate the process. You can let your little salesmen-in-an-envelope do all the selling for you, while you sit back and watch the orders roll in.

Some people are even using direct mail to send people to websites—a viable option if you still want to use Internet marketing. You can point people toward a video, or offer a free gift to get them to come online and consider your offer. So even if you're dedicated to Internet marketing, don't overlook direct mail as an adjunct to what you're already doing.

Ultimately, it boils down to ROI: Return On Investment. Within certain broad guidelines, it doesn't matter how much money something *costs* you; all that matters is how much money it *earns* you. While direct mail is more expensive than most forms of marketing, it also does a more complete job of selling if you do it right—and therefore you'll sell more of your products or services, and consequently make more money.

But even those involved in direct mail often miss the boat. Everybody seems to want to do it on the cheap by mailing postcards; and while postcards sometimes work well, sometimes they don't, because you need to do a more effective job of selling than they allow. Don't just throw some postcards out there, and decide direct mail doesn't work if you don't get the response you want. Nothing could be further from the truth!

You've got to test your marketing methods in order to find out what works best so you can make direct mail work for you. Frankly, the fact that fewer people work with direct mail these days is a tremendous benefit to those of us who do. It means there's less competition in the mailbox. That makes it even easier for the best prospects to raise their hands and prove they're qualified. Let them feel like they are coming to you—and *then* let your salespeople go after them and close the deal.

Direct mail is the ultimate form of marketing, because it's salesmanship perfectly harnessed and duplicated. It's the entire process a great salesperson goes through, put into an envelope (or onto a postcard), and it goes out there and does a very effective job of selling.

Every effective marketing secret and strategy is based, to one extent or another, on building relationships with the customer. How else are you going to establish a strong enough connection for them to get to know you well enough to give you money consistently over a long period of time? There are very few businesses in which you can survive long-term without attracting repeat business from the same people. You've seen that in the first 12 secrets. In this chapter, we've delve deeper into that reality.

Marketing Secret #13: Target Marketing

Target Marketing is when you zero in on precisely who your customers are, based on how likely a prospect is to want or need what you're offering. Once you learn this strategy, you'll be far ahead of the competition—because most people do business in a willy-nilly way, collecting customers by happenstance. It sounds crazy, but that's how it is. In order to attract customers and sell to them repeatedly, you have to know them thoroughly, in some ways better than they know themselves.

So how do you do that? Any way you can imagine. You can ask them a few direct questions, or send everyone a quick survey. Sometimes it can be as simple as chatting with them. Find out what they really want and why they've chosen to do business with you. That way you can treat them better, they'll be better customers, and they'll stick with you through thick and thin. Also, you'll be able to use what you've learned to attract future customers.

Russ von Hoelscher was recently telling me about some work he did with a private postal and stationery store that also provided UPS shipping and rented private mailboxes. The owner said to Russ, "I wish I knew what kind of people rent these, so I could use that in my marketing." Well, it didn't take Russ long to determine that they were mostly home businesses. Rather than use their home addresses, they were using mailboxes that gave them a business address and suite number.

When Russ told the man the kind of people who were renting his boxes, he said, "Well, it's still not easy to figure out who they are." Russ replied, "Actually, it's very easy. Every month, San Diego County prints out a list of everyone who applies for a business license. This is East San Diego County. The licensees in this part of the county are going to be your best prospects."

After that, it was simple. The owner got the names from the city registrar, which didn't cost him much, and then started marketing his services to that highly targeted market segment. Lo and behold, quite a few came in and rented his mailboxes—and they also turned out to be good customers for office supplies and UPS shipping.

Not everybody has a business that's as simple to figure out as that one was. But in almost every business, you can determine how to target your future customers by becoming familiar with your present customers. Ask yourself: Why are they with me? What do they want? If you own a restaurant, candy store, or dry cleaning business, at first you may not know much more than that people often come to you just because they like your food or service, or happen to live within a couple of miles. But even that's a start, and you can out find more if you try hard enough.

For example, a dry cleaner just a few blocks down the road from Russ discovered that she should be advertising to people who use a lot of quilted bedding and similar things—a market that most dry cleaners don't go for. She started to get lots of customers for those items, so she started advertising that she specialized in them. She also discovered that many people have leather coats and jackets that most dry cleaners won't touch because they require a completely different cleaning process. When she advertised that she cleaned those, her business boomed.

Make it part of *your* business to find out why people come to you, so you can go after future business more easily. You'll know what to say to them, you'll know what they want to hear, and you'll know what to use in your direct mail or other advertising to ring their bells and get them interested.

I've always been amazed when people say something like, "I've got this product; now I need to figure out who to sell it to." They've got it backward. What they really should be saying is, "I've got this great group of people; now I need to find something they want to buy!" Targeted marketing means knowing what your customers want to buy because you know who they are. To some extent, you have a psychological profile of what they're looking for, and therefore the kinds of things that interest them the most.

It doesn't start with the product, it starts with the *market*. Always. Too many business owners and entrepreneurs somehow forget that. You can serve the marketplace once you've identified them. If you do it the other way around, you'll have a much harder time getting business—because you started from the wrong place.

If you have a group of people you're already doing business with, there are services that will allow you to do a demographic study of them. This can be useful in helping you find out more about where they live, what their income level is, how old they are, whether they're mostly male or female, etc. More important than demographic studies are the psychographic studies that tell you what they're looking for, what kind of pain they're in, what problems they're looking for solutions to. The results can provide you with all you need to know to continuously develop new products and services they'll want to buy. When you match those problems and solutions up correctly, you can pretty much ask whatever price you want for your products or services.

As I write this, my company is getting involved in a brand-new marketplace—and it's huge. There are literally tens of millions of people involved in this market, so one of the very first things we're going to do as soon as we develop our first group of customers is to make every effort to get inside their heads and learn to think the way *they* think. How? In this case, we're going to host free live events. This will help us learn about them at a more intimate level, so we can serve them in the highest possible way.

They don't know it yet, but we're going to ask them a million questions during our events, doing our best to get inside their heads and hearts. That's the key to better serving your existing customers, and then reaching out to more people like them. I'll say it again: it's all about *them*, never about the product or service. Remember that! Who are they? What do they want the most? How can you offer them something that will just blow them away? Those are things you have to learn about your customer base—and that takes time.

It seems that everybody wants the easy answers, not

realizing—or not caring—that superficial answers aren't worth much. They don't realize that you have to dig deep to reach the gold—or maybe they're just resisting the idea. But the fact of the matter is that it can take many months, even years, to get the best answers. I don't say that to discourage you, because you can earn while you learn. I'm just saying that you should always to strive to figure out the best answers to the basic questions. What do your prospects and customers want more than anything else? What kind of message can you offer them that will draw them out of the woodwork in droves? Those answers sometimes come very slowly.

And figuring them out isn't as straightforward as you might think. If you just ask a customer why he does business with you, he may give you a shallow answer, or a phony one. People often have hidden agendas... and sometimes they're hidden even from themselves. Deep down, our motivations may actually be quite different than we admit; in fact, because we want people to think highly of us, we may just out-and-out lie about why we bought something. For example, a young guy might claim he bought a certain make and model of car because it'll provide good transportation for him, his wife, and their new baby... and maybe that's even true. But maybe the *real* reason was because he thinks it gives him more prestige or sex appeal, even though he'd never admit it.

So regardless of the type of business you're in, get beyond the superficial reasons people claim for doing business with you. Unearth their true motivations. Those rarely have to do with only their needs, at least once you get past necessities like toothpaste and toilet paper. They almost always have to do with their desires.

You don't have to be a genius to figure this out. You just have to understand the simple reality that people won't always tell you what they really want; you have to infer that through their actions. If you want to get rich via marketing, serve people what they truly desire—not what they *should* want, or necessarily *say* they want.

It all comes down to basics like sex appeal, greed, personal recognition, the desire for better health and long life, and freedom from pain. There are many different ways to legitimately serve those needs. Those who succeed in doing so are those who dig and dig into why people want to do business with them, until finally they hit pay dirt. Once you do this, it's much easier to figure out how to make *other* people want to do business with you.

Marketing Secret #14:
Introducing the Three-Step System

I've already revealed the Secret of the Two-Step Marketing System, but here's something rather different. The Three-Step Marketing System will get even more people to give you more money, more often, for greater profits. This system is so simple that a child can understand it, even though few people are using it. But that's good for you, because when you implement and master the Three-Step Marketing System, you'll end up a big jump ahead of your competitors.

As the name implies, it requires only three steps.

- Attract the right people and repel everyone else.

- Build the trust of those who respond.

- Prove that you alone can give them what they

want the most.

Let's break it down a little more, starting with Step #1. That's a basic element of all marketing; even as you're drawing in the people you want to do business with, you have to push others away. Never try to appeal to everyone, because in the end you'll appeal to no one. Your marketing should deliberately turn some people off while turning others on; the strategies go hand-in-hand. If you're not doing a good job of repelling the wrong people, you're probably not doing a good enough job of attracting the right people. That can be difficult, of course, but you can achieve it through specialization, certain copywriting tactics, directly approaching only those prospects most likely to become your best customers (as I've outlined elsewhere) and by using a few other strategies.

However you go about, really put some effort into it. Experiment until you discover what best filters out the tire-kickers and undesirables. Too often, businesspeople decide they want as many customers as possible—but usually that's neither feasible nor practical. So you have to develop your message in such a way that the people for whom it's not specifically targeted simply have no interest in it. That way, you don't waste time and money on people who aren't interested in becoming your customers in the first place.

Step #2 is building their trust, so that they'll honestly believe you can deliver the goods. Trust isn't automatic in the business world; it must be earned. You have to do things to overcome the natural resistance people have to your marketing, the result of years of empty promises and bad experiences. No one except an idiot hands money to someone they don't already know or understand.

Step #3 involves proving you can provide your best prospects with the things they want the most. You've attracted the right people and built a relationship with them; now finish it off by demonstrating that you can deliver on your promises.

If you can do these three things correctly, the sky's the limit.

Like Target Marketing and many of the other secrets you'll read about in this book, it all boils down to having a solid sense of what the marketplace is, how the world is affecting it, and developing an intimate understand of the people who comprise it. I'm reminded of a fellow I know who owns a company that makes steel cacti. When I first learned about his business, I thought, "What in the world?" I couldn't wrap my mind around why anyone would *want* to make steel cacti. It's a family business that he inherited, incidentally.

Then I started thinking about it from the prospective buyer's mindset. Once I realized who they were, I began to understand why some people might be interested in buying such things. For example, some people might buy them as works of art; some might use them for landscaping purposes, or as a kind of trellis. And that's where I should have started: with the customers—because it makes more sense than starting with the actual products.

Here's another quick example. A piece of land became available not far from our HQ. I think it has good potential as a business location, though it's kind of in the middle of nowhere. But there's constant traffic past it on a major highway that stretches from southern to northern Kansas. There are college towns north of us, so this road gets a lot of traffic, especially during certain times of the year. I think of that land in relationship to the marketplace of people who drive past it, not in terms of any kind of specific business a person might put there. It would succeed best by serving the prospects who pass on a daily, weekly, or monthly basis.

So again: it all starts with thinking about the prospect, then moves on to figuring out what they want, then finding ways to deliver that to them at good value, proving to them along the way that you and you alone can provide the benefits and deliver what they're seeking.

Now, I'll admit that there *are* a few businesses that just want all the customers they can get, because the direct marketplace is tiny—either because they're limited in their extent (like a mom-and-pop grocery store in a small town) or because they serve a special niche. But those businesses are relatively rare. The rest of us have to find a way to pull in the people we need while repelling the rest.

It's not always easy. About 25 years ago, Russ von Hoelscher ran business opportunity ads in supermarket tabloids like the *National Enquirer*. These are considered secondary markets, but he thought, "Hey, it's worth a shot!" Well, he did a little legitimate business... but mostly he had to deal with the kooks that came out of the woodwork. People started sending him stuff about alien abduction, and asking him silly questions about flying saucers and the Mayan connection to the end of the world (we all know how that worked out now, don't we?), and so on. It's a lively, unorthodox marketplace, and for some types of advertising it can be a very good one—but not for our kind.

One area where I think the tabloids excel is with their headlines. Every marketer should study tabloid headlines, because they really grab your interest and get the blood pumping. You can use them as models for your own marketing, even if your products and services are completely different from anything you see in such publications.

The chief reason Three-Step Marketing works is because it's such a simple formula. As I've pointed out, marketing can get too complicated if you let it; so the more you can focus on the basics, the better. That's one reason I myself pulled out of advertising in the tabloids—because, like Russ, I couldn't attract the people I wanted without attracting the ones I didn't, some of whom were absolutely insane. You've got to be able to attract the right folks while filtering out the wrong ones; ultimately, it's not so much, "Can I make money?" that you should ask yourself, it's "Can I make money in the right market by attracting only the right people?

As for trust, I'll never forget our very first expensive seminar, for which we charged over $5,000. I was incredibly nervous, so imagine how I felt when one customer grabbed my hand and wouldn't let go. He looked me in the eye and kept asking, "Are you for real? Are you for real?" Back then, I was so scared I didn't understand what the hell he meant. Now I do. What he was trying to say was, "Can I trust you? Can I *really* trust you?"

People in every market are looking for businesses they can trust, and it's up to you to prove to them beyond any doubt that they *can* trust you.

Marketing Secret #15: The Tugboat Analogy

I got this one from the late, great marketing guru Gary

Halbert. It's called the Tugboat Analogy, and it can make you a fortune with Two-Step and Three-Step marketing. It's been worth millions to us, and it can be worth millions to you, too.

The lesson here is simple and straightforward. Tiny tugboats can maneuver huge ships in and out of port, but in order do so, they have to attach enormous, heavy steel cables to those ships. This is almost impossible to do in one step—in fact, to get those massive cables to the big ships, they start with a series of ropes. First, a relatively small rope is thrown from the tugboat to the big ship. It's tied to a bigger rope, which the people on the ship use to haul in a bigger rope, and on up in size until a big hawser is tied to a massive steel cable that they can then tighten up and tie down.

It all starts with a little step, but ultimately, the tugboat—practically a toy compared to an oil tanker or cargo ship—takes complete control of a huge ship. I think this makes a great metaphor for marketing. No matter how big your efforts eventually get, you can't start out by heaving a huge cable overboard—that is, by offering people your $6,000 seminar from the word go. You may get a few takers, but you won't make any profit.

Ah, but if you start with a tiny step, and then follow it up with bigger and bigger steps as your prospects respond, you'll build a relationship in which they come to trust you and are willing to invest more of their time and money with you. Most people try to do too much too fast. Instead, make it easy for people. Let them take a series of small steps that naturally lead to those bigger steps. Think deeply about this, starting with the end in mind and then working backwards. What's the ultimate goal or objective that you're trying to accomplish?

Last Secret, I mentioned a new business model we're trying to get off the ground. We're trying to make a $3,000 sale to a brand-new prospect as fast as possible. Our entire marketing strategy hinges on our ability do so. But we know it's going to take a series of smaller steps to get there, so we're testing a very simple starting process. In this case, we're sending out postcards and direct mail packages where we offering a free report and a free consulting service—a $99 value.

It's all tied around something we believe people in this market will get very excited about. That leads to a $99 sale, and *that* leads to the $3,000 sale. It's all tightly interconnected, and we have to be very careful with how the small ropes tie to the bigger ropes that connect to the steel cables. We know we can't just ask a brand-new prospect for three grand.

I'm even using mind-mapping software from the Internet, and I'm not exactly an early-adopter when it comes to software. But the thing is, they've made this software so simple that even a child could learn how to use it. I'd suggest you try it yourself; you can find all kinds of free mind-mapping software, and for that matter other kinds of software that also helps you plan and plot and think things through. In any case, whether you do so with software or paper or other people, brainstorm it as much as possible first.

After analyzing all the things I've learned over the years, it's clear that this approach works best for marketing. Start with baby steps, test the results, and let them lead you to greater and greater steps that can ultimately flood you with money. It all starts by getting the prospect to raise their hand with a cheap or free offer. It introduces you to them, and most importantly, them to you. This has worked effectively for us for decades, and there's no doubt it will keep working just as effectively in the future.

Bring people into your business with an exciting offer that costs them very little, giving them so much that they say, "Wow! If for $10, $99, or $199 I can get *this* much value from this company, I'm sold! Can you imagine what they'll give me if I *do* spend the $2,995?" Of course, you must provide tremendous value when you start charging people that much. Continue to provide value, value, and *more* value as the price goes up. That's how to do business if you want to be truly successful.

Now, you can probably sell $20 products all day long without developing trust or otherwise building a relationship. But if you're selling premium-priced products or services, then you *do* have to build that relationship. You have to make it easy for people to take small steps that lead to the big step of purchasing your more expensive package. You can't just immediately make that expensive offer to them. You have to wait until there's some trust built up there. People will be more likely to accept your high-dollar offers if they already have a relationship with you.

The next time you're on one of the coasts, try to catch a tugboat in action. They move slowly, but in the end they get the big boat to where it needs to go. In exactly the same way, you can move customers from non-trust to trust, from small sales to big ones.

Marketing Secret #16:
Determine What Your Customers Really Want

I've already discussed this somewhat, which just goes to show how interrelated these topics really are. But it's worth repeating: in order to maximize your profits, you have to know what your customers really want. Dig deep; get into their psyches. Find out not just what they *say* they want, but what's in their hearts.

One thing that most of us are after is personal recognition of some sort. Our world is so impersonal these days that you can do a tremendous amount of good simply by acknowledging people as human beings. People are also interested in getting rid of pain, whether it's physical, psychological, or financial. If you can ease their pain, they'll jump for joy as they give you their money. Of course, that connects directly to longevity. Even born-again Christians still want to live long, fulfilling lives before they get their ultimate reward. Keep these things in mind as you develop your business.

Here at M.O.R.E. Inc., we're always looking for what we call the "irresistible offer"—the perfect combination of products and services that carries a message so right that people simply cannot refuse it. When you've got that irresistible offer in place, then the money can flood in faster than you know how to intelligently spend it. Again, this assumes that you start with a market that's big enough. If your market is a tiny town, representing fewer than 1,000 prospects, then your success will be limited even with the most irresistible offer.

Now, I won't try to tell you any of this is easy; it can take a long time to come up with the right answers. Here at M.O.R.E. Inc., we put plenty of work into it. We have long meetings where all we do is talk about what our best customers want most, what they respond to best. We ask ourselves, "What's worked best for us before? What are other people doing right that *we* should be doing? Can we adapt those ideas for our use?"

100 MARKETING SECRETS

As I've noted before, in large part people are driven by emotions like greed and selfishness—which I'm not condemning. We're just talking about spending money here, not necessarily about behaviors that represent those people as a whole. In terms of their disposable income, so what if people only think, "What's in it for me?" Good old radio station WIIFM! And speaking of radio, there's an old rock 'n roll song from the '60s by The Doors with a line that goes, "We want the world and we want it NOW!" That's how the marketplace is—they want it all, right away.

Know whatever that means to your prospects. Learn the right combination of elements to unlock the millions and millions of dollars available in your marketplace.

The WIIFM combination always stems from a selfish set of desires, and that's fine. It drives our economy, and to a certain extent it drives the world. It can be obviously selfish or apparently altruistic, but when you get right down to it, we want to spend our money on the things we're interested in.

It doesn't necessarily have to be something you want for yourself; it can be charitable giving. Even when you donate your money to a nonprofit organization, you usually do that from some self-centered desire. We put our money where our hearts are. If we want the latest gadget or gizmo, we'll buy it out of the desire to use or be seen with it. If we want a brand-new car, we buy it because we want to people look at us as we cruise down the road, applauding us for our good taste. So when we donate to a nonprofit, we do it because we feel some selfish connection to that organization.

When you flip that around and you look at it from the marketer's perspective, you have to realize that when they look at you, your prospects are all trying to figure out how you can give them what they want better than anybody else. Do you offer the greatest service, the best product/service in your category, the best prices, or some combination of the above? How can you satisfy their desires better than anyone else?

While it's true that the triggers vary between marketplaces, it all it comes back to this core principle of knowing your prospects in an intimate way, seeing through their eyes to the things that best fulfill their desires and sense of self-interest. If you can't do that, if you can't focus fully upon the reality that it's all about them rather than you, then they'll choose to do business with someone else. If you *can* make it about them, then you start from a point a lot closer to sales than if you make it about your product or company.

Marketing Secret #17:
How to Morally Cash in on
Bait-and-Switch Advertising

To many people, the term "bait-and-switch" is an immediate turnoff, because it's associated with scams and conmen. And that's justifiable, because true bait-and-switch advertising is illegal—it's morally, ethically, and legally indefensible. But there *is* a principle behind it that you can reputably and legally use, and it can be of practical use to your business. The idea for this marketing strategy came from one of our friends and colleagues, marketing expert Dan Kennedy.

We call this model Cashing In On Bait-And-Switch Advertising because it's similar to real bait-and-switch advertising—though again, understand that we're not advocating that as such. Again, that's simply not acceptable... but this particular use of that principle is. Here's how a bait-and-switch scam works: You tell someone you're going to give them something for their money, and then once they pay you, you switch the item out for something cheap or useless. That's evil, and shame on you if you try it. But what you *can* do, completely aboveboard and legally, is sell them exactly what they want—and give them what they need along with it.

Here at M.O.R.E. Inc. we love hosting seminars and similar live events for our clients; we've probably done hundreds since we first started out in 1988. We believe these events are some of the best ways possible for us to share our marketing expertise with our clientele. We provide valuable content at these events, and usually the people who attend them end up loving them. But here's the thing: if we were to promote only the event itself, most people probably wouldn't come. Events as such are hard to sell.

That means we have to find creative ways to offer these events to our clients, so we always wrap them around an opportunity that we know they'll want to respond to. In this way, we've taken something we love to do and combined it with something they want. Once they're there, we know they'll have a good time and benefit greatly. That's an excellent way to cover both sides of the equation.

In the movie *Mary Poppins*, there is a song that goes, "Just a spoonful of sugar helps the medicine go down..." Modern pharmacists have taken this to heart by combining medicines and vitamins with gummi bears or other candy, or at least by adding attractive flavorings to make children's medicines more palatable. You can use the same principle in your business, just as we do with our popular events.

Suppose that in your business, you've got things you know your prospects and customers really need, but you have a hard time providing those things to them at a profit because they just don't want to buy them. You can use this strategy to give them what they need by combining those things with what they want, all in one acceptable package. That way, you cover both sides of the coin; and if you think about it, you're serving them in a higher way than if you were just giving them what they wanted. It's perfectly legal, moral and ethical, and it's a way you can use what would ordinarily be an unthinkable concept in a constructive manner.

Here's one way we use this method. We'll sell a great program at a great price, and then throw in a free seminar—one that would ordinarily sell for thousands of dollars. If I do say so myself, it's an ingenious way to get people to come to seminars who normally wouldn't. They'll see the offer and realize that except for travel expenses, they can attend this expensive event for free. Even the food is usually taken care of. Their response? "I'd better go!"

Consider how you can use the same method in your own business; just about anyone can adapt it in one way or another. And keep in mind that, like all the secrets I've included in this chapter, it's still based on giving people what they want. It just so happens that in this case, their desire is creatively combined with a shot of what they need. This puts a unique twist on the whole thing—a twist that's been worth some very good money to us, and can be profitable to you too.

We're giving people what they need, even while we're selling them what they want. We're incentivizing them to step up and take some medicine that will keep them healthy, even when they don't want to.

Marketing Secret #18:
Push it Until You Break It, Then Fix It

This secret comes from the billionaire Clark MacLeod, who runs a company called Telephony out of Cedar Rapids, Iowa. According to *Forbes* magazine, the secret of his success is testing things to failure: he pushes something until it breaks, and then he fixes it.

That concept leapt right out at me, and I immediately saw how it could work for any business. Admittedly, applying it requires a certain type of bold, audacious mindset. Well, back in the 16th century, a fellow named Thomas Fuller pointed out: "Boldness in business is the first, second, and third thing." The problem is, most small business people have forgotten that, if they ever learned it at all. They don't have big enough goals.

You've got to stop chasing rabbits and start hunting lions. You've got to demand more from yourself. You've got to set higher goals, push it until it breaks—and then fix it. Then push it more until it breaks again, fix it again, and repeat the process.

Keep moving forward. Success in any business enterprise stems from being more aggressive than most, being willing to undertake big things that scare you because they're so big—but that have the potential to make you much more money than you've ever dreamed of.

Here's the first of two major points I want to emphasize in relation to McLeod's secret: you never know how far is *too* far until you break it—whatever that means to you. Your breaking point may be where it all stops working, where it feels like it's going to crash, or where you feel you just can't go on anymore. Most people never go far enough, however they define it. They never reach the breaking point, so they never truly know what they can achieve. The second point I want to make is this: your best will keep getting even better. The more you push, the further your limits will expand. As you push, you develop new knowledge, skills, and abilities that can take you farther.

I realize that some of this is intangible—and yet I know that people like Clark MacLeod, people who are making huge amounts of money, use this principle on a daily basis. When McLeod says you should push until it breaks and then fix it, he's telling you to always demand more from yourself, your business, and your marketplace. Never rest on your laurels and just be content.

Most of us get too comfortable after a while. We grow complacent and want to wall ourselves up in our little comfort zones, instead of pushing ourselves and our businesses to the limits and beyond. Well, once that happens, you're in trouble. On the other hand, when you become *un*comfortable, worried that things aren't working out very well, you dig in and do more to push yourself. That's how you drive great results: don't get too comfortable. Some of the most powerful entrepreneurs in the world have discovered that even after they've made millions or billions of dollars, they have to keep pushing or they'll stall out.

And really, at some point the money stops mattering so much; it's just a way of keeping score. For people like Bill Gates and the late Steve Jobs, the accomplishment is really what matters. If they run a little scared, they push a little harder—because they don't want anyone to overtake them or wreak havoc with their businesses. If nothing else, they're just trying to stay sharp. They're not going to let themselves sit back and do nothing, because otherwise, they know they'll stagnate. In the modern business world, you're either moving forward or you're moving backwards. There's no standing still.

And yet most prefer to let things roll along, hoping they can maintains enough momentum to make it to the next downhill slope. That's the lazy way to approach things, and ultimately, "lazy" translates to "bankrupt." Nonetheless, they keep thinking, "Maybe next week will be a better week"... but they don't do much to make that come true.

Push it until it breaks; then go back to the drawing board and study it, looking for things to improve on. Be aggressive about it, and don't worry about the possibility of breaking it in the first place. Yes, you have to be careful, and you have to be realistic in some situations, not just stupidly throwing away what you've built up. But business is based on calculated risk—never forget that.

You have to push hard at everything. The reason we call our core marketing strategies "Ruthless Marketing" is because they're aggressive, the basis of a marketing philosophy that doesn't believe in sharing with the competition. It means going all out to take the largest possible percentage of the market share away from everyone else. If you're just in it to build something that's self-sustaining, just successful enough to pay your bills, then why are you in business in the first place? You'll never be a billionaire—and you'll probably never be a millionaire.

But you can be king of the hill if you put this billionaire's formula into place. "Push until it breaks, and then fix it." Now, you might find that it never breaks, no matter how hard you push it; but that's fine too. I promise you, you'll still go much farther than you would if you'd just let it do its own thing.

Be aggressive with your marketing. Go all out. Build the largest customer base you can, and take care of your existing customers as well as you do your new ones. That's where almost all your profits are going to come from. This principle, combined with all the others I've taught you in this book so far—and the ones that follow—will give your business the shot in the arm that it needs.

The late, great Peter Drucker, the world's foremost management guru, once said that the only two things in a business that make you money are marketing and innovation. Everything else is a cost. While I believe that there may actually be a few other items that make you money— particularly building a solid core of knowledgeable staff members—I think Drucker was right on the mark with marketing and innovation. Both require a dogged tenacity and creativity, and those are factors that the Marketing Secrets in this chapter epitomize.

Marketing Secret #19:
Learn to Be a Great Marketer

To be a great marketer, you have to *want* to be a great marketer. This is one of the factors that separate the wheat from the chaff, the true entrepreneurs from the wannabes and dabblers. In other words, you have to spend some serious time and effort deeply studying the field of marketing, so that you understand it fully—both in general, and in your particular marketplace. Soak up as much information in your field as you can, until you become an expert at what you do. As I pointed out in an earlier chapter, people love to buy from experts. That's one way to get a leg-up in the marketplace, especially among people who don't know you yet and have no reason to trust you or your company. If you're an expert, they'll give you the benefit of the doubt.

You should also know what your competition is doing—always. I'll never forget reading the autobiography of Sam Walton, the man who founded Wal-Mart; I learned a lot from him, and it's stuck in my mind for years. One thing that especially appealed to me was that Walton spent hundreds of hours in Kmart stores in his early days—probably longer than any actual Kmart executive did—just studying what they were doing right and what they were doing wrong. In fact, he said he'd been thrown out of more Kmart stores than any other person in history. Why did he do this? Because Kmart was his #1 competitor at that time.

It's fair to say that his company has practically destroyed Kmart today. He took the best of what they were doing well, did the opposite of what they were doing badly, and built Wal-Mart into the mercantile empire we see today. He outcompeted them in almost every market, and they were unable to adjust to the challenge. Whether he called himself one or not, Sam Walton was a Ruthless Marketer. He set out to serve the customers the best, most profitable way he could, while taking away as much market share from the competition as possible.

This is a lesson for all of us. As a marketer, you must learn from your competition, regardless of your field. If already you're the #1 provider for your marketplace, then you're the target of all of the others who want to be #1; so you have to stay on your toes. If you're not #1, find out what #1 is doing, both right and wrong, and take the proper steps forward based on what you've learned. If you do that, you can achieve major marketing success—because they're doing many things right if they're already the leader in the market. But chances are, they're also making some key mistakes. Turn those mistakes around, and you can't help but get ahead of them.

Another thing that's ultra-important is that you have to meet the customers. Too many small business owners sit in the back, overlooking the help as the help handles the customers. Instead of being remote, come out of your office and meet the people buying your products and services. Find out what they're really looking for; what are their true desires? What can you do to provide them? If you get a lot of business by phone, then you'd better handle some of the sales calls yourself, so you know exactly what's going on in your business. Steve Jobs of Apple fame used to take technical service calls occasionally to keep his skills sharp.

To be a great marketer, you have to understand your business, you have to understand the customers in your business, and you have to understand the competition. Once you develop a good understanding of all three, you're going to make a lot of money. This is such a simple principle, and yet most people just never seem to get it. Maybe that's because it's all based on learning by doing: on becoming a master marketer simply by going out there and getting started.

That's how you become the next Bill Gates or Steve Jobs: you get out there and start marketing, absorbing knowledge like a sponge, trying new things out, and rolling out big with the things that really work. Just like in pro sports, you only become a superstar by becoming a star first. You have to put a lot of work into it, and become great over time. No one has yet figured out how to turn greatness on and off like a spigot; it's something most people don't recognize anyway until they're looking back on it.

This isn't something that just happens by magic, or like a lucky lottery win. You get there because you're committed and because you're dedicated to doing what it takes to become a master marketer. Just like a superior athlete or a top actor, you reach superstardom by training and hard work and dedication. Sometimes people become "overnight successes," but usually these successes were preceded by many, many years of effort, training, and study, all focused on becoming the very best they could be. They just seemed like "overnight" successes because they were under everyone's radar before that, working their tails off. It usually happens as a result of being completely sold on the goal you're trying to reach. Becoming a master marketer doesn't happen by accident. You don't just stumble upon greatness.

Now, I can imagine some people saying, "Why would I be willing to go through all that work?" Well, how else are you ever going to make a lot of money? No matter what anyone tells you, there's no way to build a fortune without putting your all into it. This is what drives star athletes to spend 5-6 hours a day in the gym every day for a decade, pushing themselves constantly beyond their limits. If they hit the peak of their prowess, they can make millions of dollars and be set for life. Becoming a great marketer can do the same: it can make you a multimillionaire, if that's what you want to achieve.

Business is the great equalizer. I know there are problems in America, but thank God that in this country, you can still start a business for next to nothing. You can go from poverty to being a multimillionaire simply by getting involved in the game and putting your heart into it. There are plenty of people who have done so already, and there are more who are doing it right now. Great marketing is the secret that makes that happen. Marketing is all about attracting and retaining the largest possible number of the very best buyers in your marketplace. Those people are out there right now. Learning to become a great marketer will help you to attract those people and get them coming to you rather than your competition.

Everybody should read the biography of Sam Walton. He was an incredible man, a man who put his business at the heart of everything he did. His family knew that his business was his central focus. They hated going on vacation with him, because that meant they had to stop at every single discount center along the way. The kids would sit in the car with their mother in the hot parking lot, while Sam was inside with a legal pad, walking down the aisles taking notes, taking it all in and spying on the competition.

Incidentally, this kind of spying is much easier to do today, now that we have the Internet. The Internet has got to be the greatest legal espionage tool ever for the marketer, because you can easily find competitors' sites, borrow good ideas, and see what they're doing wrong. Everything's right out there in plain sight—all kinds of ideas for making tons of money, if you can adopt or adapt those ideas to make them your own, and find ways to implement them.

A few years ago, Russ von Hoelscher had the chance to meet Jerry Buss, the owner of the Los Angeles Lakers. If Buss isn't a billionaire, he's very close to it. Jerry asked him, "What do you do, Russ?" and Russ replied, "I'm into marketing and business." And Buss said, "You know something? With all the star status we have with the Lakers, from Kobe Bryant on down, the one thing I've learned is that if you want to be super-successful, you can never stop marketing."

Take it from a man who's richer than most of us put together: marketing is the thing that makes you the most successful. Even if marketing isn't your forte, if you're in business I think you should learn the difference between good and bad marketing. Now, you don't have to be a copywriter; you don't have to prepare jingles for TV and radio or write the direct mail copy. You can hire that out. But you do have to be able to tell the difference between good marketing and bad, that which will serve you well and that which will not.

Marketing Secret #20:
The Secret Desire Millions of People Desperately Want to Fill

This is a great secret, because not only do most people not realize they have this desire, but most marketers don't realize they have it either. So first, I'll tell you what this desire is, and then I'll discuss how to cash in with it. Just by knowing this, you'll be ahead of not only your competitors in your marketplace, but you'll also have an advantage over your prospects. There are only 11 words in this secret desire, and it's simple as can be—but it drives millions of people to buy billions of dollars worth of products and services each year. I promise you this will make a difference in your bottom line if you find ways to tap into it. Here it is: The whole world is looking for an easier, softer way.

Everybody wants easy answers and quick solutions. They

want to take all the pain away so they can go back to sleep. Yes, I'm telling you most of the world would rather be "asleep." They want to make bad things go away so they can get back to just existing. That may sound harsh, but it's the truth. And if you know the truth, it'll set you free.

The whole world is looking for an easier, softer way—and you can make money by giving it to them. You already know that most people will pay more for the things that they want than for the things that they need. That's why people are always looking for coupons on staples like toilet paper and shampoo and all the things you buy at the grocery store. They're always looking to get the price down as far as possible. But when they go out for a night on the town, they're willing to spend tons of money on a steak dinner and a bottle of wine—enough to feed their family for a week.

They'll go out and live it up for one evening because that gives them something they want—even though technically, it's still food. It still provides for a basic need that we all have. People want to have a good time, and they're willing to spend money on that.

Again, what people really want is an easier, softer way. They're looking for solutions, for things that will allow them to get back to their mindless existence.

That's the harsh reality. Think about the stuff we watch on TV these days—it's mindless. People don't want to think too much. They want an easier, softer way to get through life. They don't want any pain, they don't want any frustration, just easy solutions to all the things that go "wrong" in their lives.

There's a handy marketing formula call ADIA. I didn't

invent it, but I've found it amazingly useful. It stands for Attention, Interest, Desire, and Action. It's a very simple formula, easy to discuss, and really helps you cash in with this principle.

The first thing to do is to get their ATTENTION. You can do that through a headline in a sales letter or an ad, or on TV or radio—whatever you do to get people to consider your offer and the benefits it provides. How can you attract them with the promise of a softer, easier way of doing whatever it is they want?

Next, stimulate their INTEREST. Offer them a promise of relief for the pain they're in, or the things that make their life difficult—their busy schedule, their obesity, their ingrown toenail, their need to pay the mortgage. Here's where you point it out to them.

Now you need to generate a DESIRE for the benefits you offer. Build that desire in them. Finally, you want them to take ACTION—and you need to tell them exactly what action to take. Of course, that should be to order your product or service, so they can get the relief they need to get back to that existence they really like and want.

Now, this isn't something that a lot of people like to talk about, and it *is* a secret desire; even the ones who realize it in themselves rarely admit it. It's embarrassing to admit that you're only looking for an easier way of life—but we all are, even in the business-to-business market. This permeates all marketplaces. Business owners are looking for easier, softer ways to get things done in their businesses. Everyone else is looking for easier, softer ways to exist, for solutions to take away the pain or the problems or whatever frustrations they're experiencing. If you can provide those solutions, the profits will come rolling in.

People also want to make money fast. They want to be able to save money. They want to get rid of all of the pain they experience—and they want it all done now. Attention, Interest, Desire and Action are all very important aspects of profiting from this tendency. In many ways, the most important factor is Desire—because if you learn as a marketer how to build desire among your customers, then you'll get their attention, you'll get their interest, and you'll have them take the action and give you their money.

People are looking for instant results—turnkey solutions where someone else does it all for them. There's a line in the movie *Hustle and Flow* where a man says to a woman, "Look, why don't you just let me do the thinking for us?" I love that line, because it really does represent what a lot of people are looking for in real life. It's not because they're stupid, or even lazy. I think that part of it is just the fact that we're all inundated with too many choices these days. Our lives feel overwhelming.

You need look no further than the Internet for the reason. The consumer has much more power now than ever before. Yet with that power comes a ton of decisions—they're frustrated, they're overwhelmed, they're confused, and they just want you to do the thinking for them. People *always* want the result without the work. Always.

Recently, I was watching an infomercial about extreme workouts—unlike all the other exercise infomercials where you can have a great body in only two minutes a day, this is actually the opposite, where they were really working and pushing hard. They all had these great bodies, and I told my wife, "I just want the hard body without the hard work." In a way, that's what everybody wants.

100 MARKETING SECRETS

We're just now entering a brand-new marketplace. Our first test pieces were getting ready to go out to this marketplace—and suddenly we realized that the products and services we're selling don't offer enough of this "done for you" simplicity. They're not turnkey enough, not instant enough. We were actually trying to teach people too many things they didn't want to learn. So we had to revamp our product line so we could create instant, turnkey solutions.

That's what the market has evolved—or devolved—into. If you want to make a lot of money, you definitely have to move in that direction.

CHAPTER THREE

SECRETS 21-30

Marketing Secret #21:
Six Reasons Why You Must
Build Your Marketing Systems

As I've pointed out before, marketing consists of all of the things you do to attract and retain the largest possible number of the best customers in your marketplace. You get people to seek you out, make it easy and rewarding for them to do business with you, then get them to come back again and again. How well and to what degree you can do that will determine, in large part, the amount of money you make. Here are six reasons why you must have your own effective marketing system:

1. A good marketing system helps you pre-sell your prospective buyers.

2. It will attract the very best prospects and get them to come to you, while repelling the wrong people.

3. It proves you can give the prospect everything they desire.

4. It establishes your true value and helps build the credibility and rapport.

5. It sells them on your unique selling position: what's different about you as opposed to all your competitors.

6. It continues to resell them again and again.

You can make this so that it's automatic, too. How do you do it? Well, I could teach a three-day seminar showing you how to create a sustainable marketing system, and even then we would barely scratch the surface of all of the possibilities. That's the bad news: that it can take a long time to learn how to do these things. The good news is, the basics are simple, and you can earn while you learn. In fact, let me just tell you how simple it can be, and then I'll give you a tip on how you can learn how to do this yourself.

We've got a good marketing system that's out there working for us as you're reading this. We use direct-mail as our primary marketing vehicle, 52 times a year—that is, we send out a direct-mail package to prospective buyers once a week. These are people with a history of purchasing the kinds of products and services we sell. We're working with a mailing list broker who hunts down these mailing lists for us, and we send out a direct-mail package that offers the prospect a low-cost or even a no-cost offer.

Our current offer is absolutely free. If a prospect is interested, all they have to do is fill out the order form, then mail or fax it in—or, they can just call our office and we'll send them a lead fulfillment package. That package answers every possible objection about the offer. It's a *huge* package that tells them exactly why the product or service we have to offer is worth far more than the money we're asking them to give us in exchange.

But we don't stop there. We also work closely with six professional sales reps who strive to develop relationships with all the prospective buyers who raise their hands and ask for the lead fulfillment package. Our salespeople attempt to build a rapport, and to discover any objections they might still have before they're ready to buy.

We also have a series of sequential follow-up mailings that go out after somebody sends for the package. We follow up like crazy, continuing to apply pressure to buy and to prove to them that what we have is everything we say it is—and more. Once we do get their business, we continue to offer them related products and services. The goal is to get people to come back and buy from us repeatedly.

That's a simple marketing system that works like clockwork, automatically. Marketing Director Chris Lakey and I put it together. Sometimes it takes us months to create a good marketing system, considering all the initial lead generation material, lead fulfillment materials, and follow-up materials that have to go out. But once it's all put together right, it works like a well-oiled machine. It allows us the freedom to just sit back and create *more* new marketing systems.

How did we learn to do this? We observed how other people did it. The secret here is to find good marketers who have created dynamic, profitable marketing systems (whether via direct mail, print ads, or the Internet), then send away for their stuff. Do some business with them. Save all their copy and study it. The best way you can learn is by modeling your systems after those of your competitors (whether direct or indirect) who are doing a great job with their own marketing systems.

Automatic systems that are easily duplicatable are best, because then you can sell the processes. Again, that's what people are looking for: easy, soft systems. The best marketers have those kinds of systems in play, whether they're in your field or not. You may well be able to adapt anyone's methods to your field. Incidentally, the truly sharp marketers are those who are looking for comrades—affiliations with other marketers with whom they're not in direct competition. This lets them wash each other's backs by recommending each other's services to their customer bases.

Look at the whole spectrum of marketing. Don't just look at what *you're* doing; open your mind to the possibilities and think deeply about them during your marketing research time. Ponder how you can improve yourself as a marketer, and what you can do to increase your business, to take better care of your current customers and bring new customers into the fold. It becomes very exciting, almost like a game. Sadly, most business owners never do this kind of thinking; they just take what people present to them. They run ads in the Yellow Pages and maybe a little newspaper advertising, and occasionally someone will present a new marketing idea that they'll try out—but they never really consider developing unique, automatic marketing systems.

It all starts with attracting the right prospects and repelling the wrong ones. You can go a long way towards success just by doing that. By the time you've got your automatic systems in place, you've narrowed your group of prospects to the people you know are most likely to respond to your offers and become your best customers. There's no point in trying to sell to people who don't want to buy what you have to offer. We're in the direct-mail business, and I hear people talking about how the post office handles so much "junk mail," as they call it.

People will talk about how they don't like to receive all

90

that junk in the mail—and some truly *is* junk mail. Those are the things coming in that you're completely uninterested in. That's done purposefully, believe it or not. If you're the wrong kind for that particular product or service, the mailing won't interest you.

Now, that's not to say that all the "right" people are going to respond; while they may be interested, they may not have the money at the moment, or may be about to move, or they may not have time to consider the offer right then, or they may have sworn off buying things from direct mail. For whatever reason, that offer wasn't the right offer at that time. That doesn't mean you've missed your target, and in fact they may end up buying from you eventually—assuming you don't give up on them too quickly.

You've targeted them for a good reason—say, because of a purchase history, or because they're a subscriber to a certain magazine. You've reached out to them based on something you know about them that makes them the kind of person you're trying to attract. By doing that, you're automatically repelling everybody else. That's Step One of the system. You go from there by proving you have compelling advantages over all your competitors, and that you can give them exactly what they want.

If you don't start with the right person or group, if you select the wrong mailing list, your offer is going to be dead in the water—and your company's probably not going to be far behind.

Marketing Secret #22:
The Single Most Important Thing to Know About Success

It took me many years to learn this one: the single most

important thing to know about success is that the journey matters more than a destination, just like when you're taking a trip by car, plane, or boat to some special or exotic place. Just getting there is special, because you have a chance to spend a lot of time with friends or family.

Sometimes, you have more fun going somewhere than when you're actually there. Not always—sometimes when you get there, it's great too—but the journey itself is usually part of the fun, if only because of the sense of anticipation. Later, you may realize that you're better off simply having made the trip. Success is a journey like that, and it's one that you should never, ever worry about. You'll have your ups and downs, but if you keep your eye on the prize and keep moving forward, great things will happen.

All the toys—the big houses, the hot cars, the expensive boats—are great, but what it really comes down to is who you are, what you want to accomplish, and whether or not you're having fun. I've known a lot of people who were poor and unhappy, but I've also known some unhappy multimillionaires. So you've got to put things in perspective. Realize that it's probably not how much money you make that will make you happy; it's how much you enjoy what you're doing.

People say to me, "You spend so much of your waking hours on business. Don't you have other activities you like? Are you a golfer? No. Do you take a lot of vacations? No. So it's business, business, business!" Well, you know something? When you love what you do, it's not just work; it's a combination of work and pleasure.

Most people in the world hate what they do for a living,

but they feel they need to do it in order to survive and support their families. Most of us have been there at some point or another; some of us have permanently moved to that address. And the fact is, there are many people in business who are *also* very unhappy with their lives, even when their businesses are doing well. You don't want to be like that. You should be in business because you *want* to be in business. Sometimes you win, sometimes you lose; but let's face it, it's the race, the chase, that's truly important.

If you can get that straight in your head, I think you're going to be a much happier person—and eventually, a more successful person. Stay in the race. Keep thinking big. Stay curious, and always do the things you like to do as well as the things you don't like, to do but need to anyway. Every job has its unpleasant tasks that you nevertheless have to take ownership of.

If you have problems with this, learn how to fool yourself into thinking you enjoy doing some of those unwelcome tasks. Fake it until you make it. If you can do that and keep a smile on your face, you're going to be fine. As A.L. Williams, the big insurance tycoon, once said: "Just keep moving forward. Things are going to work out. Remember, all you can do is all you can do—but all you can do is enough."

It's not just about the money, or the houses, cars, and fiscal rewards you reap—though that certainly matters, especially if you've been on both ends of the wealth scale like I have. Being rich beats poverty hands down. Still, the important thing is enjoying the journey, taking pleasure in what you do and in helping people. There's a reason why the wealthiest of us are the most charitable of us. Almost half of all the money given to charities in the U.S. comes from the wealthiest 1% of the people in the nation. These people love giving their money away—even though they're held in contempt by many in government, looked down upon as nasty mongrels who are just out for themselves.

That's ironic and unfair, since even above and beyond their tax burden, they're the ones who do the most for society in so many ways—simply because they *can*. They provide jobs; they provide for the charities. So don't be envious of and bad-mouth the rich. Do your best to become one. Keep a smile on your face and a song in your heart and realize that we're here to have fun, not just to make money.

Somehow, this notion escapes so many of us. Some of the most successful people in the world are jaded and unhappy, and end up committing suicide when it seems they have everything. You hear about people who are at the top of their games, at the height of their success, who are hopelessly depressed or abusing drugs or alcohol. Even though it seems they've achieved everything they could possibly want out of life, they're miserable.

Among other things, these stories prove that it's not just about getting to the top of the mountain. While it's great to be there, and it gives you plenty of opportunities to do things, ultimately the journey matters more. What you do along the way is often much more important than what you do once you reach your destination.

You'll have your peaks and valleys. Some things may not go your way; your businesses may fail, or simply not reach the goals you've set for them, or you may hit stumbling blocks that knock you down. The economy may take a downturn, forcing you to shift gears or retool. It's all grist for the experience mill, and if you can learn even the tiniest thing, then you're ahead of the game—no matter how much it hurts at the time. The only true failure is failure to learn. It's all about what you do, how you adapt, and the way you grow and shape yourself to fit your reality.

Even the most successful entrepreneurs have experienced huge failures; in fact, sometimes a failure at one thing forced them to succeed at something else. Sometimes the money comes pouring in faster than you can count it; sometimes you're selling aluminum cans and checking under the couch pillows for enough money to cover the electric bill. Those are just points on a line, though. So while we all want enough money to fill a swimming pool with hundred dollar bills, don't fool yourself into thinking that's all that matters. There are too many examples of people who found that they had achieved everything they were looking for—and it just wasn't enough. So make the pleasure of being in business for yourself one of your goals.

You're a breed apart; you already know that. Most people look at entrepreneurs and think, "How could you possibly be happy? You spend all your time working on your business. You're never on the golf course, and I never see you at the fishing hole anymore. You're never able to go skiing with us." The fact is that most of the people thinking these things are so unhappy with their day-to-day jobs that they have to escape in order to find some pleasure in life. They can't just enjoy their days like I do. When you're truly doing what you love, you find pleasure in your work life.

Part of this is sheer attitude. You've got to learn to love even your unlovable "babies;" by doing so you can get those tasks done so you *can* go on vacation whenever you want. But you don't have to leave town to escape the pain in your daily life. You don't have to go on vacation to find happiness, because every day is like a vacation. You like doing the things you're doing, so you don't have to seek pleasure elsewhere.

In our culture, there's significant resistance to the idea that people can possibly enjoy their businesses that much. Yet consider this: many people spend hour after hour, year after year, working on their hobbies. They're totally absorbed by them, and often they get so good at a hobby that everyone commends their artistry. Or perhaps someone is a talented painter or musician. Well, most people have no problem with those people committing large blocks of their lives to those pursuits. But if you're committed to business—heaven forbid! You're a workaholic, a freak, or a greedy scumbag.

Nothing could be further from the truth. There's nothing wrong with enjoying your work and making money at it. Business is our blank canvas. We are cash flow artists creating with ideas, learning daily from our experiences on the paths we tread. You've got to fall in love with the game to truly succeed.

Marketing Secret #23:
Why You Must Become a Ruthless Marketer

If you want to make all the money that could and should be yours, then you have no choice but to be a Ruthless Marketer. This concept is at the core of our teachings here at M.O.R.E. Inc.—but please, don't misunderstand this concept. When we use the term "ruthless," we're emphasizing being aggressive in your marketing tactics: not to cheat your customers, but to obtain the largest possible market segment. If anyone is hurt, it's your competitors—and you're not in business to help your competitors make a profit.

Ruthless Marketing requires you to serve your marketplace in the best way you know how, so they trust you, depend on you, and are willing to trade their hard-earned money for the benefits only you can provide. Those benefits can be physical, emotional, psychological, financial—you name it. Your goal should be to know your prospects better than they know themselves in some ways, so you can better provide those special benefits.

Ruthless Marketing has nothing to do with being a bad person—quite the opposite. At worse, you're indifferent: to your competitors, to the people uninterested in your products and services, and to the people completely outside your marketplace. The only relationships that matter (aside from those you build within the company) are those with the people in your marketplace, and most specifically with the relatively small group of your best customers. Being a Ruthless Marketer has nothing to do with ripping people off, or doing things that are illegal, immoral, or unethical.

You're out to make the most money you can in your marketplace, within the limits set by the government. Depending on where you live, those constraints may be tight or loose; but you need to learn how to use them to dominate your competitors. Sometimes, the limitations themselves can inspire you, forcing you to be brilliant in order to maximize your success.

You're in business is to serve your marketplace and make a profit in doing so. The only way to succeed at this is to provide them with products and services they find valuable;

otherwise they'll stay away in droves, and who can blame them? Ah, but if you have a product or service the marketplace really wants at a reasonable price, many will realize that what you're selling really is worth more to them than the money in their pockets. Then the exchange happens, because both sides agree that they want it to.

Ruthless Marketing is a strategy, a mindset whereby you decide to become aggressive in your marketplace and do as much business as you possibly can. If you truly believe your product or service will help people, providing them with great value in exchange for their money, then why wouldn't you want to be as aggressive as possible in making them see the need for it?

Let's say, for example that you have a health product that helps people in a specific type of pain. Wouldn't you be doing them a disservice if you didn't tell them about it, if you didn't urge them to buy it every way you could within the guidelines of legality and morality? Let's say I had the cure for cancer, and didn't do everything ethically possible to get people to buy it from me. What kind of schmuck would I look like then? It's in your best interest *and* the prospect's to be aggressive in providing them with every possible opportunity to do business with you.

Ruthless Marketing means not being afraid of doing all you can to get as many people as possible to become your customers. Most people have a certain amount of disposable income available to them; they're going to spend it anyway, so prove to them they're better off spending it with you. Show them you really do have the solution they're looking for. In pursuit of that effort, you have every right to be as aggressive as necessary, especially when you're selling something you really believe in—something that really can make their lives better, more worth living.

If you're not being aggressive enough, you're leaving money on the table. If you're not putting it all out there, then it's your own fault you're not making all the money you want to make. That's what Ruthless Marketing is all about, not mugging people, or cheating them, or otherwise being the guys in the black hats. It's about being ruthless in your determination to be successful, and not caring what your competitors think.

Dick Vermeil won a Super Bowl as coach of the St. Louis Rams, and later he became coach of the Kansas City Chiefs—but early in his coaching career, he was the head coach of the Philadelphia Eagles. At that time, the Eagles were a struggling team. The Dallas Cowboys almost always won the division, and even went on to win some Super Bowls. Vermeil once said, "You know, when I was losing games as the Eagle's coach, I couldn't have better friends than the coaches and people surrounding the Dallas Cowboys, including the owner. They all liked me, and I always heard, 'Dick is a good guy and he's a good coach.'

"In my third year, we started to win a bunch of games and challenged Dallas for the division lead. We beat Dallas—and all of a sudden, the people surrounding the Cowboys started saying, 'That Vermeil is a ruthless SOB. That guy will do any damn thing he can to win a game.' And they didn't say it in a nice way."

Once you start doing well in the industry, whatever your industry happens to be, I guarantee you that some of your competition will start thinking of you as ruthless in any case— even if they thought you were a great guy when you weren't doing so well. But look: as nice as it is to form civil groups and drink flavored coffee together, competition is competition, direct or indirect. You can't afford to be your competitor's friend or feel the least bit of pity for his; you've got to take away his business, to make it yours.

You have to outthink, outlast, and outplay all of your competitors—period. If that's ruthless, then so be it. That's how you grow, and that's how you improve the market. If competitor's any good at all, they'll fight to keep their customers, which will force both of you to improve, which will ultimately better serve the marketplace.

They call it 'competition' for a reason. The more you believe in what you're selling, the more you find a product or service you're passionate about, the more aggressive you'll be in your marketing—and the more you'll feel good about being aggressive. The only times you feel like you might be cheating people is when you don't really believe in what you're selling— so let that serve as an alarm to you.

Marketing Secret #24:
The One Thing You Must Do
Every Day to Guarantee Profits

If you do this one thing, you'll virtually guarantee future sales and profits. It's simple, but you have to do it *every* day, seven days a week. You don't get a day off. Every day, you have to strive to do something that will bring in more sales and profits.

Now, notice that I said *strive* to; it's not always going to work. You'll have your good days and bad days. To really make it work, you need to make a game out of it. Work may be a four-letter word, but it's not a nasty, rotten four-letter word. There's a saying that work is love made manifest; and notice that love is also a four-letter word. So each day, try to have fun with it. Try to take it one step farther then you took it yesterday. Try to consistently come up with new ideas. Search for that next big thing.

If I live to be 100 years old, I'll never forget when we first met Russ von Hoelscher in person. We'd already talked to him on the phone a few times, but we didn't meet until Russ came down and spent a couple of days with us. As we were driving home from the airport, Russ said to us, "Just one idea can make you a million bucks—just one!" He said it in a conversational way, very matter-of-factly; he wasn't trying to preach to us. But I was *very* excited to hear that. A million dollars was a magic number for us then. It wasn't until nine months later that I came up with that million-dollar idea—in the shower, of all places.

But as they say, chance favors the prepared mind. Ever since Russ had told us that all it took was one good, well-executed idea to make a million bucks, I'd been hunting for that idea. Of course, Russ helped us implement that first big idea; and since then, we've been on a hunt for others. We catch them occasionally, too. But as I pointed out in the last Marketing Secret, the thrill is in the hunt, not necessarily the catch.

Recently, I was looking for a very specific type of product we could market or sell, and I found it one Saturday morning. I was so excited I called Chris Lakey right away. I don't normally call him on the weekends, since he's got six kids and he's very, very busy—but I was *so* excited. Sure enough, when he went on the 'Net and saw what I saw, he realized what I did: that it was an idea that could make us *tens* of millions of dollars, no question about it. I *know* that I can sell it, and Chris can definitely sell it, and so can our salespeople. It's something we can all get passionate about.

Salesmanship has gotten a bad rap over the years, due to a few rotten apples. But look: when you've got a quality product or service you really, truly believe in and can get passionate about, and you've got a marketplace with tens of millions of prospects—then you can go out there, share your passion with them, and make millions. It's up to you to find those things to be passionate about, though. You're never going to find them if you don't look, and you've got to look *every single day*.

And again, while the end result matters, it's really all about the hunt. Being originally from Minnesota before he moved to sunny California, my mentor and colleague Russ von Hoelscher has experience with real hunting, mostly for ducks and pheasants—so he can relate to this. Usually you head out early in the morning, while it's still dark and freezing. You sit out there in the blind with your buddies, and you're absolutely in love with it. You're just happy to be there with the guys, so if you get any birds, that's the icing on the cake.

You need to inject that kind of thrill into your business hunt. You may not end up super rich, but at least you'll be striving for the things you believe in, taking care of the customers as best you can. Life is short. I've lost some people important to me over the past several years, and things like that make you realize that you've got to do what you can, and learn to take pleasure in it.

From what I've read recently, those who live the longest and are known to be the happiest are people who have a great spiritual relationship with God. I'm not here to preach to anyone, but it's worth noting that that's an important part of longevity—and it's an important part, apparently, of being satisfied and happy, so put that in your pipe and smoke it along with the rest.

I guarantee you, as you get older, the days will start to fly by. When you're a kid, it takes forever to go from one birthday to the next; even when you're a teen, the days seem to drag. Once you hit your 20s and start getting serious, they speed up—making it all the more crucial that you accomplish something with each day. Even Chris Lakey, who's only 37, is feeling the rush—though that may be because he has six kids who keep him busy. Add that to everything going on at work, and the time really does flies! Even though we have technology here to help us now, we still haven't managed to add a 25th or 26th hour to the day.

If you don't take the time to honestly focus on something every day, then your business is going to suffer—because the days will get away from you. The days turn into weeks, weeks into months... and suddenly things are stagnant, and you wonder where the year has gone. On the other hand, if you do something every day to improve yourself or your business, you won't ever get to a place where you look back and wish you'd done something. You're already doing it. This strategy of being committed to doing something positive for your business every day is well worth the effort and time.

They say it takes like 21 days to build a habit, and this is no different. It may be hard in the beginning, but as you get comfortable doing it, you'll find yourself more and more in tune with this philosophy of daily discovering more ways to make more money in your marketplace.

Marketing basically boils down to math and

psychology, and you'll need to master both to do well at it. That requires some work, sure; but fortunately we live in an age where technology can flatten out the learning curve. In this chapter, we'll take a look at technological and psychological secrets that can help you make the math come out in your favor more often.

Marketing Secret #25:
The Unconventional Approach
to Getting People's Attention

As you may have noticed, it's getting harder and harder to get people's attention these days. They've got their deflector shields up all the time. They're bombarded with every type of advertising you can imagine: online, email, billboards, print, broadcast, you name it. The average person is exposed to advertising thousands of times a day—a ridiculous number of times. So how do you penetrate their shields and get them excited about what you have to offer? You have to be unconventional.

You should at least consider being a little wild and crazy. In every market there are some people who act that way—and they get attention. They don't always do things that are too outrageous, but they may dress or talk in a certain way. That may fit your personality and it might not, but if it does, consider it— because it really can work. We have to wake people up, so sometimes we have to do something crazy to get their attention. We really do have to be different, to be bold.

When you write copy for sales materials or ads, it pays to be dramatic. You should (figuratively) grab the prospect by the shirt collar and say, "Hey, listen to me!" Engage their

imaginations —tease them, taunt them, *compel* them to buy.
Don't do it in a gangster-type way and say, "Listen buddy,
you've got to buy or else"—unless you're just fooling around
and they know it. Just find a compelling way to point out, "You
know something? You really need what I have. Here's something
you really, really want—and I want to supply it to you. You're
fortunate I have it, and that's why you should buy it now."

Great headlines teach us how people can use dramatic
ways to sell. Many people have seen or heard this one: "They
laughed when I sat down at the piano, but when I started to
play..." That caught people's attention for that piano course of
yesteryear. "Dead doctors don't lie" was a big, attention-
grabbing headline once used for a health product. Here's one I
think is very effective: "At 60 mph, the loudest noise you'll hear
will be the dashboard clock." That was an ad for Rolls Royce
many years ago.

Here's a great headline for someone selling silver coins
and bullion. "In 1948, a dollar bill and a silver dollar were worth
exactly the same amount. In 2012, that dollar bill is worth 5.5¢
compared to what it used to be worth in 1948—but that silver
dollar coin is worth $32.30." For someone selling silver, that's
going to grab attention. So when you write copy for your
products and services, try to say something dramatic. Once
you've grabbed someone's attention, you've got a great
opportunity to make a sale. If you can't get their attention, you'll
never be able to sell them anything.

You'd think this would be obvious to all the other
marketers out there... but as you know, most advertising is
boring. It's cookie-cutter follow-the-leader stuff, and everyone
gets the same lackluster results because they're doing and saying

the same things. Then they don't understand why their sales are so low. After all, they're following conventional marketing practice, aren't they?

Sure they are, and that's the problem.

Boring advertising doesn't do the job. You have to go bold or go home. Not just ought to, but *have* to. You have to be outstanding to make people notice—like that old Rolls-Royce ad. Anyone can appreciate a quiet car. That's a big deal, especially to people who've gotten used to noisy ones. To a car buyer at the time that ad was running, that would've been a bigger deal than it is now, since today's new cars are all fairly quiet.

You need to do something to make people stand up and take notice—to make them wonder what it's all about. Just think about the people you're exposed to in the marketing sense. Which advertisements do you pay attention to—the ones that sound or look like everyone else's, or the ones that jump out at you? You can see tons of ads in the newspaper—but which ones stand out? Usually the bolded, larger, or unique ones, the ones that go out of their way to get your attention.

I'll say it again: If you want to captivate your marketplace, if you want to get their attention, you have to be bold. You've got to get out there and *make* them pay attention to you, because there are a lot of things vying for their time, attention, and money. If you don't, they'll find someone else to give their money to, just because you don't stand out.

If you asked 100 different marketing experts for their definition of what marketing is, you'd get 100 slightly different answers. But every single one would agree that a big part of marketing is differentiation. What's different about you? If they're honest, most small business owners will look at their businesses and say, "Nothing, really." If you sell chicken dinners, how do you make yourself stand out from everyone else? You create something like a special recipe of 11 herbs and spice (sound familiar?) Or you can make the lightest, tastiest rolls in town. If you want to get really wild, offer something like fried rattlesnake on the side! Then you'll *really* stand out.

The point is, you have to create this uniqueness. It's up to you. You have to do what your competitors *aren't* doing, and keep on the lookout for unfilled niches.

Here's a quick story about how one man started a small company for only a few hundred dollars, then sold it 30 years later for $1 billion. Tom Monahan of Domino's Pizza built his company with a bold, outrageous message: "Hot, fresh pizza delivered to your door in 30 minutes...or it's free." That's what they became famous for—though they eventually had to give up that slogan. By then, Tom had already sold out to Bain Capital; but let me re-emphasize that he build a billion-dollar business with it.

Consider implementing a promise like that. You may not be selling pizza in 30 minutes or less, but what realistic (yet outrageous) promise can you make to your prospects? A big promise will always get people's attention.

If you're having a plumbing catastrophe, wouldn't you want to hire someone who promised, "We'll have someone at your door to take care of your crisis in 30 minutes or less, or we'll fix it free"? Now, you can't do that unless you're absolutely certain you can get someone there, or you'll lose money instead of making it. But if you *can* do it, that'll really stand out in their minds. You really need to take advantage of bold, unconventional, unique selling points that shake up your marketplace.

We're preparing to do something like that in our marketplace as I write this. I won't go into the specifics, but it's going to shake up our market somewhat. We're offering to give away for free what other people are charging big bucks for. Our offer is unconventional— because it has to be if we expect to make the big bucks.

So look for ways you can be wild and crazy and wake people up!

Marketing Secret #26: Legal Espionage

The term "espionage" may sound a little dicey, but I guarantee you, these methods are all perfectly legal. Frankly, they're a little bold and crazy, too, just like I suggested you try in the last Secret. What I'm going to teach you about in this Secret is how to use the power of the Internet to legally spy on your competitors and steal their best ideas. All the ideas you need in order to acquire more sales and profits are already out there on the 'Net. They're just waiting for you to capture them and put them to work.

The Internet has made it easy to check on what other people are doing in your marketplace. It used to be that if you wanted to discover what your competitor was doing, you had to be willing to spend some money—to buy some things and try to get on their mailing list. Eventually, they'd start mailing you their offers, so you'd be able to tell how they handled things like follow-up and copywriting in general. Then you could take the best of what they were doing, along with the opposite of the worst, and mix it up to make something you could incorporate into your own marketing. In fact, that's still a good practice to follow, especially with your most effective competitors.

It's much easier to determine competitor strategies using the Internet. So far it's the ultimate way to do so. Now, know this: I'm not talking about *really* stealing—about plagiarizing people's copy, blatantly taking their work and calling it your own. That's illegal, and rightly so. But you *can* use their work as a model, and adapt their ideas for your own use. Ideas can't really be copyrighted, which makes what you're doing research. So when I use the term "legal espionage," that's what I mean.

Understand too that the research doesn't have to be limited to your direct competitors. Your best ideas may come from other industries and marketplaces altogether. That's one thing that makes the Internet so great as a research tool; it exposes you to all kinds of things you wouldn't normally be exposed to, and that can cross-fertilize your marketing with new ideas not previously used in your marketplace. In its own way, innovation can be as unconventional as the whackos you see on car commercials.

And speaking of unconventional, people are *really* doing wild and crazy things on the Internet. You have to just to stand out, because the average person stays on a website for only a few seconds. If you can't capture their imagination, if you can't get them to stop and pay attention to your webpage immediately, they're on to something else. And when I say "wild and crazy," I mean things that are entirely legitimate and legal—not people making illegal claims, or outrageous statements designed *just* to capture attention.

The good stuff is easier than ever to find via the Internet, because search engines are always out there, prowling the sites, and they're becoming more and more responsive. There's practically nothing happening on the Internet today that's not captured and indexed by Google, Bing, Yahoo, or the other big search engines. If it's not, then it's not something you want to get involved with anyway.

Now, in order to be outrageous in an innovative, profitable way, you have to gather massive amounts of data first. That lies at the heart of this method, because you're not being innovative if you're just recreating the wheel—even if you honestly think you're being original. Fortunately, you can gather all kinds of information just by doing simple searches related to the type of product or service you're thinking of offering.

The more information, the better. Think of it this way. I've seen Chris Lakey's youngsters playing with Play-Doh. If four want to play and they have only one canister, the Play-Doh won't go very far. If Chris really wants his kids to be creative with the stuff, he needs to buy a giant package that contains several cartons, so they all have enough to build what they want to.

The same is true of research: the more you have, the more you can do with it. So gather as much as possible before crafting your offer, just like someone researching a book. Put the best of it in a "swipe file" you can consult at any time. Spy this way on *all* competitors, both direct and indirect.

I can't count the number of times that Chris or I have been browsing on the Internet, surfing or reading the news wires, and caught a headline that made us think, "Wow! That's a great one!" Sometimes, we can find a way to incorporate it into a marketing campaign. You never know when you're going to have ideas hit you; you might even pick up a usable idea from a novel you're reading. Just about anything can trigger a discovery or breakthrough in the creative process. This works even better when you're deliberately hunting for information.

If you're not using the Internet to spy on your competitors, you're wasting an opportunity to make more money.

Before I move on, I want to return to an idea I touched on earlier. Even if you don't use the Internet for legal espionage, you can still spy on a local or direct-mail competitor by becoming a customer. If they know who you are, then have an employee or relative become a customer. Find out what your competitor is doing, especially if they're #1 in their area or field. Why are they on top? It can't just be because they're the biggest, even if they *are* the biggest—because at one time they weren't.

If there's a really super company in a nearby area, one that's making money hand over fist, it's worth traveling for a while to go there and find out what they're doing—even if they're not a direct competitor. You may still find something you can use; for example, the idea for the fast-food drive-thru window came to a McDonald's VP when he visited a drive-thru bank. There's no harm in going there and looking, so really get into this form of legal espionage too. What are they doing right? What are they doing wrong? How can you offer better service to your prospects? Your goal should always be to beat the competition; so be ruthless about your legal espionage, whether physical or digital.

Speaking of digital: recently, I directed Chris to a website I wanted him to review. Though it was very confusing—in fact, I needed his help to figure out exactly what they were doing, because it's a huge company—they did include one diagram on their website to help explain what they do. I told Chris, "We're going to steal that diagram."

Again, we're not going to plagiarize it, but we're going to adapt something very like it for our use. That's what I meant by "steal."

When you steal, you should steal only from the best. This thing called "creativity" mostly involves piecing together different ideas anyway. It's hard to create in a vacuum; so if nothing else, your espionage further familiarizes you with the existing marketplace. There are all kinds of ideas floating around making other people millions of dollars. All you have to do is combine them in a new way, and you too can make millions.

If you think this is too easy, think again. I've never said any of this was easy, and I never will. While the basic concept is easy, in practice it's complex—especially in today's overcrowded, overhyped marketplace. But the basics are easy to implement. Go on the Internet to look at the websites of your competitors. Go to YouTube, where you can watch them pitching items and services in person. You don't need to focus entirely on your own field; in fact, it's crucial to get that cross-fertilization from other fields.

Don't think of the Internet as a vast wasteland of time-wasters, as many busy people do. While you can spend hours on the Internet doing nothing, there are gems among the dross. If you're looking for them, you're doing productive work, not wasting time. As the Biblical saying goes, there's nothing new under the sun, and that's as true now as it was 2,000 years ago. But there *are* new ways to combine old things to your advantage, so look for them. That's really what this principle is about.

Marketing Secret #27:
Why People Will Buy Almost Anything

I got this idea from a book by a fellow named Forbes Ley, who tells us that people will buy anything that they believe will help them feel better about themselves. Ley is a very successful sales trainer who does huge seminars, mostly out of L.A., so it's safe to assume he knows what he's talking about.

I'll admit that when I first I read that, I thought it was BS—but it got my attention, so I wrote it down and thought about it, because the idea was so different from what I was used to. I've thought about it now for the past few years, and my attitude has changed... so I'd like *you* to think about it.

People want to feel better about themselves. It's a simple statement, yet there's so much truth in it. That desire to feel better is a kind of pain—and you already know people are willing to spend plenty on solutions to their pains.

Let's take a closer look at Ley's idea. First of all, happy people don't spend a lot of money. In fact, you don't *want* truly happy people in your marketplace. The happiest among us don't have many pressing desires to spend their money on. Among the unhappy, on the other hand, there's always some emotional pain to ease, some need to be filled.

What *is* that need? What's driving your sales? Here at M.O.R.E. Inc., we sell business opportunities. Now, you may think people buy business opportunities mostly because they want to make more money—but that's not true. They *think* it is, but what they really want is the end result: big houses, lots of land, new cars, huge bank accounts, large contributions to charity—or just having the people they love feel proud of them. It all comes to making themselves feel better about themselves.

In your marketplace, all your customers and prospects want are the benefits. That's all. The package doesn't necessarily matter. Usually, they're in some type of emotional pain, confusion, or frustration they want to clear up. They're just not happy, and they want the emotional end result they think your product or service will provide.

Now, I'll admit that when I tell you that you don't want happy customers, I'm being a little melodramatic. In one sense, "happiness" is a synonym for "satiable." You want your clientele to be pleased by your customer service, and the products or services they've bought from you, but you don't want them to be sated. Consider Thanksgiving dinner. You pig out for about two hours, and what's the first thing you do when you have a chance? You either rest or take a nap. You've eaten so much you're satiated. You have no desire to eat anymore. In fact, the thought of more food may make you queasy.

Think about it this way: you don't want your customers so full of turkey, dressing, mashed potatoes, and cranberry sauce that they can't find room for a slice of pie.

Yes, we're in business to serve our customers. But we don't want them to be totally satisfied with the first helping, because then they're not going to come back for seconds, though they may return much later when they're hungry again. So a little emotional pain, frustration, dissatisfaction, or just plain hunger drives all markets. Those who profit the most are definitely the ones involved in marketplaces where people are constantly buying products and services so that they can feel better about themselves.

My wife is what they call an early adopter; she has to buy every new electronic gadget that comes along. If Apple releases a new version of the iPhone, she has to have it. She does this because it makes her feel good about herself. I can't explain it any better than that. Does she need a new iPhone every time? No, she just wants one... and since can afford it, she buys it.

Ley has really hit it out of the park with this idea, and there are plenty of ways to express it. A few months back, Russ von Hoelscher was going through boxes of old books and magazines at his home, and found an old *Robb Report* from about 2002. It was fascinating to look through; one article in the magazine showed all kinds of luxurious yachts, great cars, and multimillion-dollar houses. The writer interviewed someone who sold the yachts and asked him, "Why do people spend so much money for these boats?"

The seller, who was apparently very rich himself, said, "Some people want to travel the world in luxury, and they really enjoy being out there on the water in these big beautiful yachts. But you know what it really comes down to? Feeling good about themselves by impressing others." I thought that was pretty telling. Towards the end of the article he said, "After all, these people want to avoid saying, 'Is that all there is?'"

And so they keep buying these toys—if you can call a $10 million yacht a toy.

If you're happy with the status quo, you're not looking

to buy something. That's true of whatever marketplace you're dealing with. If you own a local clothing store, your customers are people who aren't completely happy with their wardrobes—if they were, they wouldn't be shopping for clothes. Similarly, if people are happy with their cell phones or TVs, they're not going to be shopping for the latest and greatest. If they're happy with their waistlines, they won't be buying diet products or gym memberships.

People want to feel better in any number of ways, and that leads them to buy. It's one of the reasons they're almost always willing to spend more money for something they want than for something they need. I'm a consumer of toilet paper, but it's not because I'm unhappy in the bathroom. It's because I need toilet paper. I buy toothpaste for the same reason. I would prefer not to have to buy it, but it's something I have to buy, so I spend as little money as possible on it to get the job done.

But if I want a new book by my favorite author or the latest iPhone app, I'll willingly spend some extra money if it's something I'm eager to own—even if I know the price will go down in a few weeks. It makes me feel better. It scratches an itch.

As a marketer, your challenge is to figure out why people are buying what you sell, and what it is about themselves that they feel better about when they buy it. Then you can advertise in a way that points that out to them, using some of the formulas I've already discussed in this book, like PAS. Point out their pain, agitate it to maximize their discomfort, and offer a solution. At least for the time being, that will make them feel satisfied that they've come to a resolution that rids them of that pain.

So think all this through at a deep level. Your goal is to

know your customers better than they know themselves. That's going to be your edge in the marketplace.

Marketing Secret #28:
Why You Should Establish
Yourself as a Leader

Leaders lead and followers follow. It's been that way since the beginning of time. You have to get it into your head that if you really want to make money, you have to show some leadership. Most people are just waiting for someone to lead them; many, in fact, are eager to have someone tell them what to do. So show them why purchasing your offer is the smartest decision they can make. In fact, just give them some good reasons why your offer's worth the money you're asking, and often, they'll take you up on it.

Most people are followers. It's easy to follow, because it's easiest to stay inside your comfort zone—and it's part of the herd instinct. People also have security issues, where they don't want to think. Sometimes it gives them pain to do so; and that's another reason they're looking for leaders to tell them what to do. People fear taking risks. They may have been dependent on people since childhood, so they know no other type of behavior; or maybe they have poor self-images, or maybe they just don't want to accept the responsibility for their lives. They're looking for someone to tell them what to do.

Some people have no ambition at all, making them followers by default. They also fear failure, lack confidence, and tend to be lazy. They may want to belong to something, but they sure don't want to be part of the leadership. They're unwilling to pay the price; to be a leader, you have do the things other people don't want to. You've got to take the initiative, to take command of the circumstances.

If you're in business, you've already proven to some degree that you have leadership qualities... but I've met many businesspeople who are very poor leaders. If they could change that, they could increase their business many times over.

So think in terms of what you can do to take the lead in your market, to stand out from the mob, to be someone the community looks up to. Implement programs to put your business ahead of everyone else. Leadership isn't always easy, but it skyrockets your chances of success. Think about how you can be a better leader; make it a serious consistent part of your life, and you'll have a much greater chance of being happy and making more money. A self-directed life is much better than life in the herd. When you take the initiative to direct your life, you take control over your very being. Being a follower is just too easy. You can't allow yourself to default in that direction, especially if you ever expect to be great. If you're not willing to do what it takes to become a leader, you'll never reach the pinnacle of success.

You've only got those two options. You can't huddle in the middle ground, because the middle ground doesn't exist. You're either up front innovating, or you're doing what everyone else is doing, in the same old "me too" way. If that's your strategy, then you don't have a strategy. You have to take charge of your fate, take charge of your marketing, and never let *anyone* convince you to be conventional or conservative.

That's one problem most businesses have; they just do everything the ad agency says to do, never considering for a moment that the agency is telling everyone else the same thing. The results are homogenous, vanilla, boring—and no one stands out. Unless you *are* willing to stand out, then you'll end up in the follower category by default; and what's the point in that? You'll never be one of those people they write articles about in the trade journals, saying, "Look what this company did to innovate in the XYZ market."

If you're happy with that, fine: be a follower. Maybe someone else will step up and lead. But if you want to get more out of life, if you want to be one of those rare few who gets things done and dominates the industry, then you've got take on the mantle of leadership.

That's not as tough as you may think. It's worth re-emphasizing that most people will never be leaders because they don't want to be. Even if they do, they lack the responsibility to accomplish that dream. They'll never step up and take the blame for what they are. That's how it works, and until the species becomes more mature as a whole, that's how it'll always work. Oh, some people *think* they're leaders—but they're legends in their own minds. Nobody's following them, nobody cares what they say, and they don't have any influence over anyone.

I've got several dozen books about leadership on my bookshelves, and if I wanted to, I could go out and buy hundreds—if not thousands. So much has been written on that subject that you'd think it had been mined out, but there's still a lot to be said. I'm particularly taken with one writer's attitude on the subject: As John Maxwell points out, "You can sum up leadership in one word: influence." Leaders have influence; if you don't have any, if nobody gives a damn what you say or do or think, then you're not a leader.

That doesn't mean you should quit trying. Just don't delude yourself. You have a choice to make here: do you prefer a self-directed life, or do you want to be a follower? Do you want to take command, or take orders? I assure you, you'll always find plenty of followers for whatever they want to do, become, or sell, because most people are looking for someone to lead them.

Marketing Secret #29:
How to Become a Truly Great DRM Copywriter

Direct Response Marketing has always been our great strength here at M.O.R.E. Inc., and in this section, I'll reveal three easy steps toward becoming the best DRM copywriter you can possibly be. But before I talk about *how* to do it, I think it's important to spend a few paragraphs telling you *why* to do it. This Secret piggybacks on the previous one.

Like your advertising, this is another aspect of marketing you need to handle personally. If you really want to stand out as a leader in your marketplace, you've got to learn to sell; you can't just be a plumber, electrician, bookseller, or belly-dancer. For most of us, this means learning to be a good copywriter, someone good at weaving words into a vivid picture that convinces people to buy what you're selling. We call this ad copy, and it can include writing sales letters, newspaper or magazine ads, broadcast scripts, direct mail sales letters, even postcards. I think your best bet is to learn direct response copywriting if you want to be a leader and excel in your marketplace.

That's a brief synopsis of the *why* you should become a good copywriter. Now I'm going to give you three easy steps for *how* to do it:

Step 1: Study...

Step 2: Study some more...

Step 3: Just do it!

Let's expand on those a bit. Step 1 is to study other great copywriters, especially those selling to your marketplace. Keep a swipe file of their best work, and use it to develop a better understanding of how to craft your own copy. A swipe file can consist of a plain file folder, a notebook containing headlines, a binder of actual print ads, a collection of direct mail sales letters, or an electronic file of email and Internet copy. While most should pertain to your industry, keep the best from other industries, too, and adapt what you can. Your swipe file can get large and unruly if you don't manage it. It may grow into a swipe *cabinet*, which is fine if you can find what you need. The key here is to study what other successful copywriters are doing and then find ways to incorporate their ideas into your own advertising.

Step 2 is "Study some more," and I don't mean that in a facetious way. Take it beyond copywriting; read as many books as possible that are written by marketing experts and theorists. Focus on the realists who understand what it takes to succeed in small to mid-sized businesses, not the cloistered professors and Fortune 500 execs—unless the latter have built their businesses from the ground up, like Steve Jobs and Bill Gates. Read autobiographies and biographies by marketing and copywriting masters.

Expose yourself to as much material on marketing, selling, and (specifically) writing sales copy as possible. Attend seminars. Our company has produced several three-day events focused exclusively on writing sales copy. You can attend live events of that type, you can listen to audio products, you can buy transcripts—you can do all kinds of things, and you should try them all to see what works best for you. Some copywriters even offer newsletters you can subscribe to.

In any case, study as much as you can regarding good copywriting. Learn the core principles, then continue your education. School never closes for the copywriter. I've been doing it over 20 years, and I'm still learning. Russ von Hoelscher has been studying marketing for closer to 40 years, and he'll freely admit he doesn't know it all. Like chess, it's easy to learn the basics of copywriting—but you can spend a lifetime mastering it. All of us are constantly expanding our learning spheres, discovering new things and finding new examples to model our work after. So study, then study some more.

Step 3 is to just do it, like the great advertiser Nike has taught us. Make a commitment to write sales copy, even if you start with just a few hundred words a day. As you gain experience (and learn to type faster!) maybe you can bump it up to 1,000 or more words a day. Whatever the case, practice writing copy; you'll never become any good unless you keep at it. Constantly put your new knowledge to use. In the beginning you may not want to send anyone your sales letters, because you haven't quite gotten the feel for it. Consider this practice, and don't give up. Get in the habit of writing every single day so you can acquire the necessary experience.

Abraham Lincoln once said, "Give me six hours to chop down a tree, and I will spend four sharpening the ax." The study is the sharpening; the chopping comes at the very end, when you do the copywriting work. That's basically a 2:1 ratio, where two of the three principles are studying (sharpening) while the third is writing (chopping down the tree). The great thing about it is that as you're chopping the tree, you're *still* sharpening the ax, because practice makes perfect.

Even better, you don't have to wait to earn until you're a perfect copywriter, just as you don't need a perfectly sharp axe to cut down a tree. As with so many things, you can earn while you learn, improving as you go along. You'll become more comfortable with the processes and theories behind sales copy, finding and testing new ideas that beat the old ones. So learn to write sales copy, because it will benefit you in many ways, serving as your ticket to all the profits you want and need. Don't rely on someone else to do your marketing. Take care of it yourself.

Having said all that, I know from my own experience that many people won't put those steps into action. They don't *want* to write copy—which means they need to reach out to a copywriter. Well, folks, there aren't that many great copywriters in the world: probably a few hundred, certainly less than a few thousand. That may sound like a lot of people to choose from, but it's still a tiny portion of the overall business community. So it should come as no surprise to learn that they're very busy, which is one reason that following all three steps here can be quite profitable. And I assure you, you'll find it rewarding if you do.

But if you do nothing else, at least study hard, so you can learn to recognize good copy. That way, the next time the salesman from Penny Saver or the Yellow Pages visits you, you'll be prepared. Ten to one he'll say something like, "We'll write you a great ad. We're going to tell people your name, address, city, state, and zip, and we're going to give them your phone number, e-mail, and website URL. Now, isn't that a convincing ad?"

And you'll be able to say, "Hell no, it isn't! All you're doing is giving them contact information. I can hand people business cards myself. If I want a truly convincing ad, one I can run in magazines or newspapers, one that can capture attention and get people to respond to me, I'll go to someone who can provide more than a list of contact info."

Once you learn to recognize good copy, you won't be fooled by all the charlatans who try to sell you the same thing they sell everyone else. So it's worth doing your due diligence, so that you can tell the difference between good copy and a pile of BS.

Marketing Secret #30:
If You Want to Catch a Whale, Don't Use Minnows for Bait

Are you making this mistake with your marketing? This Secret was formulated by one of the world's greatest showmen and marketers—P.T. Barnum himself. It explains why so many marketers and entrepreneurs never make the kind of money they should. When you get right down to it, they just don't want to put in the effort required to step up their game and do the things necessary to make their business a phenomenal success. They'll put in minor efforts sometimes, but you don't get big results from the smallest efforts—and that's what these people want.

They want the hard body without the hard work. They want huge results without expending the time, effort, and money those results require. They don't care to study the secrets of good copywriting, to learn how to write it or at least recognize great work when they see it. They want to make a lot of money by spending little or no money—and that's probably the biggest marketing mistake there is. In the direct response business (the form of marketing we use), they all want to mail postcards— because postcards are cheap.

Recently, Chris Lakey and I were working with a local financial consultant who wanted our advice on what he could do to land more of the best clients, whom he called (coincidentally) "the whales." So we asked him, "How do you define a whale?"

Once he explained their commonalities, we started giving him some ideas we know are making other people huge sums of money. We told him that he had to become an expert, for example. We told him he should do some seminars and workshops, because many of the people he's looking for are managing their own portfolios. You see, the Internet has made many people feel like they're qualified to make their own decisions on which financial products will best serve them, providing the biggest bang for their buck; so they might appreciate live events in which he teaches them some of his best ideas.

We even told him about an attorney out of Salina, Kansas who does little seminars throughout this area. He specializes in living trusts; and through the process of teaching people about them, he proves that he's an expert. As a result, many of his attendees want to do business with him.

This fellow we consulted with did nothing but cold calls. Here he was, approaching 60 years old, still basically being a salesman. That's all the people he contacted every evening thought of him as. We told him, "Look, nobody's going to respect you as a salesman. You've got to become an expert, someone they'll want to look up to." We told him flat-out that cold calling was the worst thing he could do. He listened to us for about 90 minutes, and then essentially did nothing. Maybe he'll come around; maybe a year from now, he'll come back to us and say, "Okay, guys, now I'm ready to do what you told me."

The problem was, what we were telling him to do required a tremendous amount of effort on his part—and he didn't want to make that effort. He just wanted the results. He preferred to make his cold calls, because he knew what to expect... even though that wasn't much, and cold calling takes a while anyhow. He's going to keep on using a minnow for bait as long as he can keep convincing himself the results are good enough. It's a crying shame that so many marketers aren't willing to swap out that worn-out little piece of bait for something that's big, juicy, and fresh. It really is. They want maximum results from minimum effort, and that's just not how the world works. You've got to have the right-sized bait if you want to bring in the big fish—or the whales, if you will.

You also need the right gear to maximize your success. About 20 years ago, Russ von Hoelscher sometimes attended the meetings of the San Diego Direct Marketing Club with its vice president, the late George Stern. He also spoke at one of the meetings on copywriting. They did a tabloid newsletter every month for the membership, and for one issue, they were planning a front-page story called "Fishing for New Business." The illustrator prepared an image that showed people in a boat with some fishing rods going out to sea, with a huge whale in the distance. The illustrator asked George, "What do you think of this?" and he said, "That looks good." But Russ noticed that the rods they had were all small rigs, the kind used to catch bluegills.

When the illustrator asked Russ what he thought, he said,

"If they're going after that whale, those little rigs aren't going to work." Russ suggested that he outfit them with a couple of huge harpoons... and a bucket labeled "Tartar Sauce." That got him some funny looks, but the president of the club said, "That's a good idea—do it!" Hey, if you're going after the big fish—if you're targeting huge sales and trying to expand your business— then you have to think big all the way around!

Think about the bait, the type of hook and other tackle you have to use, the rig, the boat—everything it takes to get that enticing message to the people who spend the most money. They call those people whales in Las Vegas and Reno, too. They give them all the free food and drinks they want, they provide them with luxurious penthouse accommodations, and they treat them just like royalty—because they're spending the big bucks. The casinos are willing to pull out the big tackle and pile on the bait to attract their business, because they know these people usually spend a fortune.

Any fisherman knows you size your hooks and bait based on what you're after. If you're after sunfish or you're fishing in a small pond, you don't pull out the biggest lure in tackle box. That'll just scare the fish away. Instead, use little jigs or a kernel of corn on the end of the small hook. If you want to catch a great big catfish, put a sizable weight at the end of your line to drag the hook to the bottom, where they live, and put on some aromatic bait. If you're after a shark, put a larger hook on, along with a metal leader, and bait your hook with a bloody chunk of raw fish. You'll automatically exclude the smaller fish that you don't want to deal with.

It's not much different in business. Little offers catch you little fish, though you may catch quite a few. If that's what you're after, fine. But the big offers are the ones that bring in the big spenders; and ounce for ounce, they're your most valuable customers. So you have to start by knowing who you're trying to attract, and adjust your offers in an attempt to attract them. If you don't, you'll attract the wrong customers, or none at all.

If I had $1,000 for every time I asked one of my best customers, "Where do I find another 10,000 people just like you?" then I'd be a billionaire, because I say that to all of my best customers when I meet them face-to-face. They view it as a compliment, which it is—but I'm dead serious. Such people are rare, and we all need to find as many of them as we can. Don't make the mistake of thinking you can catch them with minnows. It's going to take plenty of time, effort, and money to find them and keep them.

At the end of the last chapter, I urged you to think big with your marketing. No matter what business you're in, you can't catch whales with minnows. Do you think the old-time whalers even headed out with rods and reels and hooks at all? No, they knew that to catch their prey, they needed harpoons and a lot of courage.

In this chapter, I'm going to continue with that general theme, and reveal six more secrets based mostly on being bold, doing business aggressively and audaciously, and focusing in tightly on what really matters to you.

CHAPTER FOUR

SECRETS 31-40

Marketing Secret #31:
Push the Envelope... Go Big or Go Home

I believe that what we think about a lot, the ideas we dwell on, become our reality. Which means that reality follows thought... which can be a scary thing if you're a relentlessly negative individual. But by the same token, it can bring you incredible riches. You only go as far as your thoughts can take you. If you think you can be successful, you can be. But if you think, "The deck is stacked against me, nothing works well, I just know I'll fail," then you'll be right then, too.

That's why it's not a good idea to go around talking about how bad things are. Why jinx yourself subconsciously? As I write this, economy's not doing especially well; but it doesn't help to keep dwelling on that unless you're using the notion as an instrument of change. Otherwise, avoid it in your business life.

One of the richest people in America, Donald Trump, once said, "I decided as a young man that I would be a millionaire, and of course I met that goal rather quickly. And then I thought, Why can't I be a billionaire?" The secret, he says, is to choose a profession you love—in his case, real estate—and then learn everything about it, until you know more about it than almost anyone else. Donald Trump believed he could be rich, and he became rich. The richer he got, the richer he knew he could become.

Admittedly, most people aren't interested in trying to

become billionaires. But if you're in business, you should at least be thinking constantly about success, whatever that means to you—a comfortable lifestyle, living well, or going for true riches. Otherwise, what's the point? That's your choice. Push the envelope. Know that you can be greater than you are now. I've noticed over the years that most people just want to earn a steady paycheck and get by in life. They prefer to focus on life outside work, and that's fine.

Russ von Hoelscher has a friend back in his hometown of St. Paul, Minnesota who worked as an airline mechanic and made pretty good money. But all Eddie wanted to do his whole life—and he's still doing it today, bless him—was go fishing. A lot of us like to go fishing once in a while; Eddie likes to go fishing every week, sometimes several times a week. I'm not going to knock Eddie, because that's his great pleasure in life. But if you're in business, you can't always go fishing... at least not for fish.

This requires a different attitude than most people have; in fact, it requires a more creative, bold attitude—and the bolder the better. Think big, because that's what makes things happen. Daniel Bonham tells us, "Make no little plans. They have no magic to stir men's blood. Make big plans, and aim high." President Ronald Reagan once pointed out, "America is too great for small dreams." Think of your business the same way.

Consider what you can do to make things bigger and better than you've ever done before. Don't think about just getting by. Don't just put up a sign that says "Open for Business," and sit there twiddling your thumbs, waiting for people to notice. You owe it to yourself, your family, and your employees to do everything possible to become very successful.

Hire more people, do more business, create more products and services. Go big or go home.

It's okay to pursue other dreams and goals; but if you're a businessperson, you've got to make your business paramount, at least as you're establishing yourself. What are you going to do to make your business the success you want it to be? Far too few people do far too little to achieve that end. And again, it's fine if your business goals are small. But by the same token, if you have million dollar goals, then you need million dollar plans. The money's not just going to come to you magically, even though you do have to visualize it—because visualization without action is meaningless.

Start with a specific goal in mind. Now, I don't know of many small businesspeople who say they want *less* money, who aren't looking for new customers or to profit more from their existing customers. No doubt you're reading this because you wish things were better than they are right now. Well, what are you waiting for? To get there, you have to push the envelope. Be willing to go beyond where you are right now. Little plans excite no one... but people are happy to help make big things happen.

Think about a big fundraiser that a church or nonprofit might host. If it's a plan to raise just a little money, no one's going to get very excited about it. But if you're trying to raise $100,000 or $1 million for a special project, people *will* get excited. There's energy there; there's passion, and people want to be involved. The same principle holds for business, when your dreams are big and you have to take massive action to get there.

People get excited on the customer side, too, especially when you give them what they want or offer exciting new promotions. The suppliers and vendors on the team get excited as they help the business grow. Because you're dreaming big and pushing the envelope, all these factors add up to more revenue coming into your business—and that's what it's all about.

Bravado matters; and as Donald Trump once put it, "It doesn't take any more work to think bigger." Now, with bigger thinking comes greater responsibility, so you do have to step things up a little bit. But that shouldn't stop you from catching a bigger vision for yourself, for your business, and for your life. Think it bigger and see it simpler than ever before, and all that will come.

Here at M.O.R.E. Inc., we start thinking about our end-of-the-year promotion in the summer, and start really revving it up in the fall. Before Y2K, December was our worst sales month of the year. Nowadays, it's often now our best sales month, mostly due to the annual end-of-the-year promotion. We know it has to be big. Every year we have to do something bigger and bolder than last year, because we're reselling to the same people, and they require something new. This year, the idea we adopted was so big and bold that when we told our general manager, she said, "You can't do that! You'll break the bank!"

Chris Lakey and I looked at each other and smiled. We knew we had something great, though of course we modified it so that we *didn't* break the bank. As long as you can afford it, the bigger an offer is, the more it gets your customers excited, the better. You have to push the envelope to make the cash register ring.

And another thing: your best ideas always come to you when you're in that positive state of mind that results from setting larger goals and dreaming big. If you're thinking petty thoughts and hoping for some big multimillion-dollar notion to hit you, forget it! You're never going to get any big ideas unless you're in the right frame of mind. I used to listen to talk radio while I was trying to work in the afternoon, and it was so gloom-and-doom I had to shut it off, because it was affecting my thinking. Positive thinking is an absolute necessity if you want to push the envelope.

Marketing Secret #32:
People Do What They Believe is in Their Best Interests

As I've pointed out before, the only reasonable way to increase your business is to sell more goods to more people more often for more profit. How do you do that? One way is to prove to them that it's in their best interest to buy from you. In his book *Million Dollar Habit*, Robert Ringer pointed out a strategy that I think is appropriate to this principle. It's most simply explained this way: People will always do whatever they believe, or can be made to believe, is in their best interests.

So you have to show them it's in their best interests to buy whatever you're selling. The best way to make them believe that is to believe it yourself. It all comes down to you selling your expertise or products to prospects who perceive so much value in it that the money you're asking is worth less than what your offering. Of course, this has to take place in a free and fair market, which despite some problems, we have here in the U.S.A. and throughout the Western world. The consumer has to think it's fair. If there's been a bad apple harvest this year and you're selling apples, most consumers will be willing to pay more than they would in a bumper crop year. If your new widget saves them hours of backbreaking toil every day, they'll be more likely to pay a higher price. For the exchange to be fair, both buyer and seller have to agree to that exchange.

This is true whether you're eating in a restaurant or buying wing nuts. You know the price in advance and decide whether it's worth more to you than the fee asked for it. You can decide not to buy. And remember, people are more willing to pay top dollar for things they really want than for everyday needs. The secret to making money in any market is to figure out what your prospects want the most, and then find a way to give that to them in a way that helps them decide to make the exchange.

How do you figure out what's in the prospect's best interest? The key here is something I've already mentioned repeatedly in this book: you have to know your prospects thoroughly. If you've never participated in the marketplace yourself, do constant research and ask lots of questions.

Remember, people are self-serving. They don't really care about you or your company. They may say they do, but the only real reason they do—or would be upset if you went out of business—is *not* because of altruism or any relationship they have with you *per se.* What matters is the benefits you provide. They buy from you because it's in their best interests to do so.

If you can't determine those best interests any other way, just ask. You can ask in writing via quick surveys or questionnaires, or face-to-face if you have that opportunity. Even if they don't answer directly, you can at least figure out the broad outlines by asking the right questions. Ultimately, your goal is to make people so excited about what you have to offer that they'll gladly pay the price.

Russ von Hoelscher tells me that as a kid, he was obsessed with comic books. But he had a limited allowance, so he had to make a choice about where to spend his money. He'd bypass candy, soda pop, or marbles to get more comics. Just about everyone in every market is that way; they have some things they want more than anything else, and they have to apportion their limited amount of discretionary cash carefully.

When people are really into a certain category of product or service, they'll keep buying slightly different versions over and over. Keep that in mind. Think ahead to the next product or service that complements what you're selling; because if people are willing to buy that, they'll buy related items. Mix that tendency with an enticing, mouthwatering offer, and your business will increase.

Is there anything wrong with giving people what they want? No, as long as you do so morally and ethically. In some circles, capitalism has gotten a bad rap; many see business people and ambitious entrepreneurs as greedy scumbags who are just trying to cheat people out of their money. And yes, that element exists, and those bad apples stain the reputation of everyone else. But when you get down to it, the heart and soul of good marketing is altruistic in nature, because you're trying to do everything you can to provide tremendous value in exchange for their money. You have to; that's the only way to get them to come back for more. So it upsets me to hear people say that businesspeople are being greedy when they market aggressively.

Of course they're trying to make more money. Isn't that what the American dream is about? But there's no way to do that consistently without using Ruthless Marketing techniques that, while undercutting the competition, function as a means of serving the customer in the highest possible way. Focus tightly on what people want, and give it to them. Sometimes, as with the PAS formula, you'll have to remind the customers they need help, and rub salt into the wounds a little; but ultimately, it's all for the good, even if the critics can't see it. The way you get rich in business is by reselling customers over and over again. You can't do it by screwing people over.

Marketing Secret #33:
Focus on the Few Things
That Make the Most Money

I used to be a member of an entrepreneurial group that included Ron LeGrand, one of the world's top real estate gurus. Ron is an enormously successful entrepreneur. The most important thing he ever told me was, "The less I do, the more I make." Sounds like the lazy man's way to riches, doesn't it? When most people hear that, they envision someone lying around on the couch stuffing potato chips into their face.

But Ron actually works quite hard. What he meant by that statement was that the fewer *types* of things he does, the more money he makes. He focuses on a very few high-value activities only he can do for his business, like marketing, and delegates the rest. He still works long days, but only at a few things. And I'm talking total focus here.

The other option is to do it all yourself, which in fact you can. In 1990 I came up with a name for this: the Albert Morris Syndrome. Albert Morris was a small businessman, and I got to know him and his wife well. Albert and his wife did everything in their small printing operation and photography business—and they worked 14-18 hours a day, even though when I knew them they were already into their 60's.

You see, they were doing it all themselves—without hiring any employees. I consider that a big mistake. I used to wear all the hats in my business too, so I know what I'm talking about. These days, I'm working smarter and harder on fewer things, and making more money.

So despite what the "work less, make more" philosophy may sound like on the surface, it's not about just sitting back and doing nothing. You're simply focused on the fewer things that bring you the most money, or have the potential to do so. Stop trying to wear all the hats. Put all your focus on marketing and on new product/service development. As Peter Drucker famously pointed out, marketing and innovation are the only two things in your business that aren't expenses (though I would humbly submit that assembling a top-notch team to offset your weaknesses is a third).

Start thinking about better products and services you can create for your very best customers, as well as the people you want to attract. Start building and maintaining effective marketing systems. Hire people who are smarter and more talented than you are in the areas you're weakest in—and even in some that you do fine in. That's the sign of an intelligent, effectual leader. That way you focus on the fewer things, like the marketing. Never delegate your marketing.

Focus on thinking bigger, and spend time every day on strategizing. Get up early every morning, if you're a morning person; 4:30 or 5:00 is about right. If you're a night owl, then stay awake late and do it then. Whenever you do it, the important thing is that you're focused, you're trying to think bigger, you're developing multimillion-dollar ideas, you're working *on* your business, but not *in* it.

Russ von Hoelscher likes to tell a story about one of the more successful gentlemen he knows, who was constantly looking to hire people who were smarter than him. At one point, he told Russ that his chief desire was to do fun things, so he needed people surrounding him who were better at everything in his multinational business than he was. Russ figured this fellow wasn't all that bright... but he also knows from experience that often, people surround themselves with the extremely intelligent on purpose. So they do have their own kind of business smarts.

The thing about entrepreneurs is that we tend to want to do everything—and of course, that extends to being the head honcho. The gift of recognizing very sharp people who can help you in your business—the ability to build a great team—can work wonders. I think that's a pretty exciting thought to consider, frankly. If you do that (and most of us don't!) you'll free up an enormous amount of time to pursue what you want to pursue. Some of the richest and most powerful people in business have found ways to make this work. The key is to find people to help you do the things you can't do yourself. It's just another form of strategic leverage.

Consider the millionaire athletes you hear about on TV and the radio. Some of these guys make tens of millions, sometimes even more, for a brief contract—and their careers tend to be short. How many times have you heard of a former pro athlete who's broke now, a guy who once made more than the GNPs of some small countries? They blew everything in a few short years. The ones you don't hear so much about are the ones who hired someone to help them invest their money. They end up with enough revenue after their playing days are over to do what they want to with their lives... while some of their colleagues end up as cooks and janitors.

They find people to help them do things they can't do themselves—or can't do economically. You should do that as much as you can. Again, the only exceptions should be advertising and innovation, the most creative, promotional of your duties. Your top priorities should be attracting new customers and making more money from your existing customers, period. If you have time left over, you can handle a few other tasks. But don't keep doing your own books when someone else can do them cheaper and better than you.

It's important to recognize that you don't have to do everything. In fact, people who try to handle everything on their own usually end up stumbling. As John Maxwell points out, "The smartest thing that you can do is work through other people."

Marketing Secret #34:
How to Turn 30-60 Minutes
a Day into HUGE Success

I already gave you a preview of this one, when I discussed determining whether you're a morning or evening person. Some of us can do it either way; others do best with one or the other. Most married men work the early-morning angle, because wives tend not to appreciate the late-night one.

Personally, I'm a member of the 5 AM Club. There's

something special about getting up before or as the sun rises. You're all alone in the office or the house, everything's quiet, and you can get more done. If nothing else, just sit down with a yellow note pad and a pen and start to think. Write down a problem you're facing as a headline: for example, "What's the most important thing I could do for my business right now?" That's just an example—there are thousands of possibilities. Just ask yourself a vital question and start brainstorming as you sip your coffee or orange juice. This can trigger a sort of magical process, with the ideas flowing out through your hand and onto that paper.

Start writing and keep writing. Some of what you write will make a lot of sense to you when you go back to review it—though some won't make any sense at all. And that's fine. Just write. If you fill up several pages, that's good, because I expect you'll find several nuggets in there that you can use to make your business better. Our minds are marvelous things; at some level, they're always working for us. We have to take the time to stop and listen when there are no distractions.

If you're like me, once you get to the office you have to deal with phone calls, employees with questions, noise of all types, various tasks—and you can't deal with them all and still think clearly. That's the main reason for the early morning or late night thinking, because you have to avoid those distractions. If you can do that, you'll discover things about yourself and your business you never knew before, and you'll discover solutions to make your business bigger and better.

All it takes is an extra hour a day, every day. Just imagine: 365 hours a year of focused thinking. That's nine work weeks. Even if you took time off for vacation or special events, even if you did just 300 hours a year, that puts you far ahead of the pack. Frankly, most people don't think creatively for as much as *10* hours a year. Imagine how far 30 times as much creative thought can put you ahead of them.

I guarantee you'll get some tremendous answers and end up with some great insight if you'll do this. I can guarantee it because it's helped me make over $100 million in the last 20 years—and I don't consider myself special. If I have a talent besides sheer stubbornness, this early morning thinking is it. I've never found any method of creative thinking that beats it, especially when you combine it with the principle of "as you think, so shall it be." You become what you think about constantly, though let me caution you: while there's a spiritual angle to that, it's really a means of stirring yourself into action. You can think all you want, and nothing will ever happen unless you take massive action!

Just pick a time, morning or evening, to dedicate to your thinking hour—and follow it consistently. When it's quiet, it's much easier to focus your energy on serving your customers and finding new ways to give them what they want the most. So find that time, whether it's very early morning, late evening, or even in the middle of the day if that's how the chips fall. If you don't, you're missing out on a wonderful opportunity.

Recently, I asked myself the question, "How can we make *this* amount of money every year?" By the way, that number is 3-5 times higher than we've ever before generated. Just like magic, the ideas started coming. In such a situation, the more ideas you write down, the more you get. You'll come up with answers that will surprise and shock you... and after you do this for a while, the quality of your answers will improve.

It's the ideas that lead to the money, so be sure to sit down daily with yourself and let the ideas flow.

Marketing Secret #35:
The Easiest Way to Quickly Make a Big Pile of Money

Who doesn't want to make a big pile of money quickly? In this Secret, I'll tell you two things you can do right away to prime the pump. You don't need to have a big pile of money to start with, and as long as you spend wisely and keep these pointers in mind, you can keep it up indefinitely. Now, I'll admit that there are times when this strategy doesn't work—there are no 100% foolproof moneymakers. But this is about as close as you can get.

Step One: Identify who your best customers are. Step Two: Make those customers an irresistible offer. That's it. Pretty simple, right? Well, most people aren't doing it—so it *must* be a secret. But if you've been in business for any time at all, you've already got people you consider your best customers. If you're not doing as much business as you would like to, go to them and make them an irresistible offer.

Again, you pinpoint the irresistible offers by determining what your customers want and figuring out how to give it to them.

Over the years, we've had hundreds of thousands of customers at M.O.R.E. Inc., and we appreciate each one—but only a tiny percentage represent our best customers. Some people requested information, but never made a purchase.

Some bought something, but only for a small amount of money, and there was no real connection. Maybe they spent money once and it's been a few years since they bought anything. These aren't loyal customers; and they're surely not what we'd consider our best customers.

We have certain criteria by which we determine our best customers, and we always segment that group out from everyone else. When we have a hot, new offer, we go to them first. We already have a well-established relationship, there's a high level of trust, we communicate with them on a regular basis, and they know us. We tell them, "Hey, listen. You're one of our best customers, and we wanted to let you know about a special offer. Here's how to respond." Every time, without fail, those customers are the best people to go to with a brand-new offer.

Now, we've had situations in the past where an offer hasn't worked out well even with our best customers—and that's how we know not to take it any further. But for the most part, we can make what we consider an irresistible offer to our best customers and know that the cash register's going to ring. The fax machines will stay busy, the phones will be ringing off the hooks, and we'll be mobbed with mailed-in orders, sometime even FedExed orders. Occasionally, people drive from another state to make their order in person. Our best customers respond *en masse* because of that existing relationship.

So when you need quick cash, this is almost always guaranteed to work, as long as you can introduce your best customers to a truly irresistible offer. Use your knowledge gained from experience and marketplace research to determine who your best customers are and what they want. That really is the easiest, fastest, and most efficient way to get the cash register ringing and to put extra profits into the bank—and you can do it as often as you come up with irresistible offers.

You'd think this would be obvious... yet even most well-established businesses spend 90% of their time courting new customers rather than catering to existing ones. Instead of ignoring the people who've already bought from you, tell them how special they are and how much you care for them. Offer them a discount or a little extra along with a special offer—because the better you treat them, the more money you'll make. All those businesses that do everything possible to get new people to come in through the door while neglecting their regular customers will pay a price for that eventually.

Yes, you need new customers—not just to expand, but to replace established customers who move away, leave the market, die, or just don't spend as much money. But even if you only have 50-100 regular customers, you can make a lot of money off them. And if you handle your marketing right, you'll build up more and more regular clients, good customers who deserve your best efforts. This will pay big dividends for you.

Your best customers will gladly buy from you again and again; in fact, they want to. Think about your own purchasing habits. Given a choice, do you want to do business with a new company, one you don't know, don't trust, and have no relationship with—or do you want to do business with someone you know is there for you? Most of the time, you'll choose the latter rather than the former, won't you?

Quit chasing so hard after all of these new customers, and start doing more business with the people who have *already* done business with you. Put most of your marketing

efforts into that area. Which is the perfect segue into the last
Marketing Secret in this chapter...

Marketing Secret #36:
7 Copywriting Secrets to Drive Your Marketing Message Straight to the Hearts of Your Best Prospects

This Secret is all about writing sales copy. That copy
may end up in print in a magazine space ad, or a sales letter if
you're using direct mail, or a brochure or website; or it might
become the script of a radio or TV commercial or audio
presentation. It can even be copy you give to your salespeople
to use as a cheat-sheet.

The format doesn't matter as much as the style of writing;
indeed, you should use any given piece of copy in as many
formats as possible. It's copywriting in general that you should
get excited about, because it represents your ability to turn words
into cash. What you communicate to your marketplace is what
gets people to send you their money.

I will forever be in debt to Russ von Hoelscher for
teaching me about the magic of writing copy. When Eileen and I
first got started, Russ used to come work with us on the
weekends as we developed new products, services, and
promotions. I didn't know how to write copy back then, so Russ
did it for me. He'd sit at our dining room with Eileen and I, and
we'd come up with all kinds of great ideas intended to get our
customers excited. Back then, Eileen and I were doing pretty
well—but we wanted to do better. So we'd banter with Russ for a
while, and all of a sudden, Russ would start writing. Eileen and I
would immediately shut up, because we didn't want to stop him
once he got started.

He was amazing to watch. He would write so fast and furiously that it was utterly fascinating. We'd always have a stack of legal pads waiting for him, along with plenty of pens, and of course we kept the coffee pot on all the time so we were fueled by caffeine—but we were also fueled by excitement. Eventually Russ would slow down; maybe after five minutes, maybe after fifty. He'd stop writing, then we'd drink some coffee and talk some more—and he'd get all excited again and start writing. The next Monday, we'd take that stack of legal pads and hand them to our typist, who would then type them up. We'd format them a little, put the copy in direct mail letters, send them out to our customers—and all of a sudden, look out! Here comes the money!

We went from making about $500 a day to about *$16,000* a day within nine months of starting to work with Russ. Thank God for Russ von Hoelscher, because he taught me the miracle of getting excited, writing a bunch of words that convey a good job of selling an idea to people, and then drawing in money like magic. I used to watch Russ and think to myself, "I'm going to learn how to do this myself. God, this is so cool!"

And I *did* learn to write sales copy—very well, I think. At least, I've made millions at it! I've boiled the process down into 7 Copywriting Secrets that I'm going to pass on to you as a sort of shortcut to help you get started; or, if you've already started, to provide a boost. You should definitely learn to write copy. Not only is it highly addictive and a lot of fun, it's insanely profitable. While there are probably thousands of different secrets for writing copy, these are my favorites.

First, you've got to have a hook: a headline or some other grabber to snap people out of their trances. It's got to be big, it's got to be bold, it's got to be outrageous—something huge, something shocking. What do your customers want most? How can you give it to them in the biggest way? How can you shock them? How can you knock it out of the ballpark?

The second secret is: you've got to build your entire campaign around one hard-selling point. It's got to be a big, huge promise. The third secret is to remember that it's about them, not you. I used to have a big sign in my basement that said "It's All About YOU, Isn't It?" But no, it's all about them. Your value is in your ability to constantly give the people in your market what you know they want the most. Center everything around them and how they benefit.

And that's number four: show them why it's in their best interests to do what you want them to. You've got to pile on the benefits, so the money you're asking them to give you seems unimportant in comparison to the benefits you're providing.

Number five: make them want it. Do things to increase their desire, like limit the item's availability. Make it a limited offer, or make it exclusive, just for them. Personalize those benefits you've been piling on.

Number six: drive your point home. Do something to summarize everything in one brief statement. Recently, we created sales material for our annual end-of-the-year promotion. Chris Lakey suggested I do a Q & A sheet, summarizing the entire offer in a readable format that makes it easy for people to quickly assimilate it. That helps them grasp the value more easily, encouraging them to respond.

Last but not least, do a complete job of selling. Pile the

benefits on. Do plenty of follow-up marketing. If you can, provide some salespeople to answer any objections that still must be overcome before your prospective buyers are ready to take action.

Again, I could add plenty of other items here, but I believe this provides a broad, easy-to-understand picture. To convey it properly, though, you've got to understand what good copy is about. It's fine if you prefer to hire copywriters to do the work for you, but you need to be able to tell when they produce effective work. Be sure they get the hook in there, whether it's a headline or killer opening paragraph with a powerful and passionate selling point. Be sure they drive it home and focus on the customer's interests—not yours—and close very strongly. Another thing I'd suggest is to limit the timeline, so people order ASAP, instead of just tossing your offer aside and saying, "I'll take care of that later." They may not. If they know they have to act within 10 days, they'll have that on their mind and will get to it.

Again, even if you don't take the time to learn to be a great copywriter, at least learn enough to look over your copywriter's shoulder and know if they're using these selling points I've outlined here. Why worry? Because small business owners are getting flat-out ripped off by ad agencies, by local Yellow Pages promoters, and other people who want to sell them advertising.

They forget that the ad salesmen are salesmen, not necessarily good marketers. They have no clue how to create offers that get people to spend their money, so they don't know any better when the ad agency presents them with something shoddy, claiming it's the perfect way to draw customers. As a business owner, you need to be able to tell them, "You know what? I think this would be a better headline," or, "I think this is what my customers really want the most, so let's focus on that."

If you don't at least understand the basics behind good copy, you'll find yourself in a position where you're taken advantage of by people who don't have your best interests at heart. This is a good formula, a very basic, easy-to-understand formula, to help you write and recognize good sales copy.

Marketing Secret #37:
Sell Them What They Want, Give Them What They Need

This secret is derived from a quote by A-list marketer Dan Kennedy, and it rings very true for those of us with experience in the field. When it comes to discretionary income, people are more likely to buy what they want than what they need. Realizing this early on helped me immensely in my career. When you're advertising a moneymaking program, for example, you don't just talk about the money, which is what the prospect needs; you want to focus on what that money can do for them. Discuss expensive vacations, a new house, a new car. This helps them picture what they can buy with more money; because by itself, money is just a commodity. It's what money can *do* for you that counts. Your copy will sizzle when you recognize this and include it in your pitch.

If you're a very good marketer, you'll not only sell people what they want, but you'll give them what they need as well. Now, our true needs in life are basic: we need food, water, shelter, transportation, and in some cases medical care. We all crave love and friendship, so human contact is important too. Once you've gotten all those in place, your attention shifts to your wants, some of which mesh with your needs.

For example, let's take a closer look at the transportation need. When you're first starting out, you buy economical cars that get the job done. Later, as you make more money, you may go for the less-practical cars like Cadillacs and Lincolns. Do you really need to spend $40,000+ for a new car? Of course not, but it makes you feel good; and we all want to feel good. So at times you spent money foolishly, just to get some fun from it. I know someone who bought a new banjo just for the hell of it. (He has no idea how to play it yet!) And Russ von Hoelscher's brother-in-law in Minnesota recently bought a used boat for $150,000. He struck a pretty good deal; he likes to brag, "This is a million dollar boat." His wife points out, "Yes, and you've already put another $80,000 into it."

The point is, once we've got the basics covered, we tend to spend money on what we *want* rather than what we *need*. That's something that we have to realize as marketers, so you know to stoke the fire of the prospect's desire first, to make them crave what you're selling. But in the final analysis, if you're a standout marketer, you'll do good for people when you sell them something they want, because it's also something they need.

I've learned a lot about wants vs. needs by observing Chris Lakey's interactions with his six children. He's always explaining the difference to his kids. His 13-year-old son *wants* the latest cell phone; he says he *needs* it because of the things it will do for him. Chris has to remind him that it isn't really a need. You have to recognize the difference between the two. His oldest child is a sophomore in high school, and his youngest is in kindergarten, so his six run the gamut in between. Each of their definitions of *need* is different, but they all think they need things they can't live without.

Part of his job as their dad is to continuously remind them they don't really *need* those things, they just *want* them. He tells them that if they just want something, they need to find a way to save their money to buy it for themselves, or wait until Christmas or their birthday, when Chris can buy it for them.

This is a reality all marketers must face. If you sell only things that people need, you'll find business a lot tougher than if you sell things people want. So sell them what they want and give them what they need when it's feasible to do so. People will spend as little as possible on what they need, so the opportunities for profit are minimal. If I need toilet paper, I'm likely to buy the cheapest variety that fits my needs (and is still comfortable!). If I'm buying shampoo or toothpaste, why spend more than the minimum necessary? How often do you see a toothbrush and say, "I want that! I've gotta have it!" Now compare that to the number of times you've said the same about a car, an article of clothing, or even a baseball card.

When people buy based on what they want, you can demand a higher price for your offer—and you'll likely find a bigger marketplace for it. You can make a LOT more money on wants than on needs; but if you can combine a true need with a want, one that supplies the benefits people really want with those that will improve their life, you're all better off.

A car is a good example. When I'm buying a car, there are certain things I look for that would be totally boring from a sales standpoint. Safety features are a good example; few salespeople make a big deal over those until they knew the customer is truly interested in them. Then they're all out. The truth is, there are probably dozens of essential things about any car that no one knows or cares much about, things that are there because they must be and make practical sense. But a salesperson won't bring them up when trying to close a deal, because they want to sell the things people want the *most* about that car.

If you're selling a car to a young single man, for example, you'll emphasize how fast, sporty, and sexy it is, or its awesome stereo system, or the cutting-edge satellite radio. If you're selling the same car to a soccer mom, you'll emphasize roominess, gas mileage, and safety features. But in the end you deliver that whole vehicle to both. It comes with not only the things your prospect wants to buy, but also all the things that they need as well. You deliver both the wants and needs simultaneously.

But let me re-emphasize this again, because it's so very important: *the money is in what people want, not in what they need.* That's where your biggest orders will come from, and what drives repeat business with existing customers. Sell to their wants, and you can give them what they need; don't try to sell them their needs, or you'll find that they won't respond positively.

Here's a great real-life illustration of this concept. For decades now, our parent company has sold low-cost business opportunities. We basically show people how to get rich in mail-order. When we had our very first expensive seminar, we'd been in the business about eight years. The seminar sold for about $5,000, and we were a bit afraid of that cost, because at the time it was a lot of money to be selling a seminar for in our market (things have changed radically since). We had over 100 people there. At one point, we were upstairs mapping out our strategy, and decided we were going to start the event off *not* by talking about making millions of dollars right way, but about building up to that point gradually.

We were going to tell our attendees, "First, focus on making $100,000 per year. Then shoot for $250,000. In your third or fourth year, aim for $500,000. By your sixth or eighth year, you can hit that million dollar mark." We decided the best approach was to manage their expectations, to give it to them in a blunt "tell them what they need to hear" way. We forgot about the value in needs vs. wants.

When we went down there and laid that message on them, you could have heard a pin drop.

After a pregnant pause, I said, "Okay, then—how many of you want to make millions of dollars *right now*!?" Everybody started clapping and shouting, and the event began with a splash. You see, they wanted to get rich instantly...as unrealistic as that was. They wanted to go to sleep that night and wake up millionaires. Although we weren't promising they actually would do that, we were there to show them that they *could* become millionaires. Needless to say, we had to take it easy from a legal, ethical, and moral standpoint; we couldn't promise things we couldn't deliver. But the fact was, we *were* there to show them what they wanted the most...while what they *needed* was our first approach. Most of those people had never made as much as $50,000-100,000 annually before; they were dreamers. Thank goodness we woke up fast.

Look—if we all bought *only* the things we needed, we'd all be driving cars that got about 40 miles to the gallon, we'd be living in beat-up mobile homes, and we'd be wearing old clothes. Obviously, that's not the way things are at all.

As Robert J. Ringer once said, "If you want to make a

comfortable living, sell people what they need. If you want to get super-rich, sell people what they *want*." The people at our seminar could have learned to make $1,000 a week or more easily. But I learned my lesson. People don't want to make $100,000 per year. They want millions.

So we decided to talk about making millions, but teach them how to do the things that would make it possible for them to start out by making the $50,000- $100,000 they needed to start with. Making millions immediately wasn't realistic, God bless them; but then, all of us are unrealistic in some aspects of our life. We want what we want.

We found that it was best to talk about the huge amounts they *could* make, stress that there were no guarantees they would, and then get back to showing them what they needed to know: how to make a nice income they could build upon. It was a great lesson for all of us involved.

Remember: *your job is to give people what they want*. But there's no reason you can't sneak in what they need, too, when you provide their wants.

Marketing Secret #38:
How to Double Your Sales and Profits in a Year

Once upon a time, there was a groundbreaking fellow named Harry Cunningham. Now, Harry had a super-easy strategy—call it a secret, if you will—that pushed his business profits through the roof. You can incorporate it into your business as well if you haven't already, but most people aren't— which is why focusing on this strategy can be a windfall for most businesses.

So who was Harry Cunningham? He was the man responsible for starting Kmart, which he built into making the biggest discount retailer in the country before Wal-Mart took away that title. It began when he took over a failing store in Gross Pointe, Michigan. Then he incorporated this brilliantly simple strategy that ended up doubling that store's sales...and suddenly it wasn't failing anymore. So how did he do it?

Easy. He had his sales clerks make a note anytime a customer requested something specific. They'd write it down on an index card, and Harry would find a way to get that item into his store. It's amazing how the simple ideas are so often the most profound. The person who owned that store before Harry could have done that, but didn't.

In fact, there are a lot of simple ideas out there that people could use to transform their businesses—but not too many people are using them. Sometimes you hear a marketing secret and say to yourself, "Eh, that's not really such a big deal." But the reason that it's a secret is that *no one is using it.* Harry's strategy was profound because it made his store a one-stop shopping experience. That had an amazing and immediate impact on its profits, just because he gave people what they wanted. All he had to do was ask. Isn't that the simplest thing? But what a profound impact it had!

How can you incorporate this kind of strategy into your local business? You can just ask, too, but it's even better to anticipate what people want in advance. I like to use what I call the "perfect world scenario." In a perfect world, if it were possible to give your customers the thing they wanted the very most, what would it be? You may generate lots of crazy ideas doing this, but, sometimes those crazy ideas *can* work.

Sometimes they're not workable, but you can accomplish the next best thing.

One of the things businesspeople tend to suffer from is pessimism. We consider the worst-case scenario instead of the best. So we shoot down ideas, sometimes thinking we're just being realistic, especially if these ideas are new or untested .But how do you discover new things if you haven't thought about the situation from that perspective before, or at least checked to see if it might work? If you're in a rut, you can't just shoot down a new idea when someone offers it. Stop fearing change, even when it might force you out of your comfortable behavior set. That attitude won't put you ahead of the pack. At best, you'll be among them, where you'll all be snapping and slavering at each other.

Open yourself up to the perfect world scenario and let the ideas flow. Sure, you'll have to come back later and figure out which ideas are workable, while realizing that even if some aren't workable now, it may become workable in the future. When an idea is in its baby stage, when you're just planning and thinking about all of the things that could be, let it alone for a while. You never know what it could grow up to be.

If you've got sales clerks, encourage them to ask customers if there was anything they were looking for they didn't find. Maybe they just didn't see it, or maybe you haven't thought to add it yet. Maybe you can order it right then and there for them. You can do surveys, if your business model supports them. However you handle it, let them tell you what they want—and then set out to give it to them.

My friend and mentor, Russ von Hoelscher, used to own a small chain of bookstores in San Diego County. He'd owned a couple of stores in Minneapolis/St. Paul before moving to San Diego, and says that while he gave his Minnesota customers what they wanted when they asked, he didn't make as much of an effort to find out what that was as he did in San Diego. That's when he decided to put a suggestion box in the store. He knew he could make money on bestsellers, and he liked science fiction, westerns, mysteries, and historical novels, so he had all of those. He also had a moderate romance section. After he put that suggestion box in, it didn't take him long to realize that the customers wanted lots more romantic novels. He started to pile in the Harlequin, Dove, and historical romances. Russ had no personal interest in them, but he wasn't his own customer, and they became bestsellers in the store.

Regardless of what your business is, I recommend a suggestion box—even a virtual one if you're mostly online. Let people make suggestions about what they want to buy. It's easy to set one up. Once a week you can open it and take out the suggestions. You can enhance this, and get more people to participate, if you offer a weekly drawing. Russ started with $25 worth of books and took it up to $50 worth by the end. Your customers will love this, and tell you exactly what they want to buy from you.

You can lose a fortune if you ignore this principle. Take Henry Ford, for example. He revolutionized the automobile industry—he created it, really. His Model T was the first affordable car, making it possible for virtually everyone in America to own an automobile. They sold so many that at one point, it seemed like everyone had one. Then, *bam*, the market changed. All of a sudden, people didn't want cars that looked identical—so they started asking for simple variations, like different colors. Ford's response was the famous, "They can have

100 MARKETING SECRETS

their Model T in whatever color they want, as long as it's black." Frankly, that reminds me of Marie Antoinette's comment when told that the poor were upset because they didn't have any bread: "Let them eat cake." Some historians argue that she wasn't being nasty when she said it; she was simply raised in privilege, and had never eaten a meal that didn't include both bread and cake. She couldn't conceive of the fact that when people couldn't afford bread, they certainly couldn't afford cake.

But in the end that comment got her beheaded in the French Revolution, just as Henry Ford's flippant comment got him beheaded in the very market he had created almost from scratch. He tuned out to what the market wanted, which opened the door for GM and other competitors to offer people cars that allowed them to differentiate themselves from everyone else, to make their own personal statements. Ford lost millions because he was resistant to change. I see this happen all the time. I've even been guilty of it myself. Your market is constantly changing—and you've got to stay on top of it.

Marketing Secret #39:
The Hard-Sell Advertisement

Back in the 1950s, legendary marketer Rosser Reeves created a marketing method that works even better today: the Hard-Sell Advertisement. Its purpose is to cut through all the clutter people face daily and drive that sales message home. For example: he created a commercial for Anacin, the headache tablet, that was soon called "the most hated TV commercial in the history of advertising." You'd think that would have hurt Anacin, but here's the reality: when he started working with that account, they were selling $18 million a year worth of the pills. Within 18 months, he tripled their sales.

This is a secret you can use to dramatically increase your profits, and it all boils down to simply selling your products harder. With marketing, the only thing that counts is *results*. It's all about who buys your products, not who doesn't. That Anacin commercial may have annoyed the hell out of people, but it struck a chord with them—and they remembered it when they had headaches.

So many advertisements produce zero results. They're cute and funny, and they're meant to peddle brand awareness—a complete rip-off for small business people. They may work for Coke and Anacin, but they won't work for you, no matter what medium you use. Your business is too limited. Accept that and move on.

You have to use the Rosser Reeves approach to draw in customers. *Your* goal must be to cut through all the senseless clutter, to drive your sales message home. That's truer now than ever before, because the market is more saturated than ever. It's over-hyped, over-crowded, and the average consumer has built up a huge resistance to sales messages. As you go about cutting through that resistance, you can't worry about upsetting people. But many people do, which is why don't do a harder job of selling.

If there's one word I think is more important than any other when it comes to this subject, it's *disruptive*. Your marketing has to be disruptive. You have to be willing to offend people, to follow up relentlessly, to be extremely aggressive with your marketing. Worry only about the people you're trying to sell to; forget the others. Who cares if they find your ad offensive? You're out to make money. You have competitors after the same exact people you're trying to attract, so you have to be more and more aggressive.

Many years ago, one of the greats of advertising, Claude

Hopkins, took over the account for Schlitz beer in Milwaukee, Wisconsin. Schlitz was struggling, but it had potential, and Claude Hopkins did a whole series of ads and commercials for them. In them he told people exactly how Schlitz beer was produced, starting with the use of deep well water and going through all the meticulous things the brewers did to bring that beer to the public, including the fine ingredients they used. At one point someone said to him, "But *all* modern brewers do the same things we do." Claude Hopkins replied, "That may be true, but they're not telling people that."

Schlitz went from being poorly known to being the bestselling beer in America. But eventually someone else took over the account, and they decided they'd had enough of the advertising that had made Schlitz famous. They decided to change the thrust of their ads to the old slogan, "The beer that made Milwaukee famous." Today Schlitz is still produced, but it's not even in the top 20 best-selling beers, much less #1.

Good marketing can build up a company or a brand—and bad marketing can kill it. You have to be careful how you advertise your business, or else you won't have any. So it's important to consider this strategy. A lot of the brilliant advertising we see today—the good, hard-hitting direct-response marketing and some of the most successful TV and radio ads— owe their success to the strategies Rosser Reeves was using back in the 1950's. The results really *are* the important part, so stop worrying about offending people. Worry instead about the people you'll attract.

It's important to remember that the *only* thing that matters in the end is whether the ad makes a profit for your company. You need to pull in your best prospects and repel everyone else.

If you're not doing that, your advertising isn't working. A mediocre or lukewarm response won't do it. You need to generate some buzz, drawing in some people while pushing away the tire kickers, the half-interested, the lookie-loos. Part of the reason Anacin is so well known today is because of the hard-sell commercials Reeves created for them, the ones that turned so many people off—because they also *sold* a lot of people. He increased sales from $18 million to $54 million in 18 months. That's phenomenal!

The object of the game is to make as many sales as you can. Don't worry about offending the wrong people; sometimes, even offending the right people can be good. Sometimes the people who are the most upset are the ones who buy the most. Every single day of every week, we see people go from hot to buyers. The reason they buy is because they're frustrated; things aren't quite working for them, and they're looking for solutions in the form of your product or service.

Many people are coming to you upset anyway—and your product or service may be the one thing that brings smiles to their faces.

Marketing Secret #40:
Understand Why People Do What They Do and Want What They Want

As a marketer, it's crucial that you understand human nature as intimately as possible. The better you understand your customers and prospects, the better your profits; it's that simple. So develop a complete understanding of what people want or need...and again, focus on *want*. Know that the top two motivators of the buying public are greed and fear of loss. People mostly buy what they want, but they'll also go to great lengths to preserve what they already have.

Some people are motivated by power and superiority. Some want sex. Others are just lazy, and that motivates them in surprising ways. Love is always a big motivator; the same goes for the desire for recognition. Pride and ego are very powerful. Some people are so bored and feel so empty that they're searching for something or someone to turn their life around. Pain, both physical and emotional, motivates us to do all kinds of things, some of which aren't even good for us. Then you have the emotional distress, anger, anxiety, frustrations, and confusions that make people do things they later regret. People always seek immediate comfort and security. Finally, we do many things out of habit—again, sometimes to our detriment.

Many people just want attention—and they especially want to be appreciated. That's something you should definitely play to, because it often makes them feel good enough to favor you with an order. Anything you can do to make someone feel better about themselves is a powerful marketing tool. We are, each and every one of us, flawed human beings—and we all have some of these desires and feelings we need to be healed of or helped with. We need someone to show us what to do to make our lives better. Well, good advertising does that...or at least, it's perceived as doing so. That gets a person's business.

Consider the psychology behind each of these common denominators. We can observe what people do, and often why they do those things are obvious. Sometimes they're not, but you still have to try figure out the why. If you can discover why people are behaving a certain way, you're more likely to determine how to get them to respond to your offers. If I'm trying to help someone stop smoking, for example, I can see that they smoke; that's an observation, but the *reason* they smoke is what I need to get at if I'm going to find a cure for that obviously self-destructive behavior.

Similar, it's easy to see when someone is overweight...but knowing why helps you get to the cure for it. Maybe it's a glandular issue; or maybe they live in a land of such plenty it's easy to overeat (that's mostly our excuse for it, here in the U.S.!). But there's probably a psychological component in there somewhere. So before you promote your offer, attempt to understand the behavior you see, and how to sell to it. Why are they doing what they're doing?

The common denominators I outlined earlier in this section really are key here; they're all basic to human nature, so I encourage you to study them closely. Again, they include:

Greed
Fear
Power
Superiority
Pain
Emotional Discomfort
Habits

These can all help you figure out why people in your marketplace are behaving a certain way, so you'd better address those things in your advertising. Why does someone want to buy a boat, a new car, a specific house, your widgets, or the fashions you sell in your clothing store? Knowing the Why will help you advertise to them, using just the right marketing tools, offers, and hooks to draw their interest. If the Why isn't obvious, dig deeper.

In fact, it's a good idea to keep digging even when it *is* obvious.

If you had to focus on only two of these, make them greed and fear. I know that may sound a little ruthless, but it's reality. Look no further, because most things people do can be traced back to greed and/or fear, and *maybe* the desire for power or superiority.

Remember that story earlier in the chapter about our seminar customers not just wanting to make money, but wanting to make millions of dollars effortlessly? That's greed. We never for one second promised them that they *would* do that, but we did have to address what they really wanted. They wanted the dream to be real, and that's what we had to give to them. Knowing Why is vitally important in all your marketing endeavors.

CHAPTER FIVE

SECRETS 41-50

Marketing Secret #41: The Danger of Thinking Big

Many of the biggest thinkers also happen to be the biggest losers.

Right about now you may be thinking, "What!? I thought this was a positive book! Now you're telling me that thinking big can make me a big loser? What the heck is *that* about?" Well, Of course, the title was mostly a teaser to get your attention—but it's still true.

With this secret, I'm going to tell you about a question that leads to an amazing answer that can produce instant sales and profits. Here's the thing: any fool can think big, and most fools do. So there's nothing inherently positive about thinking big; in fact, it can be downright dangerous. It's what you think about and how you think about it that matters. *Of course* you want to dream big and have big goals—but most people do that. Yet what are they doing to make those dreams a reality?

Nada. Let's be honest here. Most big thinkers are just being delusional, because there's no way they'll ever be able to bring their goals to fruition. They have no plan of action to make it happen. You can sit around all day long and dream big dreams, but without a plan of action, you'll go bankrupt. Despite what some celebrities keep insisting—people who are ALREADY rich, by the way, often because they worked hard for what they have—just wishing for things doesn't make you successful. You have to couple those big thoughts with a solid game plan for achieving the desired results.

I started out this section by telling you that there's danger in thinking big—and so there is. But many things in life are dangerous. Simply getting into business increases the chance that you'll fail in business...just as living increases your chances of dying. The reality is that the only way you'll ever succeed big-time is to dream bigger, think bigger, and try to accomplish more than anybody else is willing to. I recommend you read *The Magic of Thinking Big* by David Schwartz. It shows you how to combine big dreams with the right plan of action. Schwartz's book is an old one (it was originally published in 1959) but that makes his ideas no less valid.

You don't get bigger by thinking small, folks. Small thinking generates small results. Sure, sometimes big thinking does lead to bad things; you may experience negative outcomes as you try to grow your business. Life's never going to be perfect. But you have to dream big anyway...because so many people don't.

Here's a story from *The Magic of Thinking Big* about a chat David Schwartz had with a recruiting specialist for one of the nation's largest industrial organizations at the time. Remember, this was more than 50 years ago. This woman interviewed young people for jobs in her industry as they were preparing to graduate from college. She said that most days, she interviewed 8-12 students, all from the upper third of their class. She wanted to determine through the screening process each student's motivations for coming aboard, to find out if they were the kind of person who, after a few years and some training, would be able to direct major projects and do big things within the company.

She told Schwartz, "I must say that I'm not too pleased with the personal objectives of most of those that I talk with. You'd be surprised how many 22-year-olds are more interested in our retirement plan than anything else that we have to offer. Their second favorite question is, 'Will I move around a lot?' Most of them seemed to define the word "success" as synonymous with "security." Can we risk turning our company over to people like that? The thing that I can't understand is why young people these days would be so ultraconservative and so narrow in their view of their future. Every day there are more signs of an expanding opportunity in this country."

Here she was, talking to young, bright people ready to graduate from college, people with their whole adult lives ahead of them—and they were worried about security instead of opportunities. What her company was looking for was someone who was hungry, someone with big dreams that went beyond protecting their little nest egg and retirement plan.

That's really what this principle is all about. Yes, thinking big can lead to negative results. You can lose it all, or you might spin your wheels. But what are you going to do to try to turn those big dreams into reality? Your plan of action is what gets you there. Thinking big is good—but you have to think big *and* smart.

The con artists on Wall Street and elsewhere like to target wealthy, intelligent people. They tell them they can make tremendous riches by investing their money a certain way, with unheard-of returns. You might think only dumb people would go for that...but dumb people don't have much money, do they? They know people so well they can sell even a genius a bill of goods. Some, like Bernie Madoff, take in billions of dollars with their scams. That's caused by people thinking big, but thinking greedy.

As I outlined in the last section, greed is a prime motivator in the marketplace—but it can get you in trouble. When someone says, "Invest a $1 million with me, and next year you'll have $2.5 million. I've done it for others and I'll do it for you," that should be a red flag, even in a bull market. You'd think that smart, wealthy people would say, "C'mon now. I know how to get 5-10% annual return on my money easily—but you're talking about more than doubling my money in a year!" But they still fall prey to these scams.

Even being careful with your big dreams is no guarantee. Many people who dream big and smart still fail. The important thing is not to give up. Some of the world's biggest successes have failed multiple times. Knock them on their ass 10 times, and they'll get up 11 times. That's the kind of big thinker that you need to be; don't confuse greed with tenacity, because that will lead you straight to disaster.

The Magic of Thinking Big, which I first read 30 years ago, changed my life. It's still in print for a good reason. I've seen a lot of wild-eyed dreamers—I've been one myself—and this book can help separate them from the real entrepreneurs, or at least teach the wild-eyed what entrepreneurship really is.

What separates the dreamers from the doers is a plan of action, and the willingness to stick with it long enough to see it come true.

Develop as many different strategies as you can. It's nice to dream, but while you're dreaming you should strategize and create contingency plans for anything that might go wrong. You should be willing to test a lot of different ideas to find out which ones work, because you never really know what will. You have to factor in all the potential problems, obstacles, headaches, and challenges.

The wild-eyed dreamer always thinks everything will just fall together for them. It very rarely does. That's magical thinking, and you need to avoid it.

Marketing Secret #42:
A Five-Step Formula for Powerful Promotions

This formula can be your #1 secret to getting the very best prospects in your marketplace to do business with you, and it takes just five simple steps.

Step #1: Focus on the marketplace, *not* the product or service. **Step #2:** Write your sales material based on the biggest wants, hopes, dreams, and fears of your target market. **Step #3**: Make the biggest, boldest believable promises you possibly can. **Step #4**: Throw in a ton of specific facts and figures, to make it seem even more real. **Step #5**: Use your sales material as a template for your fulfillment material.

This formula mostly applies to information products or services, but any business can use parts or all of it—so let's go over these steps in more detail. **Step #1:** Make it all about them, *never* about you. Mention yourself only to emphasize your ability to provide what they want the most.

The time for you to create your sales materials is when you're still at the height of your passion. This is integral to **Step #2**. Selling is a transference of emotion and belief, so crank it out while you're hot. Don't put together a product or service first and

169

then worry about how to sell it. Focus on how you'll sell it *first*. The item is secondary.

Step #3: The bigger the promise, the bigger your sales. Remember the perfect world scenario I discussed earlier. If you could give people anything their hearts desired, what would it be? How would you do it? Pretend you could conjure whatever their hearts desired, like magic. Then find a way to come as close to that as possible.

In **Step #4**, prove that it's real with facts and figures—a preponderance of evidence, if you will. Pretend you're an attorney, defending a client accused of murder. What would you do, especially if you honestly believed he was innocent and you had to save his life? You'd come up with a preponderance of evidence demonstrating his innocence. You have to do that with your sales materials too.

Finally, rewrite your sales materials and use them as part of your fulfillment. I know that that's a little tricky, and it means different things to different people, but the main thing about **Step #5** is that your sales materials are the most important thing part of the process. Later, after you've already gotten their business, constantly remind them that you have and *are* giving them the things you promised to in your sales copy.

This is a simple but powerful formula, and Step #1 is the linchpin that holds it together. *Never* forget that the marketplace is more important than the product or service. I don't know how many times I have to say that to people, but it seems so hard for them to understand. Too many people fall in love with their own offers; but you have to be realistic here, focusing tightly on the marketplace. Your focus must be on who you're selling to, not *what* you're selling. Write all your sales materials first, based on the client's biggest wants, hopes, and dreams. If you were a marketing god, what would you say to them? How would you convey that message?

Once you've made every effort to make the biggest promises you can, use your finished sales material as a template for serving it up to them. We've created quite a few audio products that way. We write the letter first, then use it as the guide to the product. In the fulfillment we make sure we cover all the promised points. You can do that over and over again while developing products and services that your market wants.

Think of it as a recipe. If you follow the recipe, you get the desired result. There are different ways to follow this particular recipe—but if you're careful, you'll always end up with something tasty and popular.

Marketing Secret #43:
Don't Run Your Business by Committee

While large businesses are often run by Boards of Directors, that approach doesn't work for the small business (and some say it doesn't work very well for the big ones, either). Look: a business isn't a democracy. When it comes to politics, we want leaders who believe in the American way and free enterprise and everything that makes this country great. But in a small business, you need a true, clear-cut leader who makes the final decisions. He may do so based on advice he gets from other people and sources, but he has to be something of a dictator in many ways.

Everybody who works with you or knows you—your

friends, family, hired help, even the barber down the street—will tell you how to run your business if you let them. You have to learn to say, "Thanks, but no thanks," because to be a successful leader, you must *lead*. Pay attention to experts, especially any you hire to help you; and yes, do listen to good advice from your spouse, relatives, and friends. But be very careful about what you classify as good advice, and always make your own decisions.

It's frustrating to deal with people who hem, haw, scratch their heads, and say, "Well, maybe we should do this, or maybe we should do that." I've noticed that such people aren't usually very successful, because they lack the ability to stand up and make a decision on their own. I've seen this happen many times in my marketing career, and so have my colleagues. Here's an example of what I mean, courtesy of Russ von Hoelscher.

Years ago, in addition to his biz-op and marketing business, Russ also owned several other businesses, including the bookstores I've already mentioned, a movie theater, and a newsstand. He got to know a fellow called "Big Gene" who sold business signs like "Open for Business," "No Smoking," and the like. Big Gene's brother-in-law and sister actually made the signs, and their business did well in the San Diego area. Russ got to thinking, "I wonder if this guy could make signs cheap enough that we could put together a nice color brochure and get into the sign business nationwide." Russ knew of another sign company that had advertized in the biz op magazines years before, and thought it could work.

Russ made the pitch to Gene's brother-in-law, who seemed excited by the idea...but for some reason, decided he had to run it past his wife and two employees first. Well, he came back days later and said, "No dice. They hated the idea." When

Russ asked why, the sign-maker said, "Well, we'd be shipping signs, and shipping is a big hassle." Russ told him, "It's not *that* big of a hassle—and I can handle that for you." Then the guy said, "Well, my wife and the employees just don't want it. I'm for you, Russ. I think this is a great idea. I think we could make a lot of money, but the guys working for me and my wife say no." That just ticked Russ off no end, because the sign man was letting his employees decide how to run his business for him!

We've all run into this before, instances where business people have other people around them who just say, "No way!" to growth. Russ also tells a story about a man in New York who made great cat food. Well, he let his wife screw everything up. She tried to tell him exactly what every bag should look like, and that her cat should be on the bag, and on and on until it became a huge hassle. They nearly got a divorce because she wanted to take over the business, even though he started it.

Look: if you're going to run a business, run it. Make your own decisions. You can have great people working for you, and sure, you should listen to their input—if and *only* if it's applicable—because it may help you make the right decision. You can also listen to your spouse, but ultimately *you* have to make the decision.

Don't let your implementation dictate your marketing, as the sign-maker did. If you have a little difficulty in the implementation, that shouldn't have any bearing on whether you strike a deal or not. Yes, we all listen to what other people think. But you have to run a business more like a dictatorship than a democracy. *You* must be the one making all of the decisions, because ultimately *you* are the one responsible for your business. You can't be a good business owner if you're constantly second-guessing yourself. Sometimes your decisions work, sometimes they don't. Live with it. The worst thing you can do is be wishy-washy, always asking for peoples' opinions and never making a decision on your own.

There's a famous quote from the 16th century that goes, "Rule with an iron fist in a velvet glove." I've always loved the contrast there. You have to take charge, be responsible, and accept accountability for success or failure. The buck stops with you. It's easy to blame other people, but true strength comes from what I call TTR: "Take Total Responsibility." Only when you assume responsibility do you gain any power. It's too easy to blame other people and make excuses—and people who are great at making excuses are lousy at making money. The two are incompatible.

Another lesson from Russ's story is that when considering any kind of new strategy, most people focus on the potential headaches and hassles instead of on the money they can make. And sure, the pain's there—but why see everything from the bottom up instead of the top down? Having been on both ends of the scale of riches, I can assure you that poverty sucks rocks. It's hugely better to have to deal with a few challenges and make money hand over fist than to wonder where your next meal is coming from. Don't talk yourself out of success!

That's the difference between entrepreneurs and those who have what I call an "employee mentality." People with the employee mentality *always* see things from the bottom looking up, looking up through all the trouble and pain any business faces, while the entrepreneur sees things from the top down. They perceive the business in a more conceptual way, going for the gold and ignoring the dirt they have to screen through to get it. They refuse to be bogged down by the details. That's what leadership is all about—and that's what makes entrepreneurs great leaders. They're visionaries. They're moving forward, and tend to attract other people who want to come along for the ride and who love the excitement, the thrill of it all—and, of course the profits.

Marketing Secret #44: The People You Should Fear Most

Looking at the title to this marketing secret, you're probably thinking: aha, the government! But that's not who I mean. While there may be reasons to afraid of the government (can you say "IRS?"), I'm leaning more toward the kind of people you can trust in business. Who do you look to for advice and help? You have to figure that out in order to know who to be afraid of.

I covered this somewhat in the last secret, when I warned you that *you* have to be the decision-maker for your business. No matter where you look, there are people all around you offering advice. Some will offer good advice, but many will lead you completely astray. The group of people I'm going to discuss next is the group of people in that last category you can trust the least. Maybe you're surrounded by these people already and don't know it.

This may sound a little off, but bear with me here, because I have some caveats you'll have to consider carefully before you dismiss this group out of hand. The people you need to be the most wary of are **experts**.

Right about now you might be thinking, "Wait a minute. *You're* an expert." Yes, but in my opinion, there are two types of experts. The problem with those in the first group—and that's most experts, period—is that they're *almost always wrong*. Consider your weather experts. They're wrong constantly; it seems the only time they're ever right is when the weather is actually happening. If they say it's raining right now, you can trust that, because you can look out the window and see that it's so. They may tell you it'll be hot in the summer, and yep, they're usually on the mark there. But if they tell you it will rain next week, how often are they right? Not that often. Past that, they're guessing.

Sports experts are also often wrong, and these are people who've spent their entire careers studying their subjects. I'm fascinated with football and college basketball, and as you watch these games, the experts often predict the scores...and then you see what their records are so far this year, and they're lucky if they're batting .500. C'mon, now—a monkey with a dartboard can be right half the time. So you can't trust weather experts or sports experts...and you can't trust most business experts either. Back in 1899, Charles Duel, the Commissioner of the U.S. Patent Office, declared, "Everything that can be invented already *has* been invented." He really missed the boat on that one. Consider electronics, CDs, and lasers, just for a few examples. In 1963, Thomas Watson, the Chairman of IBM, said, "I think there's a world market for maybe five computers." Some of us have five computers in our own homes! This next one is really good: Decca Recording Company rejected the Beatles in 1962, saying, "We don't like their sound, and guitar music is on the way out." Are you *kidding* me?

Even Orville Wright once said, "No flying machine will ever fly from New York to Paris." Chris Lakey, has been on several flights from the U.S. to China, and that's much farther than a trip from New York to Paris. Airplanes fly between New York and Paris daily—even though the co-inventor of aviation said it would never happen.

All of these prognostications by experts were wrong. Experts are *always* missing the mark. So be very careful about which experts you pay attention to. Ignore the pundits and the talking heads; the only people you should pay attention to are those who are out there doing what you want to do, or who've already done it. Forget those who lack experience on the front lines, or who haven't been where you want to go. The experienced experts are the ones who've lived to tell about it and can share their stories and success with you. And even they aren't always right!

Suppose someone comes along who has never accomplished anything in the field he's offering advice on, though maybe he's earned a college degree in it. That doesn't make him an expert even when he calls himself one, so you have be very cautious about listening to what he has to say. If, on the other hand, someone offering advice can point to genuine experience and accomplishments in your field, their advice is worth listening to. Even then, you have to weigh it against the needs and demands of your business.

Those are the people you can trust, and they don't always call themselves experts. They're just people out there doing it. There's an old saying that goes, "Those who can, do; those who can't, teach." The "experts" who were never successful doing something—or never actually tried—are those who can't. They're theorizing or teaching classes about it. The rest of us get out there and do it.

So fear the experts, especially the self-titled ones. At least do your due diligence and check them out. Find out if they've gotten the results they're recommending; and if they have, can you take what they're doing and run with it? If so, take their advice. Otherwise, you're wasting your time and money.

Here's a good example. Once upon a time, Russ von Hoelscher and his colleagues Dan Pointer and Harvey Shelton hosted a self-publishing seminar in San Diego. Russ spoke mostly about writing the sales copy, while Dan Pointer took the audience step-by-step through how to write and promote a book. Back then, Dan was recognized as a leading teacher of self-publishing, and he's still held in the highest of esteem. Harvey Shelton was a printer who was looking for self publishers to do business with. They spoke to a group of about 70 or 80 people, and among them were two English professors from San Diego State University.

The professors approached Russ during a break, and scolded him for "massacring the English language" in his sales literature. Russ asked them what they meant, though he had a hunch already. One said, "You use phrases like 'you gotta do this.' Gotta is *not* an English word, and you have about a dozen or more words here that are absolutely in the wrong place."

Russ replied, "Gentleman, I realize you're from academia and probably smarter than I am, but you have to realize that we're not here to teach you English Composition. We're here to teach you how to make money. When you're writing sales copy, you don't have the luxury of worrying about rules, and you shouldn't—because in the real world, people don't use proper English. We have to appeal to people in the real world. Can you understand that?" One admitted that Russ had a point, but the other said, "No, I don't buy it. If you're going to teach people how to write, you've got to use proper English." Well, try that and see how much money you make.

So sure, some people are experts—but their expertise won't make you a dime.

This is one of my pet peeves, actually. When I peruse books about small business in bookstores, I often find that the people who wrote them don't have a *clue* about operating small businesses. Often they've never owned their own businesses, or they're business professors who've never left academia and don't know jack when it comes to earning real money. In other cases, they're trying to teach you strategies applicable to Fortune 500 companies, which are useless on the small-business level.

I've got one right now that was written by an "expert"...and I feel truly sorry for anybody who reads any of his books. This one is called *The 12 Secrets of Business*, and not *once* does he mention the words marketing, selling, or advertising. None of his secrets have anything to do with actually selling anything, if you can believe that. I've got the cover of that book on my wall just to remind me what *not* to do.

Business is based on marketing, period—selling and reselling to people over and over.

There's a business professor on a TV commercial who says, "If you want to be successful in business, the key is this copy machine." Excuse me? Business success reduces to how well you can make copies? Ridiculous. A copy machine is just a tool. *Don't let the experts lead you astray.* Find people who are making it big and have already been where you want to go—and listen to them. Those are the only experts that count.

100 MARKETING SECRETS

Marketing Secret #45:
Five Secrets from Advertising Legend David Ogilvy

If you don't know who David Ogilvy is, you can Google him. The man is a genius, one of the greatest advertising experts who ever lived. In this section, I'll share five of the best secrets that I pulled out of one of his books.

Secret #1: What you say is more important than how you say it. **Secret #2:** 99% of advertising doesn't sell much of anything at all. **Secret #3:** The consumer is not a moron. She is your wife. **Secret #4:** Don't bunt. Aim out of the ballpark. **Secret #5:** Hard work never killed a man. Men die of boredom, psychological conflict, and disease. Indeed, the harder you work, the happier and healthier you will be.

Let's look at each of these items in more detail. First of all: what you say is more important than how you say it. You have to get inside the heads and hearts of the people you want to attract, especially those you want to become your very best customers. Who are they? What's most important to them? You can't just ask that question on the surface once and expect to understand; you have to keep asking it repeatedly, and take it to heart. Try to become them, just like a great character actor. Think of the best character actors you know—people like Jack Nicholson or Meryl Streep. They play their roles so convincingly because they become the characters they're pretending to be. They move you emotionally.

I honestly believe that in order to say the right things to the people you're trying to attract, you have to almost become them. You have to think like they do, you have to see what they see; and only then will you be able to create the kinds of messages that drive them wild with excitement. Try to get behind the eyeballs and under the skin of your best customers, then spend a lot of time fine-tuning your marketing message.

The second point is that most advertising doesn't sell anything. The better you understand this concept, the better off you are. Most advertising is a joke, designed to be cute and clever and make you laugh—but that's not supposed to be the purpose of advertising. Don't ever make that mistake. Advertising is supposed to sell things. Most advertising doesn't bother, which should boost your confidence—so open your eyes and wake up a little. How are your competitors handling their advertising? Are they doing a good job of selling their products and services? In almost all cases, they're not. Make sure that yours does. Emulate the few competitors who really have it going on—and try to beat them. Save those sales materials in a swipe file, to help you develop your own advertising that sells.

In his third point, David reminds us out that the consumer isn't a moron. You've got to respect the people you do business with, which often means getting up close and personal with them. The older I get, the more I believe that; it's one of the reasons I love doing seminars. During a seminar I hug my customers, I listen to them, and I spend good, quality time with them—or at least, I try to. I think that whatever business you're in, you should be spending face-to-face, eyeball-to-eyeball, belly-to-belly time with your customers. Get close enough to smell their breath. Don't be afraid of them at all.

I'm convinced that a lot of people are attracted to the DRM business because they *don't* want to have personal contact with other people. They love the idea that they can do business with people they'll never have to meet. But that's a completely wrongheaded approach. Russ von Hoelscher got us involved in seminars right from the beginning; we've had several hundred since 1990, and hosting them turned out to be one of the smartest moves we've ever made as a company. I'm very grateful to Russ for getting us involved, because it allows us intimate contact with our customers. You can't do that over the telephone or Internet.

In his fourth point, David talks about aiming out of the ball park. You have to go for the gold—think, dream, plan, and even pray bigger. I love this quote from Babe Ruth: "When you hit the ball over the fence, you can take your time strolling around the bases. You don't even have to run. You can just skip or strut." Look for the things that are going to produce the biggest profits and sales for you, letting you skip and strut.

The last point is the simple reality that hard work won't kill you (except in a few extreme cases). I know you can get burned out. I've been burned out myself, and it's not a productive place to be. I've learned that I have to push myself but pace myself. Push but pace—that's one of my mantras. I think David's point is that rather than killing you, hard work does just the opposite. Find a challenging business you're totally passionate about. If you're not passionate about the business you're in now, get out of it and get involved in something you *do* have passion for.

Now, there are times when you rebel against hard work. It can take me a while to get motivated; but once I'm into it for a while, I stay with it until the job is done. That's a lesson we can all learn from. When you start a job correctly, you're already half there. Oh, you may have to stay with it for many, many more hours, but when you make that commitment to do it, you've made a tremendous stride in the right direction.

I'm always surprised and excited by how many people in the DRM business are in their 70s or 80s, and still going strong. Many of my colleagues feel the same; Russ says that he's especially motivated by a couple of people in San Diego, one of whom I know, who are in their 80's but still working hard because they're passionate about what they're doing. I'm convinced that if you love your business and you're motivated to stay with it, to keep trying to make it more successful, it's going to help you live longer.

We now know that the people who live longest are those who have some motivation to keep going. When you're considering the next big thing you want to do in business, this should be one of your motivations. Keep that in mind regardless of how old you are. If you're passionate about your business, if you love what you're doing, your chances of success are far better. As the years go by, you'll have a reason to continue to live, work, and achieve, because that's what we do when we really care about our work.

Before we move on to the next secret, I want to re-emphasize that the consumer is *not* a moron. Too often, business owners try to second-guess the customer. Ultimately, in a free market economy, the consumer sets the tone and decides what's going to sell and what isn't, within certain limits set by the government and big business. The consumers tell you what's important to them, and you respond to that. Consumers are actually very smart about what they want, so pay very close attention to what they're saying.

And again, don't bunt; aim out of the ballpark. Dream big. Most bunts don't accomplish much beyond the occasional base hit. Even a successful bunt, in baseball terms, is only used to move a runner over; and almost always, you yourself get tagged out and end up back in the dugout. So aim big. If you always try for the big hits, sometimes you'll hit grand slams, sometimes you'll hit a home run, sometimes you get triples, doubles, or singles—and sometimes you'll strikeout. Babe Ruth led his league in home runs *and* strikeouts. But you'll always end up with bigger and better things. The average length of your hits will be longer, because you're always swinging for the fences.

It's always easiest to play it safe, to keep your business small and manageable. A lot of businesses get by just by doing that; it's all they want. They never expand or grow, never try to do big things; they exist in a small bubble. But the ones that make history are the ones that dreamed big and took massive action to try to accomplish their goals.

Marketing Secret #46:
A Fast, Powerful Checklist for Writing Copy That Sells

The very first thing you need when writing good, top-selling copy is a great headline. That's especially important for print ads, but use the principle in sales letters as well. A headline must grab the reader's attention—grab him by the throat and pull him in so he starts reading the rest of the copy, which should be simple and straightforward. I don't care whether you're writing to high school dropouts or Ph.D.s: make it easy to understand. You don't want people to mistake what you're saying in any way.

Next, pile on the benefits to enhance your offer, especially if it's an expensive one. Lots of free bonuses can help justify a higher price, so jazz things up and make it exciting. Keep them reading by using different styles of type, bullets, graphic teasers—anything that keeps the reader enthralled. Then make a list of all the objections people might have, and answer them preemptively, right there in black-and-white.

Put personality on every page; make it exciting. And be sure to build a legal defense in your copy. If you're writing about a business opportunity that can help people make up to $25,000 a month in profit, it's not wise to say, "You *will* make $25,000 a month." You do not know what a person's going to do or how hard they'll work, so you have to use words like *possible, potential, the power to make,* etc—not because you want to beat around the bush, but because there are legal ramifications if you tell someone they can make so much per month and they don't. Even if they don't try, they can come back and say, "You lied to us in print!"

You also have to give people a reason to take action immediately, which you usually do through a limited offer. Set a deadline—for example, 15 days from the day you send out your sales letter—and make it the cutoff date. Tell them if they want to take advantage of your special offer, they'll have to respond immediately. That works like magic, because an offer available for anybody at any time loses a lot of its power.

Once you've put together your sales letter, read it out loud. You might be surprised to hear things that just don't quite sound right, so that you need to tweak the text a bit. Many of us use this trick, and you may find that it's very helpful to you. Next, make it look different from the average sales letter. Experiment with various envelopes, in terms of color and design. You may very well come across a combination that works ten times better than all the others, for reasons that aren't obvious.

Every time you write any type of sales copy, make sure

you follow all these rules. Are there some that work better than others, that are more important? Of course. I think the idea of answering potential objections in your sales text is arguably the most powerful point I've mentioned here. Most of your sales letter may end up addressing the objections, though it usually doesn't happen that way. I also think it's especially important to read it out loud. It's amazing how many times you can read over something silently and it looks fine—but then when you read it aloud it doesn't sound right.

That's important to discover, because many people read the copy "out loud" in their heads; that is, they think it as if they're hearing it in normal speech, with all the overtones and cadences. If you find yourself stumbling over certain words or pronouncing them the wrong way, the readers may do the same. Also, many times when we're reading our sales copy mentally, we'll read something that's not there because we know what it should say...even if there's a missing word or two.

If you want to take it to the extreme, record yourself reading aloud; it's easy to do these days with something like an iPhone or iPad. Then listen to it, and you'll hear even more things to fix. It's important to ensure there are no stumbling blocks in your copy. You don't want people to get hung up when they're reading it to themselves; you want it to flow smoothly, and for them to move from one point to the next seamlessly, without any confusion, hang-ups, or stumbling blocks.

And another thing: if you can avoid it, don't farm your copywriting out to other people. Sure, let an expert like Russ von Hoelscher go through it and make suggestions; but realize that this is a skill you need to learn. It took me eight years to get it right—but I made money the whole time, so you can learn as you earn.

Let's look more closely at another item I'm particularly fond of: the second, what I call the Pile-On. In this day and age, when the marketplace is hugely overhyped and oversaturated, you really have to pile on the positives. Every offer has to be bigger and bolder than the one before. The consumer is looking for an irresistible offer, not just a good one; they want something they can't say no to. They don't want cheap things; they want expensive things for low prices. You create that perception of value with a Pile-On offer. They'll get this, plus this, this, and this. Spend a lot of time working on your offer.

Last December we presented our customers with our annual end-of-the-year offer, which we built up as big as we could. But then, when we got down to San Diego a couple of weeks before and did a seminar, all of a sudden it was crunch time—and Chris Lakey and Drew Hansen, my Sales Manager, came up with four new things to add to what I already thought was an irresistible offer. I didn't think it could possibly *be* any better than it was, and yet they found a way to make it better! Now we're taking their ideas and expanding them to other offers. *Always* look for ways to pile it on.

Marketing Secret #47:
Why You Should Be Begging for More Problems in Your Business, Not Fewer

Read that header again. You may think it sounds crazy...but I know from experience that having more problems than you like can drive you to make more money than ever, assuming you handle the situation correctly.

100 MARKETING SECRETS

Part of the reason this works so well in business is that most of your competitors spend their lives trying to avoid as many problems as possible. That's no surprise; it's human nature to want to live a comfortable life, so we do whatever we can to avoid even the slightest discomfort. Some of us take it to such an extreme that we run away as fast as possible when trouble arises. We can spend our entire business lives doing this.

Ah, but if you let them, problems can actually be useful, because they spur you into taking massive action for your business. They can put you under tremendous pressure to perform; and *that's* why you should seek out more problems that will create even more pressure. Those problems lead to profitable solutions, as I know very well from experience. Our most profitable quarters have resulted from facing down and beating specific problems that were weighing us down. Through that trouble and discomfort came the action necessary to try to break free from the problem, along with a big-money solution.

I'll admit that the process isn't especially fun; no one sane enjoys facing constant problems. At the very least, it's acutely uncomfortable. But that agitation spurs us on to the massive action we need to make our breakthroughs...and then later, when the problem is past, we can enjoy the profits that result!

Think about it. When things are going well, you tend to relax into complacency. You don't really plan on it; it just happens. You get lulled to sleep, and your business becomes mundane as you lose the passion and energy you've accumulated. Sometimes you end up just working hard enough to make it through your daily routine. One thing leads to another, and your business just ends up doing its thing. On the other hand, when faced with a big problem, you're alive and your energy is heightened, and you put all of your passion and attention towards fixing that problem. That may result in a breakthrough and an ensuring flood of cash. So don't see problems as a negative, even though they're sometimes uncomfortable. See them as opportunities for growth! Welcome those problems, welcome those challenges—not because they're fun, not because they're easy, but because growth happens when you're facing them head on and inventing solutions.

Here's a Russ von Hoelscher solution I've used many times. Get up early in the morning and say a little prayer or meditate. Then get yourself a cup of coffee, sit down, and take a piece of paper. At the top of the paper, write down the #1 problem you're facing. Recline a bit and start letting the thoughts come through. Don't pre-judge, just let the ideas flow. You'll be amazed, as I am so often, at what great ideas you get from this simple procedure. It works like magic when you focus totally on the problem.

Approach your problems as life-giving energy sources. Here's why you should: life is action, movement—and problems spur you into action. You need to run towards the things that other people run away from. Too many people go through their whole lives trying to avoid problems, never achieving any real success.

Marketing Secret #48: The 12 Paths to Power

There are two sides to becoming powerful. The first is being able to act effectively; in fact, the definition of power is the ability to act. The second side of power is staying out of other people's control. That's a big one in itself. Here at M.O.R.E. Inc., we've identified 12 paths to power:

Path #1: Know yourself intimately. I believe this one is the most important. Many businesspeople overestimate their chances of success and wildly *under*estimate their chances of failure. This is especially true of wild-eyed, optimistic entrepreneurs. That's another reason to get up at 5 AM with that blank piece of paper and try to think through things from as many angles as possible. Know your strengths and weaknesses, and say no to what I call "open-ended ambitions." People who are very ambitious—and I am one—tend to want it all, just like that Jim Morrison song that goes, "We want the world and we want it now!" That's open-ended ambition, and it's a recipe for disaster. You have to know what you *don't* want as well as what you *do* want.

Path #2: Be an information filter and a knowledge sponge. Keep searching for the truth. Keep trying to figure out what makes other people tick, and why they do what they do. Greater knowledge of yourself and the world around you gives you a wider range of actions to choose from.

Path #3: Get it together. Focus on what you want. Many people want it all, so they're not very powerful. This reflects what I was saying about open-ended ambition.

Path #4: Live an upright life. Honesty really is the best policy. One of my favorite quotes is "To thine own self be true." I've said it to myself thousands of times when I didn't know what to do. If you're true to yourself, you can't be false to others.

Path #5: Take a shot. You can't win if you don't play. Dream big dreams. Go for the gold. Take massive action: start moving in a lot of different directions, and figure things out as you go.

Path #6: Hang in there. Persevere no matter the pain, as

H. Ross Perot once said. You'll find that those who make it in this world are the ones who hang in there longer than everybody else.

Path #7: Pick doable objectives. Don't waste your time and energy fighting losing battles.

Path #8: Don't make a big deal about being the boss. Be humble. You need other people to help you win.

Path #9: Don't motivate other people to oppose you. They say that friends come and go, but enemies stay forever. Don't make people any more jealous than they already are if you're super successful already. Don't strip someone down and cause them to seek revenge. I've made that mistake too many times.

Path #10: Put your adversities to good use. Adversity contains the energy you need to succeed. I've already discussed how problems spur you to action. It's up to you to decide what to do with that action.

Path #11: Calm down. Open-ended desires lead to nothing. Be satisfied with what you have, and then keep pushing. So pace yourself and push yourself.

Path #12: Think win-win. You empower yourself by empowering others. As Zig Zigler once said, "You can have anything in this world you want, if you help enough other people get what *they* want." Think about how you can help other people while helping yourself in the process.

Those are the 12 paths to power. I urge you to reread them and think about them deeply—especially Path #4, live an upright life. To thine own self be true; realize that in your little universe, you're ultimately #1. But let's consider Path #3 in a bit more detail, too. You really must get it together and focus. It's easy to lose track. Given this helter-skelter life we all live, we're constantly bombarded with everything from good to bad to sports to music to other people, the Internet, the signs on the highway, the radio, the TV, and everything else that pulls our focus off anything important. I sincerely believe you have to take the time to focus on what matters, a time when you're alone and can put everything else aside. For morning people, that may be very early; for night owls, it might be very late.

Get rid of all distractions; just allow things to come to and through you as you focus on that aspect of your business life. Those who can learn to focus will be very successful, because there are just so many things happening in life that leave us *un*focused. The better you can focus, the better you can solve a particular problem or suite of problems you're facing. This particular path will serve you well.

I'm also especially fond of Path #9. It's a bit different than the others, because it's more of a philosophical strategy; but I think it's important to realize that there are times for gloating, and times when you should be very careful not to gloat, so you don't create enemies where they don't exist. For example: Chris Lakey is very interested in politics. Naturally, he gets into a lot of conversations on the subject, especially during the height of election season. As a result, he tends to be very cautious in what he says, because he can create enemies just because of his strong political beliefs and tendency to think that he's right (his words, not mine!). As a marketer, this Path especially rings true for him. No matter what you do, you'll encounter enough opposition already without making more—especially if you're successful and your business is growing. Competitors may think you're doing things you shouldn't be, or they may simply be jealous of your success. So never motivate them to go above and beyond their normal reasons for not liking you. Don't give them extra incentive to seek to dominate you in the marketplace. You don't want them to use Ruthless Marketing against you—keep those strategies for yourself. Just let your success speak for itself, and don't give them that added bonus on top of it.

These are our 12 paths to power. Are there more paths? Yes, of course there are—but focus on and master these first.

Marketing Secret #49:
Seven Steps to Mastery of Your Marketplace

If you follow these steps, a thunderstorm of money can rain down on you and your business. Can you handle that? If not, you'd better stop reading, because these steps are like the combination of an overstuffed safe: once you learn how to open it, money just falls out. Really, these are seven steps to freedom—because when you do business the right way, you have the freedom to do what you like, and that makes life a joy.

Without further ado, let's run through these simple steps.

Step #1: Give the customers what they want. It doesn't get much simpler than that. Again, that just seems like common sense, but somehow, many businesspeople don't really understand it. They ignore what the customers want; basically, they offer what they like, and hope enough other people want it that they'll make some money. Well, they've got the formula precisely backward. The real money lies in selling people what they want. We all know customers have needs and wants; and believe me, they'll spend a lot more for their wants than on their needs.

Sometimes it's hard to tell what their wants are. Sometimes the customer won't tell; and even when they do, they may not tell you the truth. They may not know themselves. But you've got to figure it out to master your marketplace. Maybe that means reinventing your business or dropping some products from your product line, launching new products in their place. *Mastering your marketplace means giving people what they want.* The bigger that need or desire is, the more money you can make.

Step #2: Create offers that make them salivate. That's the crave factor. If you're not creating offers they want to respond to, then why are you in business? This goes above and beyond just having something available for sale. You have to create an offer. Package it neatly, put a bow on it, make it presentable so they want to respond. Make them crave it through the best copy you can get. If you can't write it yourself, hire someone who can, because the competition in all media these days is truly fierce.

Step #3: Maintain good sales margins. When in doubt, raise your prices and focus on your best customers and prospects. No one ever went out of business from making too much profit. These are tough times, and trying to sell things on the cheap or appeal to everyone can get you in big trouble. Wal-Mart has been able to get away with it so far by selling at big discounts, but even *their* business is down recently. That's scary, because Wal-Mart is the largest, most successful retail business in the world.

Step #4: Continually improve your follow-up marketing methods. You must rain mail on your prospects. You must keep in touch with buyers on a regular basis, because you want to turn them into long-term customers. Invite them to do more business with you more often. Sometimes people ask, "How do I know how much mail is too much?" Our response is, "Whenever it stops being profitable, stop mailing."

Most people stop following up too soon. You may be able to mail 4-5 follow-up letters to people, or you may be able to mail 15-20. If they're still responding and you're still making a profit, why would you stop? Most people don't get this right. If they follow up at all, they do so far too infrequently. Even if you're not in the DRM business, you have to have some way of following up on the leads you've captured. Whatever it is, keep at it. Pursue them relentlessly, as if their life depends on them buying your product or service. If you focus on the benefits you're able to deliver, you should feel totally confident and comfortable doing so.

Step #5: Constantly strive to know your customers better. This is key, because if you don't know your prospects well, you won't be able to sell to them. This goes hand-in-hand with Step #1, selling them what they want. The only way to know what they want is to know them better than they know themselves. People lie about things; they even lie to themselves. If you're a really innovative marketer (and you should be), then try to figure out exactly what they want at all times and under all circumstances.

Step #6: Plan all your marketing campaigns so you can make a profit even with bad percentages. In other words, arrange things to make money even when response is poor and people aren't coming into your store. One of the problems we entrepreneurs have is that we think too much of our promotions, overestimating how well they're likely to do. Try to get away from that mindset; spend some time thinking about worst-case scenarios. If you can make a profit even when the numbers stink, then you're onto something. That's why it's important to get a good price for everything you do or make, because you never know when response will fall. When it falls for someone who's doing business on the cheap, they're in a world of hurt and often go bankrupt.

Step #7: Continually test. This is most marketers' least favorite activity, and even we experts sometimes don't do it as much as we should. But it is *vital* to your success. Constantly seek to replace ideas, systems, and promotions with bigger, better, stronger ones. Testing is the only way you develop even better promotions. So once you have something that's working, keep looking for ways to improve it.

If you're in the mail business, run controls against the main piece you know is working, trying to beat it with new tests. Always look for ways to make something work better than it works now. We usually do head-to-head tests, so if we're mailing 10,000 pieces of mail, we might mail 5,000 of our control and 5,000 pieces of a new idea we think might work better. Sometimes that means reinventing the offer in a major way; other times it means testing a new headline or a new hook, angle or offer in an attempt to get them to respond in higher numbers. You see, what's working now will eventually *stop* working—and you've got to have somewhere to go after that, some new offer to attract customers.

These seven steps lead to mastery of your marketplace. Of course, we could add others; but these are seven critical ones, the ones you have to push at if you want to master your market. Most marketers will tell you that's what they want; but the reality is that all too often, business owners are just doing the bare minimum to get by. They exist in their marketplace, but aren't striving to master it.

They may not even really think about their business as being in a marketplace. They have whatever they do, and of course they have customers, but aren't really thinking about their marketplace as something they could master, or even do a better job of reaching. They just do what they do, the days and the weeks flow by, they limp along as a business...and they never really try to get better at marketing.

Mastering their market is a completely foreign subject to them. All they're thinking about is how they're going to pay their bills and survive. They're just following the follower, never even trying to think outside the box. They fact that they haven't spent any time thinking about mastering their marketplace is actually good news for you, because it means your competitors are very easy to beat when you follow these seven principles—especially the last two.

Learn to make good money with bad numbers. Crack the world of possibilities wide open and think outside of the box. Test rigorously and religiously—even things that are a little outrageous. You never know what's going to work the best, so you need a lot of ideas. Try to answer the question, "What if everything fails? What will I do then?" Lay out five or six of your best strategies—and then ask, "What if they *all* fail?"

Ultimately, your goal is to take a small amount of money and see how far you can stretch it. If you can make a profit on little or no money and the market is big enough, the sky's the limit when you roll out in a big way. These seven steps are crucial in accomplishing that—so consider deeply what it takes to dominate the marketplace you serve, to truly give the people in it what they want and need.

Marketing Secret #50: Why Idiots Get Rich

Have you ever wondered why so many apparently uneducated people make huge fortunes, while many of the smartest people in the world struggle financially? Why isn't it the other way around? Shouldn't you be more successful the smarter you are? Shouldn't your income be higher than a high school dropout's, any high school dropout's? How can you have so many undereducated millionaires, and homeless geniuses?

Before we go any farther, let me remind you that I, T.J. Rohleder, am one of those undereducated millionaires. I dropped out of high school and never went back...and my companies have grossed more than $120 million over the past 24 years. I'm not telling you this to brag—though I'm proud of the fact—but to point out that it happens, and I know what I'm talking about here.

Obviously there's some factor involved that's not being figured into the equation. What is it that makes some so-called "dumb" people more capable of making money than smart people? Now, I want to emphasize that this isn't meant as a knock on either end of the intelligence spectrum. It's just an observation: many smart people struggle financially, while many less intelligent people make money hand over fist. Why?

I think that the "secret" here is not that book smarts don't translate well into the business world—which some people would happily argue about for days—or that hard work without talent beats talent that doesn't work hard. I think that many of the "idiots" who succeed do so because they don't know that they *can't*—at least according to the experts. They just go ahead with a strategy they believe in and find a way to make it happen. Often, smart people let their intelligence and education get in the way, talking themselves out of doing things that might otherwise let them make a lot of money. They figure out all the reasons why something won't work, why the numbers won't be profitable, and why it's not a good idea to try—so they don't. An uneducated person may not see the obstacles; they'll just decide they want to do something, then go and do it.

When you look at personal stories of the rich and famous, you'll see that while many *are* of high intelligence, quite a few were high school dropouts, or otherwise poorly educated or from the lower classes. Even Einstein was only so-so in math at first (despite "common knowledge," he never failed math or was kicked out of school), but he eventually built himself into the world's top physicist.

Many of the world's greatest business successes weren't always considered the sharpest knives in the drawer. If they went to college at all, it often wasn't an Ivy League school—and yet they started businesses and built them into successful enterprises. In some cases, this was partly because they didn't worry much about why or how something couldn't be done; they focused instead on how it *could* happen, and all the things they needed to do to make it successful.

That's why "idiots" get rich. It's not about education or socioeconomic status.

One of the greatest things about living in the United States is that you can get ahead from wherever you start in life, as long as you work hard and catch some breaks. You might have to go get a business license or file paperwork, but you can take an idea and run with it to whatever degree you like, within certain broad guidelines. Therefore, the smartest people *in the end* aren't necessarily the smartest people *in the beginning*. The brainiacs usually talk themselves out of things, while the "idiots" just go out and do it. They accentuate the positive, and don't try to convince themselves it can't be done.

In other words, the idiots who get rich aren't really idiots at all.

There's no question that a person who is driven, who won't settle for anything less than success, is more likely to succeed. You can knock down a person like that 10 times, and they'll get up the 11th and try again. Look at Thomas Edison and other great inventors, and all the failures they went through for their few successes. People chastised them and told them they weren't going to succeed. It took Edison thousands of tries to find the right filament for his light bulb, but he did it. Similarly, the Henry Ford story is the story of a single-minded person who was dedicated to putting America on wheels.

Even during his heyday, people made fun of Ford because of his lack of formal education; and sometimes he'd reply that he didn't have to be smart—that he just had to keep people around him who were. He didn't care what the capital of North Dakota was; he could have any of 20 young men answer the question in minutes. He deliberately surrounded himself with capable people. He always had access to any information he needed because of that. So when reporters threw trivia at him, he had people to deal with it. He had no need or desire to remember it himself.

Now, I'll admit that outright idiots and the mentally

incompetent don't get rich. But those who aren't well educated but who are often driven to be successful, and are single-minded in their pursuit, can achieve great success.

One of my personal heroes is Ray Kroc of McDonald's fame. He didn't create McDonald's; that was done by the two McDonald brothers in San Bernardino, California. When he first ran into the McDonalds in 1952, he was in his early 50s and his sales business was going broke. The McDonald brothers were his customers, and he noticed that they kept ordering multiple milkshake mixers. Well, he wondered why, so he jumped on a plane for San Bernardino to check them out. He was impressed by the popularity of their restaurant and their business plan, bought them out, and the rest is history.

Forbes magazine has published a book called *All the Money in the World*. There's a chapter in that book about all the multi-billionaires who started out uneducated, broke, and without silver spoons in their mouths. Many of them claim that had they been educated, had they had all of those other advantages, they might never have succeeded as they did. There are plenty of very successful people on the Forbes 400 list that never graduated from college, which I've always found very inspiring—because I didn't go to college either. Just study the success stories, and realize that success *does* leave clues.

CHAPTER SIX

SECRETS 51-60

Marketing Secret #51:
The Amazing Secret of Selling Money at a Discount

All of us should be in the business of what I call "selling money at a discount." That simply means that you have to do things to make it clear that your prospect is getting hundreds or even *thousands* of dollars worth of value for every $100 they give you. The better you can convince them that the potential benefits far exceed what you're asking them to pay, the better off you are. Just remember, people don't want cheap things; they want a lot of value for a little money. It's up to us to create those beneficial selling environments, and I'll teach you how to do so in this secret.

First of all, remember that it's never about what something actually costs you to produce that matters; the value lies in how it benefits you and your prospect. You can write a million-dollar secret on a McDonald's napkin, but that doesn't mean the secret is worth just the few cents that napkin and the ink it was written with cost to produce. If necessary, make that point or answer that argument in your sales copy.

Next, never compare apples to apples—always compare apples to oranges. That is, compare what you're offering with things that are far more valuable. There's enormous power in the right comparison, because you can never fully understand, appreciate, or really know about anything until and unless you have other things to compare it with. It's up to us to educate our prospects on all the reasons why giving us their money will help make them even more money.

Create a sense of urgency to get people to purchase right away. At M.O.R.E. Inc., we have a brand-new advertising service we're selling to local business owners. It has a huge value for a very low cost; and we have some interesting, exclusive features built into it that help create a sense of urgency, so our prospects don't just say, "Just call me back next month," or "I'll think about it." Here's the headline of our sales letter and postcard, and the opening line in our telemarketing script: "How to Quickly Get Dozens of New Customers for Almost No Cost." We're sending that message because we know the business owner doesn't give a damn about our advertising program itself; they're already getting pitched by other advertisers trying to get them to cough up money. The only thing they want is more customers for a very low or no cost.

We're promising them the potential to get dozens of new customers who will continue to come back and buy from them. Those customers will be predisposed to do more business with them in the future because of the way this program is structured. We're rolling out the service at a dollar per day, and pointing out that they can potentially make hundreds or thousands of dollars in lifetime customer value for each dollar they spend. So if we do our job right, we really are selling money at a discount—and they're going to jump at the chance. It makes the amount of money we're charging for the service seem absurdly low...and it is, really.

This method works even for businesses that don't directly involve selling money at a discount; depending on your market, you can also offer them more comfort, peace, better looks, better health, or something simply good and delicious. It's always about what we have for them, even if it's a service that just brings relief from what they're dealing with—pests, plumbing problems, bad electrical work, or pain. The idea is to offer something that the prospect needs to make life more bearable and happy, something that, to them, is worth more than the money that you ask for.

I think this ties in well with the Seven Steps to Mastery I discussed earlier. The #1 point I made in that Secret was that you must sell people what they want. The best way to focus intently on selling money (or any other commodity) at a discount is to give customers and prospects what they want the most. If they want or need something desperately, the value goes up in their minds when counted against the money you're asking them to spend. For example, if I haven't eaten in three days and I've just stumbled upon your hamburger stand, and it just so happens that I have a lot of money in my pocket, $10 is inconsequential if you can provide the best burger in the tri-state area and if I can get some fries and a Coke with that. In fact, $100 would be acceptable; I'd be happy to make that exchange if I were starving. Water might be even more valuable...but I think you get my point. If you match what you're selling to what your prospects want the most, you'll have an easier time getting them to see the value of what you're offering. You're then in a position to make a much greater profit.

That's why it's so important for you to do your homework before you get to this point: you have to know your prospects and marketplace well enough to be in a position to offer them something of great value to them. The more urgency there is in their need or their want for what that you're offering, the more likely it is they'll pay what you ask. You need know your prospects well enough to make that connection. Otherwise, there's no urgency there. That drives down the price, pushing them toward flipping to the other position, where they view their money as more valuable than what you're offering. You certainly don't want that, because then you won't make the sale. You job is to know and understand, even if only instinctively, where that tipping point is.

Marketing Secret #52:
Leverage – The Real Secret to Building Wealth

The lever is a simple machine for amplifying force, and it works very well. Back in Ancient Greece, Aristotle said, "Give me a long enough lever and a place to stand, and I will move the world." The concept of leverage, as the amplified force is called, applies very well to business—and the richest people in the world use a *lot* of leverage. The best thing about leverage is that you get other people to help you make money. In some businesses, that may be as simple as working with your customers to get referrals, offering special compensation or gifts for every referral they bring in.

Russ von Hoelscher once worked with Vince Bartaloni, the top real estate salesman in El Cajon, California for years. He had a whole army of people telling their friends and relatives about how good his service was. Once he sold a house to someone, he made that person into a salesperson for him—and of course he rewarded them in some way. This is something all businesses can do, and you should consider it.

Some business people tell me, "I'm working my ass off, but I'm not making much money." The thing is, you have to realize that hard work does *not* equal wealth. If it did, people who dig ditches, work food service jobs, and pick up garbage would be rich—and they're not. So working smart, rather than just hard, is the best way to go. You want to create multiple streams of revenue that run through your business. Positive cash flow gives you tremendous leverage, and there's nothing like getting a whole horde of people to help you make money.

That's one of the benefits of multilevel marketing, whether you love it or hate it. The successful companies, some of which have gone on to become billion-dollar enterprises, have hordes of salespeople out there beating the drum and selling their products. There can be thousands of them in a downline, which means that you don't need to work hard if you have all those people working for you. Your share of what they earn can go right through the roof, if those people are serious marketers.

Whatever your business is, get people working on your behalf. This might involve hiring sales staff who work on commission only, so you don't have to pay them unless they produce. At a very simple but important level, it's also about turning your customers into testimonial builders, people who encourage their relatives and friends to buy—which means extra profit for you. Once it's in their hands, you can sit back and enjoy a big boost in your business. Leverage is crucial if you want to make real money.

Let me re-emphasize: it's not necessarily working harder that matters, but working smarter. We've all heard that, but few of us really believe it; we think, "If I work harder, surely I'll be rewarded for it. If I bust my tail on a day-to-day basis that's going to translate into success." And sure, there's a great deal to be said about working hard and being dedicated to your craft. But the truth is that when it comes to making money, it's not the *quantity* of work that you do that matters, it's the quality. Productivity at the right things is what ultimately determines the level of success you achieve.

100 MARKETING SECRETS

When discussing the benefits of direct mail at our live events, we often talk about the difference between sending a salesperson out to make that sale versus sending a sales letter. A salesperson can only knock on so many doors in a day, and may make a few sales. We can be a lot more productive if we write a letter that says the same thing the salesperson would say, and mail it to those same houses. Actually, instead of being able to visit only a few dozen or hundreds of homes in a day, we can mail to tens of thousands if we want to, all over the United States or the world.

Our sales message will hit all those doors within a few days of each other, depending on where they're going and where the business is located. Because of the huge numbers involved, direct mail gives us massive leverage over the alternative. We get more productivity out of less work.

Leverage is something you have to acquire and use to your advantage, no matter what your business is. If you can't find ways to leverage your time, energy, and resources, you're limiting your ability to make money. If your time is billed based on the number of hours you're working, then if you want more money, you have to work more hours. Well, there are only so many hours in a day—and you have to sleep, eat, and do other things during some of that time. Leverage allows you to go beyond getting paid directly for the efforts you're making, and start getting paid for other things in ways that aren't related to you having to work hard.

We're developing a new strategy that's fairly simple on the face of it. Our goal is to have 1,000 salespeople working for us nationwide, responsible for an average of one sale a day each. The strategy involves just a few round numbers, though some would say it's a lofty goal. Maybe so, but it's a good example of leverage and how it should work—and that's what this is all about.

The idea is to find something that works and then roll it out as big as you can. The richest people in the world have the same amount of hours in the week that you have: 168. In many cases, they're no smarter or talented than you are; they simply have a lot of other things besides their time making money for them. You can do that too.

Marketing Secret #53:
The 6-Step Million-Dollar Sales Letter Formula

This formula, when used successfully and correctly, can practically guarantee large profits—yet only a few people know about it, and of those, only a handful are actually using it. The 6-Step Million Dollar Sales Letter Formula will help you hone the craft of writing sales copy, and even better, guide you as you learn. Writing good copy is critical, because it's one of the best ways to increase your sales and profits, no matter what business you're in. So let's take a quick look at the six steps:

Step #1: Sell them something revolutionary and wild to get their attention. This is where you make a bold, strong promise to get them to pay attention to your letter. The thing you have to remember about direct mail (our specialty) is that you're usually catching people over their trashcan as they're sorting it out. They're trying to decide whether what you have to say is kept or goes straight into the trash, and you want them to feel like your letter is important enough for their attention—that you have something urgent and beneficial to say to them.

Usually you accomplish this with an intriguing headline,

although you can use some of this strategy on the envelope. Now, there are a couple of theories on envelopes. One is to go completely commercial, so it's totally obvious that there's a marketing piece inside, and to go all out to convince them they need to open your letter and pay close attention to it. The other option is to go with a plain envelope that looks like it's from a normal, everyday person. In this case, you could use a handwritten font and not put a return address on it. You want it to look like a standard first class letter, something that perhaps came from a friend or has something in it that's otherwise important to them.

The very first impression they get from the letter should be a bold statement about why they need to pay attention to you. Usually this is where you make your #1 promise or claim. What will you do for them, and why should they pay attention to the rest of what you have to say?

Step #2: Offer them a variation of something that's already successful. Maybe it's another of your products, a competitors' product, or something else they're familiar with that will help them understand what you're offering. A story about someone's success with this familiar product or service may help them, because you're talking in a language they understand. Key your language to the type of person you're speaking to; if you're speaking to a farmer, tell a story a farmer can understand. If you're selling to golfers, use a golf story.

Step #3: Point out the problems with whatever it is you're talking about in Step #2. If you sell golf equipment, the problem might be that all the putters on the market don't putt straight...at least, for the prospect. What they need is your new putter, which always putts straight. But first tell them why existing putters don't work so well. That gets the problem on their radar screen and agitates it.

Step #4: Tell them about your new discovery, and how it eliminates all of those problems you've already outlined. "I just created a putter that putts straight every time. Even if you're a horrible golfer, my brand-new putter is going to help you get the ball in the hole in fewer strokes." As they say, you drive for show and you putt for dough; if you're a golfer, you know that putting is the most important part of the game, and *your* putter will solve all their problems. "So, you've been wanting to throw your putter in the pond? Me too. That's why I invented this new putter, and now all of my problems are solved!" This is where you really start talking about your offer and why they should want it instead of the other, similar offers available.

Step #5: Show them what it will be like to use your product or service. Help them envision life as a better putter. Talk about all of the games they're going to win, and how they'll be the envy of all their buddies. Every time they play for cash on the course, they'll take home the kitty. Their game will be so improved that all their friends will be amazed.

Step #6: Your final step is the close. Tell them what you want them to do—which is to buy your product or service. By now, they should be imagining how life would be without it, or thinking about the complexities of trying to figure how to get those results on their own. Remind them they can keep putting the way they always have, and keep getting the same golf scores they're used to getting. Tell them that other putters on the market may be cheaper, but they won't be happy with the results. Build one vision of life if things continue as they are now, as opposed to what happens if they buy your offer.

100 MARKETING SECRETS

I've talked about golf putters throughout this secret, but this works for just about any product or service in any field. Whatever you're selling, these are the steps that will help you sell more of it. It starts with a big bold promise and ends with the close. Those six steps are very formulaic; you can just go down the list, and incorporate each into your copy. If you've never written a sales letter before, start by writing down each of those points, then elaborate on them—and pretty soon you've patched together a letter. It may not be long or impressive, but it's a good place to start. You'll find that if you keep using this 6-Step Million-Dollar Sales Letter Formula, you'll keep getting better and better at it.

To reiterate, the first step is especially important: to make that promise, to make that bold statement, to have that great headline, no matter who you're writing to. That bold statement tells them *exactly* what you're promising to do, making your best pitch right from the get-go. And again, the close is always critical. Some people are afraid to close—to be blunt enough to ask for the sale—and so they never become good salespeople. Good salespeople know how to close with power, and you must do the same. Telling them precisely what you want them to do, what they *must* do to take advantage of your special service or your exceptional products—whether it's to send in their check or money order, or to call up with their Visa number, or to come to your store on Thursday.

Incidentally, it's important to use testimonials when you can. They must be 100% honest, too. When you do a good job for someone with your services, or your products are cherished by a customer, ask them if you can use their name in a brief testimonial. Third-party reviews will really help you. People expect us to say great things about our businesses, but they're truly more impressed when someone chimes in and says that they were very pleased with the service, or very happy with the product.

The Six-Step formula is one that my company has used repeatedly to generate millions of dollars worth of sales for our own products and services. It's a recipe for success that always works if you follow it to the letter, and you can still earn plenty of money while you're learning and perfecting it.

Marketing Secret #54:
Why You Absolutely, Positively
Do NOT Want Happy Customers!

I realize the title of this secret may confuse you; you may be thinking, "Of course I want happy customers. Happy customers are going to come back." But as the song goes, it ain't necessarily so. If they're *too* happy, if they're utterly satisfied with what they got from you and never need a similar product again, they may just move on. You see, people buy in a vacuum; and as soon as that vacuum is filled, they stop buying. You want customers who will keep coming back again and again.

Our parent company was built on a marketplace of people who are basically unhappy. I didn't realize this when Eileen and I first started our company, but only because I wasn't taking my own experience and multiplying it by all the other people in the same market I'd bought from for years. There's a general frustration in our marketplace—and that description fit me to a T back then. It's their unhappiness that keeps them coming back. They're looking for some product or service they believe will make them happy, but it almost never works out that way.

Because happy customers stop buying, you have to find

marketplaces with huge needs, marketplaces where there are never-ending problems that you and your products or services can play some role in helping them solve. But the day you solve those problems for good is the day you basically put yourself out of business.

One of my good friends once told me that the bureaucratic framework of the medical profession doesn't want you to get completely well. That was a wild idea to me at the time, but as he explained, "If you get well, you're going to quit taking their drugs and buying their services because you don't need them anymore. They just don't want you to die." Now I'm starting to think that he may be right. They want you healthy enough to keep coming back, but that's about it.

In the last six months of my father's life, I drove him around to various doctor's offices and medical facilities, and there would always be a wheelchair waiting for us. I would pull my car up and put him in a wheelchair; he didn't even have to walk, as long as I was there to wheel him in and out. That's all those people care about. I know that sounds a little cynical, which was why I thought my friend's idea was over the top when I first heard it... but now I believe there's a lot of truth to it. The drugs are meant to keep you just healthy enough to keep coming back for more.

There are so many examples of marketplaces that are unhappy...and basically, people buy because they're unhappy or frustrated. They're usually in some sort of emotional or physical pain that causes them to buy. They're looking for solutions—so you need to start with those problems. Find a hungry marketplace where people are desperately looking for solutions. I've already told you about the new company we're starting that provides low-cost local and online advertising programs to small business owners. We're very happy with it, and one of the reasons we are is because we know that small business people have a *lot* of problems.

If you're reading this, you're almost certainly a small business owner yourself, and you know what I'm talking about. It's one problem after another—seemingly a new one every few minutes, some days—and it never ends. Small business owners are often frustrated, confused, overwhelmed, burned out, and in great emotional pain. Quite frankly, it's one of the reasons we like this marketplace. It's filled with problems we're trying to solve on an ongoing basis, problems that will never be completely solved. We sell an advertising service that produces results; and we know from experience that when people drop our service, they won't get the benefits they want anymore, so they stay with us or come back when they leave. We don't want our customers to be fully satiated, and neither do you.

My first business was a carpet cleaning business, so every time it rained or snowed I used to rejoice because I knew my customers' carpets were getting dirty all over again. No matter how much Scotchgard or other fabric protectors I used, I knew I'd be right back there soon. So stop believing you want completely happy or satisfied customers, because *they don't buy*. You want customers who are happy enough, but also want to keep coming back to you. Look for marketplaces with the enormous problems that will never end, and then provide services that will also never end.

Is there any business that might want completely happy customers? Maybe a restaurant, since people will always need to eat. If they love your food, they'll come and "fuel up" there often. And I suppose it could also happen with a massage parlor or hairstylist—any business that counts on repetition. But that's not how most businesses work. You don't want them happy; you want them upset with something that you have the solution for. I realize this is a somewhat controversial idea, but I hope you can see why it's a good approach for many business owners.

I think that there's a difference between customers who are unhappy with you and customers who are unhappy with the status quo. You definitely want your customers to be happy with the quality of your service and product, and you want them to be satisfied with how you're serving them. But you *don't* want them to be happy with the way things are going in the general sense, because that results in satisfaction, which results in complacency—or at least a lack of an interest or desire in your solutions.

If I'm hungry, I'm more likely to look for a restaurant than if I'm completely full and satisfied. So the restaurants want you hungry; they don't want you to be satisfied. They want you to be happy with your meal when you end up eating there, but they don't want you to lose that hunger. They want you to be back in a few hours or the next day.

In general, people will become less interested in doing business with you if they're satisfied with the way things are going for them. If they have no reason to seek out improvement, why should they spend their money with you? A certain percentage of the population will be in that category already. They won't be good customers because they're happy all the time. They're good to go, all's well, and they don't seek out solutions. On the opposite side of that is an entire class of customers that has a whole host of dissatisfactions, so they seek out solutions that will help them with those dissatisfactions.

Those people are your best prospects. The more dissatisfied they are, the more likely they'll continue letting you provide solutions to them. You also need to have a fresh new group of unhappy people coming through your business on a regular basis, so look for a market that has plenty of them. The greatest marketing ideas in the world won't make you money if work a marketplace that isn't extremely lucrative. Finding and catering to those markets is a big part of the secret to overall profitability.

Marketing Secret #55:
How to Take Your Game to a Whole New Level

This secret breaks down into four different strategies:

Think bigger and bolder than your competitors do. Most of them are thinking small and timid.

Understand things about your market that they don't. Why do people buy? What are they *really* searching for? What do they want the very most? What are the unconscious desires that drive your marketplace? Your competitors are pretty much blind to all that. They've never thought things through at a deep level; they're following the follower.

Stay deeply committed to being the very best company in your marketplace. Most of your competitors are just trying to get by.

Focus all your resources into those few areas that stand the greatest chance of making you the most long-term profits.

There are many things you can do to accomplish these strategies; that's the good news as well as the bad. That's why you've got to apply as much leverage as possible to the few things that make the biggest difference to your business. You may think this sounds hard, and Thank God it is! If beating your competition were easy, then there would be a lot more people doing all this. To truly succeed, you have to be willing to do the things that they're *un*willing to do.

In most cases, your competition doesn't understand the marketplace at all. They don't really want to make the effort. They're not committed to becoming the best they can be, and they don't bother to focus on those few areas that bring in the most profits. It may not be easy to turn those attitudes around, but doing so is what brings you the *real* money.

This entire attitude boils down to thinking bigger and bolder, because most people are focused on how they're going to get through the day, and that's it. You have to go beyond that. Get away from the business itself and start thinking about what you can do to work *on* your business instead of just working *in* it. You'll separate yourself from most of your competition simply by investing the time required to decide how you can make your business bigger, better, and more profitable.

I saw an interesting interview with Donald Trump on the Business Channel recently. As you may know, he had some help getting started from his father, who was already in real estate; but the Donald decided to go in a new direction and build really mammoth buildings—some of the largest, most elaborate casinos and luxury hotels in the world. He put together some ideas and then decided to make it known that he was the man who could get things done. He didn't have as much capital to work with as most banks want, but he was able to convince them to invest millions of dollars in his ideas. This shows you how important it is to be a big thinker. Now, he's gone bankrupt a few times; he's been up, he's been down, but he's back up today. He's worth a billion dollars and has properties all over the world. That illustrates the value of big thinking.

The second part of this strategy is also critical. You *must* understand things about your market that others don't. Do your homework. Keep learning. Most people either don't bother or don't have the time. Make the time, especially when it comes to understanding the basics. Most people are selling things they think people need, but they often forget about what people *want*—they're forgetting about the psychology that makes their customers buy. It may not be what they think it is. You have to be willing to take the time to discover what they *really* want.

Then of course, you must stay totally committed, totally focused on improving your business. Those who achieve magnificent things, who become very rich or famous, or make a big contribution to the world itself are those who focus tightly on their dreams. They take the time to think about what really matters, get deep inside the dream, and go straight for the end results they're after.

You have to beat your competition at their own game. If you're not striving, at best you'll end up somewhere in the mediocre middle. To excel at your game, you've got to be in a position to do things bigger and better than everybody else. If this was easy to accomplish, then everyone would be doing it— and no one would shine. Well, folks, that never happens; there's always someone who stands head and shoulders above the rest, because frankly they just want it more.

It doesn't matter what field of endeavor you're talking about—athletics, academics, professional fishing, or business.

There will always be people who excel, while others just get by and the rest struggle to survive. It's going to sort itself out that way automatically, no matter how hard you try to level the playing field. So you need to improve your game if you want to do better.

Traditionally, one way to do this is by going to college. Now, while I may get some negative feedback for saying so, I have to admit that I believe that by most standards, college is a waste of time and money these days. Everyone's getting a degree, and those degrees aren't always worth the paper they're printed on. College educations don't teach you how to succeed; they just bury you in debt. Most business degrees don't even show you how to run a real business; they're oriented toward administrating large corporations, a whole different kind of animal, and are rarely taught by people who've runs businesses in real life. They're just not as useful as they were 40-50 years ago.

Now that just about everyone has a college diploma, you need an advanced degree to get ahead—and there goes even more of your life. The value of a college degree has been watered down. The point is, college degree or not, you can't do what everybody else is doing and expect to get better results than they get. You'll only be average—and is that what you really want? Of course not. You want to take it to the next level, to increase your income, excel in business, dominate your competition. You want to be the one everyone looks to as a standard, the one everyone else wishes they were. To accomplish this, you have to take your business above and beyond what it is now. You have got to commit to doing things that nobody else in your marketplace is willing to do.

Think bigger and bolder. Understand things about your marketplace that your competitors don't understand and aren't even willing to learn. Deeply commit yourself to being the very best possible, and totally focus all your attention on the few areas that bring you the best return on investment. Do all that, and you'll definitely up your game.

It doesn't necessarily take a lot of work. Most business owners are weak, you know, and never make the least effort to do anything it takes to excel. They're happy to just muddle through life. They may be great people, but they're not good marketers—so you need to take advantage of that fact. If you want to excel, that's where you have to start. Begin by being better than they are, and just keep pushing from there.

Marketing Secret #56:
The Instant Cash Flow Solution
for Every Business Problem

This Secret covers one thing you can do every day that will solve the vast majority of your business problems, if not all of them. At the same time it can dramatically increase your cash flow, which should definitely be one of your goals. Once you attain and retain a river of cash flowing into your company, 99% of your problems will be over.

Now, I say that like it's simple—as if you can just snap your fingers or wave a magic wand, and all your business problems will vanish. It's not *quite* that simple, but to be honest, it mostly is. More money coming into your business gives you more choices, especially in regard to the things that you normally couldn't without that money. To ease your burdens, you simply have to start by bringing in more cash.

The worst thing in the world for your business is to

struggle financially, to be in a position where you can't pay your bills or where most of your time and energy is spent on just staying afloat. The more you struggle, the more time you spend thinking and worrying about the necessities—and the last thing you need is to go to the mailbox and find another bill. Each expense is like a big cinder block weighing you down, forcing your focus downward and inward to working *in* your business and not *on* it.

So, how do you get your cash flow situation right? The most effective strategy is to spend more focused energy and time on a small number of things that you know can increase your sales and profits. This echoes one of the strategies from Secret #55; you can see how interrelated many of these secrets are. Now, every one of us has the same number of hours in our day and week, so 'time management' is a misnomer; you have to learn to manage yourself and how you slice up your time. Again, if your business is struggling, you spend a lot of that time putting out fires, doing things that consume energy and take a lot of time. To really succeed, you have to fight for focus and commit to doing things that carve out the time necessary to innovate within your business, and to think about all the ways you can bring in more sales and profits.

I often say that I belong to the 5 AM Club—which simply means that I get up very early every day, at least an hour before everyone else, and spend time focusing on business strategy before the phones start ringing and people start bugging me. You should do the same, spending this meaningful time focusing your energy on things to create more cash flow in your business. You know the bills are going to be there no matter what; what can you do to work around them? How much money must you make before you can wake up on the first of the month and think,

"Well, all the bills are paid—everything beyond this point is profit.""? This is especially necessary when times are tough. You've *got* to find time to focus, to put your energy into things that bring in more money.

Think about ways you can get more business from your existing customers. When you're really struggling, that's a great time to make them an outrageous offer. You don't have to tell them your business is down; just do something crazy that gets the phones and the cash register ringing.

As with so many of these secrets, the process starts with intimately knowing your customers, so you can make them a killer offer they can't refuse. These people already know, like, and trust you, which makes them much more likely to do business with you. So make them an excellent offer, knowing what they want based on the kind of benefits they're looking for, and they'll come through for you. They're the lifeblood of your business. You just have to spend the time to think about what they want.

One of the worst things you can do is to get mired in that negativity that arises when things are going poorly. Don't focus on the bad. The bills are still going to be there even if you put them off a day, so stop worrying about them and spend some time focusing on activities that can bring in the cash. Get that money flowing in. Even if it doesn't fix all your problems, maybe it'll give you some freedom not to think about them for a while, so you can enjoy some of the success you experience when your cash flow is high. Maybe you can pay an accountant to worry about your money problems later.

Al Davis, the former owner of the Oakland Raiders, used

to say, "Just win, baby." When it comes to business, the equivalent is to just get the cash flow flowing. How you do that depends on your business, and nobody knows that business as well as you—or at least, they'd better not!

A good friend of Russ von Hoelscher's was telling him recently that business had been very bad lately. He works with publishers, especially small presses and self-publishers, and that business is going through a lot of changes. He decided he'd better start calling his previous customers, to see if he could help them with anything. So he started making some phone calls—and lo and behold, he had one of his best days ever.

The lesson here is to stop waiting for people to come in the door, or to write to you, or to call or email. Get in touch with them yourself. Going back to existing customers you have a good track record with is a great way to stimulate business. Another way to drum up business is to offer substantial discounts, even on things that cost you so much you're hesitant to lose money on them. Well, you need the money, so cut the price rather than leave them to gather dust or go to waste. Offer huge discounts—50%, 60% or 70%. Just go to your customers, especially those you haven't heard from for a while, and tell them you just wanted to check in and see how they're doing. Pitch that special order. Be proactive. That's the way to get the cash flowing.

Marketing Secret #57: Operation Money Suck

This one ties in well with the previous Secret. The idea here is to suck as much money out of your marketplace as you possibly can. Target every cent of disposable income your prospects and customers can afford to spend. This may be the most important thing you can do to get the money that you need right now. It's such a simple concept, too—all you have to do is invest some time and put it into action.

Think deeply about how you can draw more money out of your customer or prospect base. That's the exact opposite of what most small business people are doing, because they're so busy they don't really take the time to consider how they can increase their income. Their focus is diverted in too many directions.

I alluded to this earlier with my 5 AM Club, but if early morning isn't for you, then do it late at night—whenever you're undisturbed and at your best. During my hour in the morning, I think constantly about how I can make more money, and take plenty of notes outlining my ideas. For my entire life, people have accused me of being greedy. But let's get real: I think about money a lot because money is what makes it all happen. And honestly, I'm not as obsessed with money as some people think I am. I'm obsessed with building a business, making payroll, and being as debt-free as possible. That's it. I'm trying to grow and expand and do something substantial with my life, something that helps not only me but other people as well. I don't have expensive tastes, I don't drive very expensive cars, and God knows I dress like a street person half the time.

I'm focused on building a substantial company, and that takes money.

Money is the oil that greases the business process. It's absolutely necessary, and it has to come from somewhere. The money you want to make tomorrow, next week, next month, next quarter, or next year is all going to come from what you're working on right now, today. That's a point most people just can't seem to get their heads around. You have to focus on the future *now*. Spend as much time as possible thinking about how you can make as much money as you can right now, next month, next quarter—and also looking for great strategies that will put you ahead of the game.

I like all the baseball analogies applied to business. As Babe Ruth once said, "Focus on hitting those home runs, and then you can just walk around the bases. You don't have to run." As long as you keep hitting it over the fence, you don't have to scramble. You can just wave to the crowd as you jog around the bases. In business, you'll never get those home runs unless you constantly focus on the money, almost to a point of being obsessed with how you're going to make the biggest bang for your buck.

People who practice Operation Money Suck always look toward the future. Now, be forewarned: just because you have big goals doesn't mean it's all going to happen for you, but the likelihood is much greater when you *do* have some serious goals in place. Just setting those goals and being totally focused on making a lot of money is the closest thing you've got to a guarantee.

In Oliver Stone's first movie, *Wall Street*, Michael Douglas played Gordon Gecko, or GG as he was called in the movie. There's a speech he gave in that movie that consisted of a seven-minute long, one-camera shot in which he proclaimed, "Greed is good." If nothing else, find that speech on YouTube and watch it. It's very good, very instructive. You might be accused of being a greedy dog when you're into this Operation Money Suck, but somebody has to bring in the money. If it's your business, it's up to you.

One thing I have to re-emphasize here is that you have to relentlessly pursue your existing customers if you expect to make long-term profits. Most businesses seem to focus primarily on new customers, and while that's an important part of being in business, it's only a part. You have to take care of your present customers as well; in fact, they're more important than the new customers in most ways. A wise business person understands the lifetime value of a good customer. The profits get higher the longer you can retain that customer.

If you've slacked off on your existing customers, bring your emphasis back to them. That's where your real gold lies. Make attracting new customers a secondary goal. That's still necessary, because you have to replace existing customers you lose for whatever reason; these processes go hand-in-hand. But don't emphasize attraction over retention. When it's working properly, that cycle of attraction and retention will bring a fresh stream of new customers, some of which will become long-term customers.

When you need to make money immediately, your customer base is where that's going to happen. You already have a relationship with them; they already know, like, and trust you. That's a much faster path to a sale than focusing only on attracting new people. With a new customer, you have to build the relationship from scratch. That takes a while, and you may lose money doing it. When you approach an existing customer, they already know who you are. When they receive your letter and see your return address, they're already willing to open it because of the existing relationship. It's almost like receiving a letter from a family member; it goes into their "to read" pile.

Now, when I call this Operation Money Suck, I'm being a little tongue-in-cheek. It's just a logical extension of working with your existing customer base by making them offers they can't easily refuse. They know you're in business to make money, and you know that your cash flow comes from serving them. Do so as irresistibly as possible, so they can immediately see the value in what you have to offer.

Everybody in every marketplace has disposable, discretionary income; otherwise they wouldn't be in the market in the first place, because they couldn't afford to be. Discretionary income is the money left over after they pay all their bills and buy all the other things they need. That amount may be small or large, depending on their earnings and needs or desires. Some will want to save it; others will want to spend at least some of it. So why shouldn't they spent it on your products and services? Your job is to make your benefits seem so much better than everyone else's that they can't help but want to give you some of their discretionary income. That's all marketing is, really—and that's what Operation Money Suck does.

All you're asking for is their discretionary income. You don't want them to starve or lose their house; you just want the extra money they can *afford* to spend to help keep the economy tricking along. Do your best to brighten their lives with the best possible benefits you can offer, and they'll be happy to trade their money for those benefits. That's what Operation Money Suck is all about. It's not about ripping people off, or greed for the sake of greed. It's actually the opposite, because the best way you can suck and re-suck the largest amount of money out of your customer base is by serving them in the highest possible way and giving them the highest value, through products and services that make them extremely happy and ready to come back for more.

Marketing Secret #58:
Enthusiasm is Your Key to Riches and a Happy Life

Many people want to receive a regular enthusiasm jolt, so

they go to various seminars where they can hear a great motivational speaker, or they read books on motivation. Good people to read or listen to are Tony Robbins, Mark Victor Hansen, and Tom Hopkins. However, the key here is to stay motivated 24/7, and that can be tough. It may not seem like you get much from the effort, but it's something like air conditioning on a warm day: You may not notice it, but as soon as it shuts off, you feel it right away.

So don't let that motivation cut off. Now, I realize that when things are down, the economy is hurting, or you're having problems with your life or business, it's hard to stay motivated. But you have to remember how important it is, because when you're motivated, you're *alive*. You're accepting life as it comes and you're eager for more of it. There's a lot of beauty on this planet, and there are plenty of wonderful things about being born in America and having a chance to be in business and to do great things.

Enthusiasm is a skill you can learn. You sometimes hear people say things like, "I'm sick and tired of this!" Actually, their subconscious minds pick up the *idea* that they're sick and tired, so they often act that way. Watch what you say, since the subconscious takes in and holds onto what you express. This can be a blessing or a curse.

A good way to think of enthusiasm is that it ends with IASM, an acronym for "I am sold on myself." Tell yourself, "I believe in myself. I'm a good person, and I believe I can do great things. I believe I am here for a purpose and want to achieve that purpose, while being the best person I can be." When you're sold on yourself, and sold on the fact that you can expect to accomplish great things, you can stay enthusiastic most of the time. When you're ill or just aren't feeling enthusiastic, tell yourself, "This too shall pass." It's important to look at the bright side of life. Yes, there's a lot of darkness and misery in this world, but you have to maintain the perspective that says, "I want to be a blessing to the world. I want to do great things and be willing to help people who are having a hard time." That's the key. Stay enthusiastic even when it's difficult.

Often, how you think becomes a part of how you act. Now, I'm not one of those people who believes that you can just think about success, and all of a sudden you're successful, or that if you can just think happy thoughts, everything will be fine; you have to couple action with thought to achieve the outcome you desire. But I *do* think there's a direct relationship between the way you think and the way your mind puts those thoughts into practice to create reality. If you think and act like you're sick, you're going to be sick. If you think positive and act positively, you'll feel positive. As Henry Ford once said, "Whether you think you can or think you can't, you're right."

So the right frame of mind is essential to success. Remember the IASM rule: "I am sold on myself." If you're *not* sold on yourself, if you don't have passion and enthusiasm for what you're doing, you won't be as productive as you might otherwise be. You have to sell *yourself* on whatever you're doing before you can sell others. That's true in all aspects of life.

If your business isn't getting you excited, maybe it's time to make a change. Maybe you need to consider selling out and getting into another business that you *can* get excited about. There's no point in struggling every day in a business you hate. There are other things you can do. You can work for someone else for a while, if you need to. Whatever you do, be in love with it—or don't do it. Life is too short to spend time on something you're not passionate about. Once you find something with good cash flow potential that you can get excited about, run with it and make it your passion, and you'll find that necessary enthusiasm.

Nobody is born enthusiastic. You have to manufacture your own energy, practice getting excited. One of the quotes I have hanging on my office wall reads, "Generate your own energy. The power plant does not *have* energy, it *generates* it. You have to generate your own happiness, power, motivation, enthusiasm, and passion." It's not something that just comes to you.

Practice getting excited every day. Search for things to get excited about. One of the best definitions of happiness I've ever heard so far is that it's always having something to look forward to. I love that quote, because with business you *always* have something to look forward to!

Marketing Secret #59:
The Only Two Things You Need in Your Business

Management guru Peter Drucker once pointed out, "Marketing and innovation are the only two things in business that make money; everything else is an expense." Most people have heard of Drucker: he's a legend in business management circles. He was instrumental in making General Motors more profitable in the 1940s, and he did so by carefully analyzing everything they did from the inside. That led to his famous quote.

Marketing is the sum total of the things you do to bring in sales, including advertising to attract new customers and transacting more business with existing customers. The framework you put in place to do that is your marketing system. We help our clients get into marketing systems that automate most of these factors. Automation is hugely beneficial in marketing. For example, when done correctly, direct-mail marketing is superior to even the best door-to-door salesperson. We especially teach DRM, where you send out sales letters to make your entire sales presentation, along with follow-up systems to convert leads into sales, associated with ongoing systems to keep doing more business with existing customers.

Innovation includes invention and creativity—the process of doing things differently than everyone else. This goes back to what I discussed in an earlier Secret, in terms of doing things that other people in your marketplace just aren't willing to. If you have something that you've created, and it's working to bring in new customers and excite your existing customers, and your competitors notice that and are jealous of what you're doing—well, that's the kind of innovation you're looking for. You want them to go nuts because they can't figure out exactly what you're doing. Or even if they *can* see what you're doing, they can't duplicate it. It's a little mysterious, an unknown quantity just off the radar. You have to do things that make people stand up and pay attention—especially the people you're trying to sell to. Innovation will result in more business.

Everything besides marketing and innovation is an expense. I could include a long list of all the things that make up the other category. You know what they are in your own business, though maybe they're a little different in other businesses and marketplaces. Whatever they may be, they don't bring in the revenue or the sales. So spend your time on marketing and innovation; let other people focus on fulfilling your business's other demands. That may mean hiring people to take care of your accounting, or using a fulfillment center to send orders to your customers. If you'll focus on innovation and marketing, you'll find yourself bringing in more revenue with less effort. You'll have more happy customers, and fewer cash flow problems.

The people who really get innovation and marketing are the ones who make the most money, because the simple fact is that most businesses have little time for innovation, and almost no time for marketing. A few years ago, Russ von Hoelscher had an opportunity to speak to the late Dr. Gary Buss; he asked Russ what he did, and when Russ told him marketing, he responded with, "Boy, that's where the action is."

He then went on to say, "I made money in real estate, and then I took that money and bought the Los Angeles Lakers, and it's been a tremendous success. But even with the great players we had, like Magic Johnson, Shaq, and Kobe Bryant, we had to constantly market. I did everything I could to get the Hollywood crowd involved, because I knew that if those Hollywood types would come to games and sit at courtside, it would be a big plus. You can have a great team, you can have a great business, but it can go away quickly if you don't know how to market."

I was really impressed to heart that, and it really drove home this concept that it all comes down to marketing and innovation. Oh, there are other significant things you have to do; don't get me wrong. You have to have someone to take care of the financial part of the business and run it day-to-day. Personally, I'm a terrible business person, so I know the importance of surrounding yourself with people who can handle the everyday affairs. The bottom line is to never, ever forget marketing and innovation.

So far, I've read the book *Steve Jobs* by Walter Isaacson several times, and I've listened to the audiobook as well. This book was published right after Jobs' death. There's a part in the book where some of the people who were closest to Jobs said that there has never been a CEO who spent as much time so completely focused on the marketing and advertising of the business as Steve Jobs did. I thought that was very instructive, because after Jobs came back to Apple in 1996, during those 13 years before he stepped down and then passed away, he made Apple the most profitable company in the world. He did it partly through marketing, partly through great innovation.

One of my heroes is the late, great Ray Kroc. During the 1960s, when fast food was taking off and suburbia was spreading rapidly, there were hundreds of different companies trying to knock off McDonald's. One day a reporter came up to Ray Kroc and said, "You have hundreds of competitors now, popping up everywhere. What are you going to do about all these competitors?" Ray replied, "We're going to innovate faster than they can copy." There's a lot of wisdom in those words.

Constant innovation makes you the competitor everyone is trying to beat. You're always looking for new and better ways to do everything, and that's tied directly to the marketing itself. Marketing is all about how the customer views you, what the customer thinks about you, how excited they are about doing business with you and about buying the products and services you develop. It also includes your ability to connect with them, to create bonds that keep them coming back again and again for as long as possible. Think about that. The most innovative companies are also the ones doing the best job of marketing—and vice versa.

Marketing Secret #60: Your Key to Power and Position

You may find this Secret a bit controversial, because your

key to power and position is to create the illusion that your prospects and customers need you a hell of a lot more than you need them—and that's considered by many to be somewhat manipulative. But think about the flip side of that: the idea that you need them more than they need you. If they know it, that's a recipe for disaster. Neediness and dependency is never a turn on. Even if you *do* need their business very badly, you can't let any of your customers know that—or they'll run. You're in position of weakness. Instead, you have to create the opposite illusion: that you have something they want in the worst way.

There are many great metaphors and analogies that you can use in marketing and business. Consider the world of dating: it has much to teach when it comes to attraction and retention. Look at a woman who has several different men after her, and at all the power she has. Now, granted, this probably works with men too, but as a man myself I know it only from this angle. Popular women have the power in the relationship. There's a great little saying from the dating world that goes, "Run until they catch you." It's all about power—who has it and who wants it. Whoever wants it more is the loser in the situation; that puts them in a position of weakness. That's Negotiation 101. You always have to pretend like they need you more than you need them. You have to make it seem like you're in a position to walk away from any deal. That's a position of strength.

There's a famous marketing expert who used to tell a story about his early years, back when he was struggling. He was desperate and going broke. He could barely pay the mortgage, he was having trouble putting food on the table, and he had bill collectors after him. He was in deep financial trouble. Yet when he got a good prospect on the phone, he never wanted to sound too eager. When the new client would say, "I'm ready to do business with you. What does your schedule look like?" he'd be looking at a blank schedule—yet he refused to sound desperate.

Instead, he'd say something like, "Well, I'm totally booked this week; I can't get you in at all. I think I have an opening three weeks from today." This actually heightened their interest in doing business with him. So yes, in some ways it's manipulative. But so is dating. It's a game that you play to heighten your advantage, so you can play from a position of strength. If people think you're desperate or needy, that's not an attractor factor in any sense. Who wants to do business with somebody like that? We run from those people—we avoid them. The people we run towards, ironically, are those who claim they don't need us.

There's actually a psychological theory that if two people are together, the one who loves the least has the most power. But there's also the other side of the coin: according to the psychologist Dr. Kinsey, "The one who loves the most experiences the most pain and the most pleasure; while the one who loves the least experiences very little pain and almost no pleasure." So there are two ways to look at that concept. From a business standpoint, the idea that you're so busy that a customer is lucky to hire you is a plus. The same thing is true if he has to pay premium prices for your products. Your goal is to make him want what you have more than he wants the money in his pocket.

I've always thought, for example, than an emergency plumber might just be the most profitable service there is. All of a sudden your toilet or sink explodes, and you need help right away! You call the plumber at midnight and he says he'll come over for a certain fee. You say, "I don't give a damn how much you're charging, get your ass over here!" Again, the power comes when the money isn't nearly as important as the service or product—no question about that.

That's an enviable position to be in, if you're the plumber. When someone is chasing you, they're willing to pay the premium. If, on the other hand, they feel chased, your price goes down. They know you're in a desperate situation and will take advantage of it; that's basic economics. Now, that desperation can be real or perceived, but their perception is, "They're going all-out for my business. I can make any demand I want and I will most likely get it. So this is what it's going to take."

I'm not telling you to stay aloof, but don't chase ambulances either. That's pathetic and verges on the unethical. You have to market, but don't go out hunting business like you'd go out hunting quail. Let them come to you—or at least perceive that they have.

Now, here's where it gets more difficult: you want to chase them without them *knowing* they're being chased. As an aggressive marketer, you want to let them know you exist, that your business is there for them—so you don't want to be passive. You want to actively promote and encourage them to do business with you even when it doesn't seem you're doing so. Mostly you do that by using two-step marketing, where you let them identify themselves as your prospect. We've gone over that in detail in previous chapters.

Otherwise, the main strategy is to give them the perception you're not readily available for them. Don't let them think your appointment book is wide open; if they ask you when they can meet with you, don't say, "How about now?" Make them wait until next week, so it seems you're busy and much sought-after.

By doing this, you might risk losing the business—but

you also may end up with a happier customer who feels like they're chasing you. Maybe you can call back in a few days and say, "I have a cancellation, so I thought I'd offer the slot to you first." Whatever the case, you want them to feel like they're winning by getting you to agree to provide the service. That's where you're in a position of power; your prices can be higher, and you'll end up making more sales and profits. As crazy as it seems, your customers will be happier in that scenario as well. It's win-win for everybody involved.

People want to do business with the person they think everybody else wants to do business with. When you have something people want badly, you've got all the power. Again, I know that's somewhat manipulative, but *all* selling is manipulative. It's their money, you want it, and you're playing a game to get it.

In my very first sales job, my sales manager taught me something that's stuck with me for 30 years. I didn't think much of it at the time, but I often think about it now. In every sales process, in my closing technique where I'd make the customer an offer, I'd say something like, "Now, if I can work this out with my sales manager, will you do the deal today? Because I'm not going to go try unless you say yes."

I'd get up from my desk, and I'd walk over to my sales manager's office, where there was a glass window where my customer could see me in front of his desk. It looked like I was discussing the deal, but I was just in there shooting the breeze. I was a cigarette smoker back then, so I was usually smoking. Sometimes I'd wave my arms and the customer would think, naturally, that I was in there arguing—but I was actually in there because my sales manager told me to be as part of my closing technique. And it worked.

It's all about creating an illusion. We teach our phone sales people to do something similar—to tell the customer, "I'm going to go see if I can work this out. If I can, are you willing to make the deal?" Then they get up from their desk, stretch their legs, go get a cup of coffee, and come back five minutes later. It makes people feel special. People have to feel like they're getting a good deal, and they have to feel that what they're getting is really top-notch.

CHAPTER SEVEN

SECRETS 61-70

Marketing Secret #61: More, More, More!

A gentleman named Jeffrey Gittlemore created something called the More, More, More rule, and it's quite brilliant. Here's how it works: The more you believe, the more you will achieve and the more you will sell. That makes a lot of sense, right? The more you believe in what you're selling, the more value you provide to others, the more people will come to know and respect you, and the more they'll reward you with their business. The more enthusiastic you are, the more you will sell—there's no question about that.

This reminds me of the pitchmen at carnivals. These people are among the best sellers in the world, even though they're not making the best money in the world. The folks selling kitchen gadgets that slice and dice and do all sort of crazy things, or cool sunglasses, or special toys—those guys are true pros, people who could probably make a fortune selling other things if they weren't stuck with the carnivals and state fairs. They're fun to watch, and you can learn so much from them—because when the rubber meets the road, they make things happen. That's the secret of any great salesman.

Salesmanship in print is the same as face-to-face salesmanship, except for one big difference: we can make thousands or even *millions* of "sales calls" in a brief period of time, whereas even the greatest salesman in the world can only see so many people in a day, week, month or year. That's the advantage of using direct mail and other forms of DRM, including the Internet, to reach people. If you do try DRM—and I recommend you do—realize that the more you study sales, the more you'll know how to react in any sales situation. There are plenty of good books on this subject; for example, anything by Elmer Wheeler, a classic salesman from that past, is absolute gold.

And speaking of more—the more you follow-up, the more sales you'll make. It's all about *more, more, more*. Giving more and getting more, because you believe more and because you're doing everything you can more often. If you do this day after day, week after week, year after year, you're bound to see spectacular results. Never stand still. Do something every day to improve your business, even if it's something small. When you combine all the small things, big, wonderful, record-breaking things will happen.

Of course, the opposite is true as well: If you're unwilling to do more, then you're going to get less out of life. This applies to all facets of daily existence, both personal and business. If you exercise more, you'll be more fit. If you eat more, you'll be heavier. The more you work toward success, the more successful you'll be.

It doesn't always follow, though, that just doing something more results in more things happening. For example, just hoping more for good things to happen won't help if you're not doing things to make them happen. Similarly, if you're using poor technique, you can work hard and never get any better results. I could shoot baskets all day at the free-throw line, and if I keep using poor technique, I'll keep missing. Despite the old saying that "Practice makes perfect," that's true only when you're practicing the right way. What the saying should be is "Perfect practice makes perfect." As long as you're practicing using proper technique, you'll get better and eventually master whatever it is you're practicing—as long as you put in the time to practice. If you want to accomplish big things, you have to *do* big things. The more you're committed to the principles of success, then the more likely you are to achieve that success...again, as long as you're using proper technique.

There was a car commercial on TV recently in which a kid was playing baseball with his dad, and he was throwing the baseball incorrectly. If you've ever thrown a baseball, you know you lead with your opposite foot. If you're right-handed, you step forward with your left foot and point your toe towards where you're aiming. Well, this kid is starting off the wrong foot and the ball is going all over the place. You wonder where this kid went wrong—then they show the dad throwing the ball back to him, and the dad is using the same terrible throwing technique. He's encouraging his son to keep throwing it incorrectly...and so the kid keeps getting bad results. That's a good illustration of what happens when, despite your best intentions, you practice wrong: you're never going to achieve good results.

If you want to be a master of DRM, you can't take massive action in the wrong direction; that'll get you no closer to achieving your desired results than doing nothing at all, and may actually hurt you worse. If you want to be a good Internet marketer you can't use the wrong technique when it comes to selling online, either, or you'll never get anywhere. Whatever you do, it has to be the right thing before you leap into action. Sure, once you do get it right, the more you do it the better you'll become at it. But you have to start with the right technique in mind in the first place.

Massive action is generally a good thing, because you

hustle around, trying all kinds of things and going in a variety of directions, covering all the bases in an attempt to bring in more sales and business. But still, it helps to know which directions to focus your attention on, so it becomes easier to home in on the things that work the very best. The small business owners who hustle most aggressively will come out ahead. That's no big mystery; more is better. The big mystery is why more businesses don't apply this concept.

You have to test a lot of different things to find out what works best. When you find those things, lock onto them, roll them out with more and greater effort and resources behind them, and then continue to tweak, fine-tune, and improve upon them. Then you make an awful lot of money, and people scratch their heads, thinking that somehow you're special—even when that's not the case. What you're *doing* is special—and it's just something other people could be doing, but don't bother to.

Marketing Secret #62:
Throw Away All Your Leadership Books

Most business leadership books are absolute trash. They rarely work; typically, they're oriented toward Fortune 500 companies and written by people who don't have a clue about how to lead one of the regular, everyday businesses that make up 99% of the business sphere. In this Secret, I'm going to tell you about the *real* secret of successful leadership—what you should be doing if you want to be a leader in your field.

Nowadays, it's the "in" thing to be a leader, and sure, there are certainly things you can identify with those who claim leadership. But you have to wonder: why are people always talking about how to be a leader? Why aren't they just out there leading by example, showing us instead of telling us?

Some people seem to think that everybody is capable of being a leader, is a leader, or *should* be a leader. Well, here's a news flash: if everybody's a leader, then no one is. To be a leader, you need followers; and in any case, you can't have everybody occupying the same space in society. There's nothing wrong with being a leader, but you actually have to be out front to claim the title. You're never going to get anywhere if all you want to do is achieve income equality or a level playing field, which won't happen anyway. Utopian ideals don't mix with business reality. If you want to distribute income and leadership equally, get out of business, because you'll be eaten alive by your competitors.

There must be and *will* be a leader in every environment and situation. Even when people start out entirely even, someone will eventually take the lead. It's a natural law that some people will do better than others. Some will create wealth with the money they have and leverage it into greater wealth. So what makes that person a leader? Well, a true leader is good at persuading people to do what they want them to. They have something to say that makes people rally around them and give them their support, in the form of labor, social prestige, or money. This is true of secular, religious, and business leaders alike. Sometimes the leaders are benevolent; sometimes they're dictators.

If nothing else, business leaders have to convince people that their products or services are good deals for them. They can successfully pitch their product to an audience and get those people to respond.

The point is that when you think about leadership, *don't* think about some nondescript thing that people can't really quantify, and don't entertain any politically correct ideas about what qualifies someone to be a leader. You're a true leader only if you've learned to persuade people to follow you or to do what you want them to do. Jesus Christ was a true leader. Ronald Reagan was a true leader. So were Mao and even Hitler, though we don't like to bring him up in polite conversation. Some of these people were born with natural charisma; others developed it.

It's your duty as a marketer to use your creativity, inventiveness, and skills like public speaking and writing copy to enhance your leadership skills, whether or not you're a natural leader. This results in increased sales and profit, because you can persuade people to buy what you're offering. Learn to be a good persuader, and you'll find yourself more successful than you'd be if you followed any of those leadership books. They're a dime a dozen. Forget them. There's no question that great salespeople, great marketers and good copywriters are great leaders, because we persuade people to take action and buy our products we want to sell. In fact, most leadership is about selling—even politics.

Back when Andrew Jackson was a general—before he became president—he had a great saying: "I lead, you follow, and everybody else gets the hell out of the way." You have to take the reins, because no one else will just give them to you. But let's be real here; most people are letting the business reins flop around loose. Dive on them and take charge of your market, especially when no one else will! Become the very definition of leadership for your market, and keep pushing that leadership in everyone's faces.

Sometimes I watch World War II documentaries. I've mentioned Joseph Stalin, the Russian dictator. He was a charismatic leader, but not an especially good one. When the

Germans attacked Russia in 1942, several of his generals ordered the Russian army to retreat. He went to the front lines, gathered his generals together, and told them, "Any general who doesn't stand and fight to the last man, or who retreats hoping to save himself, will die. I will kill you if the enemy does not." That form of leadership is persuasive, yes, but it leaves no other option than to do what the leader wants. We marketers are pure persuaders, and that's a more valid form of leadership.

John Maxwell once defined leadership as influence, and I firmly believe that your ability to influence other people is what makes you a real leader. Lots of people *think* they're leaders, when no one is actually really following them. A specific position doesn't automatically translate into leadership. Leadership isn't a title, whether the title is CEO or President of the United States. Yes, people who serve under you may do what you say when you order them to, but if you're not a true leader they won't follow you when you turn your back, and they may find ways to sabotage you. If you're a true leader, then you're influencing people, providing real value in their lives You're singing the song they want to hear, and they *want* to follow your lead.

Years ago I read another quote that went, "Good leaders are good followers." When I first read it, I thought it was nonsense. How could a good leader be a good follower? But in the years since, I've given that quote a lot of thought, and I've seen the wisdom in it. A good leader understands his followers very, very well. There's a push and pull there. Good leaders know how to admit when they're wrong; they go to their followers and work with them, listening to what they have to say. And it's doubly true today, as business leadership trends toward more of a one-to-one working relationship with the rank-and-file, where leadership supplies the vision and the rest of the team provides the strategy and execution. A good leader empowers his people.

The reason I know that most leadership books are crap is that I bought too many back in the 1990s; leadership was a very popular subject then. In most of those books it's difficult to pin down what the author is even getting at, because everything is so homogenized. Toss those books away—or at least put them on the shelves to collect dust—and remember that true leadership is based on your ability to influence and persuade other people. This is a learnable skill that you can develop over time.

Marketing Secret #63:
Sell Products and Services That are Guaranteed for Life

Some products and services will *always* make you money, and in this Secret, I'll show you how to spot them instantly —and how to start getting all of the money you can out of them. The basics of this Secret are easy enough: you constantly search for the products and services that provide the largest gap between the perceived value—which is what the purchasers think they're getting—and your actual cost. That means you're looking for items where the average prospect either doesn't know or doesn't care about your cost. In those situations, the actual cost can be dirt cheap, but that doesn't matter as long as the item provides a high benefit level.

It's not always easy to find such products and services to offer; in fact, it can be very difficult to find just the right combination. You need to understand that from the very beginning. You may end up doing a lot of experimentation before you hit on the right formula, but it's worth the effort. Most small business people are working way too hard for far too little money, partly because they're misapplying this concept. They often sell products and services that are more like commodities, which typically offer very little profit. Worse, they're selling products where it's easy for the average prospect to determine what their cost is.

I say, let the giant corporations sell those types of things. Let them fight over the razor-thin profit margins. They can afford to. We SMBs need to look for products and services that have the highest possible profit margins and perceived value in the minds and hearts of the people we're promoting those products and services to.

The ultimate high perceived value/low actual cost ratio is in information. Knowledge really is power—and you can usually buy cheap and sell dear. I challenge you to go to Google and search on the words "information marketing." Do the same on YouTube. Spend a couple of hours watching videos and going to websites. The more you study information marketing, the more excited you'll be. There are all *kinds* of ways to make money, and an endless number of information products and services you can sell.

Even if you sell traditional products, you can always add information services or products to your line-up. By providing these along with your original products, you can charge more money. People are getting a higher value when they receive these products or services, so they expect to pay more. It doesn't matter one bit that it might cost you an insignificant amount to provide that information. As long as people perceive that the value is super-high in relation to the benefits you're offering them, they don't care what your actual cost is. You especially have an edge when you develop proprietary information products and services.

Here are just a few types of info-based products and

services you can sell: newsletters, books, booklets, pamphlets, special reports, audio programs and their transcripts, video programs, workbooks, courses, CDs, DVDs—the list is huge. You can license out various aspects of your business. You can sell distributorships. You can provide consulting services and warranties. You can do seminars and workshops, and hold a variety of events.

Even if you decide not to go the information marketing route, look for value-added services you can add to your product mix to boost sales. My wife runs a pet boutique. She sells all kinds of things, mostly for dog lovers: clothing and jewelry for dogs, gourmet treats and premium quality dog food, and of course everything possible that a dog can chew on or play with. But their big profits lie in their dog grooming; that's what keeps the customers coming back more than anything else. People hate to groom their own dogs, so that service drives that whole boutique. Take away that grooming, and suddenly you're not giving people a reason to come back into the store. Basically, it's a value-added service to go along with the products that she sells in her store—but ultimately, it drives business and generates profits.

Look for similar value-added services that you can tie into your business. I recommend that you strive to become an expert in your field by developing a wide range of information products and services you can sell for generous profits. Typically, they're inexpensive to produce and yield profits well beyond their actual cost. This does *not* mean you're taking advantage of people, because the *information* is the product. You're not just selling the paper and ink a book or pamphlet is printed with, or the CD an audio product is burned on. You're selling valuable knowledge.

I remember a seminar held in Orlando, Florida several

years ago by Ted Thomas, who discussed all the advantages of information marketing. He's made a lot of his money and wealth through information marketing in the real estate field, and pointed out how great it was, and how you could produce the product for such a low price compared to the selling price. Then it came time to sell his package: a bundle of videos, audio products, and big manuals he offered for $995. A woman raised her hand and said, "You just told us how cheap it was to produce this stuff. How about a big discount?" He thought about it for a minute and said, "I'll admit that it isn't that costly to produce this stuff...but it did take me 25 years to learn what's in here." Everyone got the point.

Something like that happened to Russ von Hoelscher once when he was in Spokane, Washington years ago, speaking at an Al Gollasal seminar. He was discussing all the advantages of information marketing, and the big mark-ups you can get that you can't get anywhere else, when a guy stood up and asked if he could say something. Russ told him yes, and the man said, "I work at local theater here. We sell popcorn for $5, and it costs us 15 cents!" Russ replied, "You have a point there. You have a captive audience, which is another situation where this kind of mark-up works well."

There are ways you can incorporate information and value-added products and services to the marketplace you serve, whatever it may be. This very book, and the audio program it's based on, are both information products. Russ, Chris Lakey, and I spent weeks pouring our hearts into revealing a hundred of the best ways for small businesses to make money. Then I had it converted to book form. We can put a certain amount of value on all that work, plus the production cost for delivery of the content—CDs, paper, ink, etc. But the reality is that its value is higher than all those things.

When you read this or listen to the original audio, you're receiving the combined experience of the three of us, which amounts to over 70 years total, and includes all the knowledge we revealed when discussing these strategies. If we were to put a price tag on this particular product of, say, $10,000, we could make a valid argument that the information revealed here is worth that much. Now, of course it didn't *cost* you $10,000 to purchase this...and if somehow it did, I want my cut! But I think you get my point. You can (and must) charge a lot more than just the production value of a product.

Consider this: if I had an actual, workable cure for cancer and I printed out the formula on a laser printer, how much would it be worth? The cost of the paper plus the toner and electricity? Of course not. All that may be worth only a few cents per page, while what's printed on that paper could fetch millions of dollars. Those who need it would pay any price I asked. *Don't confuse something's production cost with its value.*

A deed to a house consists of just a few sheets of paper, but it's worth tens or hundreds of thousands of dollars. There is a *huge* potential difference between cost of production and value, and you have to understand that, and how to strike the proper balance in order to maximize your profits without losing your customer base.

Think about how you might incorporate an information product of some kind into your existing business, whatever that might be. Suppose you own a landscaping service. My landscaper does a lot of work, and I've thought before about how he could increase his business by becoming a landscaping expert on paper or audio. He could produce a book, write a report, dictate a short audio program, or something simple like that. He could distribute that product free to generate more business, or sell the product itself. He could reveal all his strategies for having the perfect lawn.

He could even hold events where he teaches people what he knows about it. For example, he could charge as much as $100-$200 dollars for an annual spring event in which he teaches people *all* of his best strategies. They get to spend the day with him and learn how to craft the perfect garden and yard. This could enhance his ability to make money as a landscaper. He could also use information products as lead-generation tools, for example by distributing a free guide that tells people like me how to do it all on my own. By teaching the many things it takes to do it yourself, he could be selling himself—that is, showing people why they should really just hire *him* to do it all.

That's just one example of a business you can use this strategy with; and truthfully, you can do it with any number of businesses. Be creative. Think about how informational products can increase your sales and profits and generate new revenue streams. If you can't come up with anything you like on your own, look at what other companies are doing—and not just your competitors. Keep your eyes open everywhere for unique, innovative marketing ideas. When something strikes a chord, find ways to use it in your business. Become a detective, adapting the best ideas you find out there.

You find what you look for in this world. As long as you stay open and receptive to new ideas, you'll see plenty of innovative marketing methods in use. They're easy to spot, because most marketing methods are so boring they cause those that aren't to really stand out. Keep your eyes and ears open. Try many different things. Think outside the box. Hell, throw the box out the window.

Marketing Secret #64:
Proven Ways to Get More Profits From Direct Mail

Direct mail is one of the most profitable ways to market, though it's also one of the most expensive. If you're thinking about doing direct mail marketing, whether you've done it before or this is your very first time, you've got to consider a few things in advance. What is your budget? Who is your target market? What's the competition doing? Needless to say, you want to promote something a little different and a lot better.

Then you have to think about what type of appeal is most likely to motivate the people you're mailing to, whether they're existing customers or new prospects. Consider the action you want the prospect to take. Never send out direct mail without telling the prospects exactly what you want them to do: call for more information, get their credit card out, or come into your store. If you tell them what you want them to do, you'll get better results. In addition to that, you'll want to raise prices, so you can afford to send more direct mail and do more promotions. Consider that as a value-added touch; because that's what's important here. No matter what your service is or what your products are, think of ways to add value so you can raise the price and lower the cost of promotion.

Although direct mail isn't cheap, it's very dollar effective, because it produces such wonderful results if it's done the right way. Of course, you also have to consider the mailing list you'll use. You may need a list of people who are within a few miles of your store, or you may want to try a list of people from all over your city, state or nation, depending on what you're trying to sell and the range you want to reach out to.

You must also consider ways to make your offer more powerful. That's what makes the sales soar. So many offers are so dull that they have little or no chance of getting people interested enough to buy. You have to make it exciting and fresh. There has to be something in that sales letter that makes people say, "Wow! I'd rather have this than the money he's asking for it." Or "This sounds great. I've got to get over to this shop as soon as I can." Always strive to improve the impact of your direct mail. Stress benefits, not just empty words about your company.

Practice reading your copy out loud. This is a technique I learned long ago from one of the late Gary Halbert's newsletters. He said that if you read your copy aloud, even though your potential customer will be reading it as a letter, you'll find things you like about it and things you don't, and you can make positive changes. Consider reinforcing your letter with a flyer or brochure if and only if your product needs one to highlight it. There are some products that look great in color, like landscaping. If you're sending information about how you're going to help people with their landscaping, sometimes a color picture will help—but for many forms of direct mail it's not necessary.

Make your letters as personal as you can. Don't write to some amorphous "Dear Potential Customer." Always write your copy as if you're writing to just one person. You may be sending out 10,000 letters, but you want each to feel as if it were aimed right at the person who reads it. Of course, today it's easy to personalize your letters, in the salutation and throughout the body; try that and see how people respond. Also, keep in mind that good direct mail copy consists of short sentences and paragraphs. Also, don't forget a call to action: tell them exactly what you want them to do. Use testimonials if you can. People expect us to be all gung-ho about our products and services, but if they see other people making positive comments about them, that's very helpful.

Any good direct mail letter should also include a postscript that summarizes what you said and repeats the call to action. If possible, offer a guarantee for anything you're selling, because that reduces or eliminates the risk, and people really love that. You also want to write a letter that's very easy to understand. Use simple English at about an eighth-grade level. If you do all this, especially if you make the product or service sound fantastic, you'll have big results.

Let me re-emphasize that I'm especially in favor of raising your prices, if only so you can spend more on promotion. Most marketers tend to do the exact opposite, either because they think they won't get any orders if they don't, or that the economy just isn't good enough to support a higher price. Then they contribute to a race for the bottom as they try to keep their prices lower than the competition. There are 101 excuses for lowering the price on a product.

On the other hand, when raising your prices, you may reach a price ceiling beyond which your customers will no longer respond. But most businesses never do, because they never try raising their prices. Remember, when you price toward the upper end of what your market will bear, you can do more creative things with your marketing to try to attract more customers. Your additional revenue covers the costs. You can spend more money to attract your customers and still make better profits, because you were more aggressive with your marketing and ended up with more customers.

More customers equals more chances for repeat business or sustainable long-term growth. That's an important point to keep in mind—so always think about what you can do to charge more. Maybe you can bundle several products and services together to create a bigger package that you can price higher, so your average ticket price goes up.

Do all you can to increase the size of every order that comes to you; that may be the most effective strategy for making more money with direct mail. Here at M.O.R.E. Inc., we occasionally put an option for an upgrade right on the order form. Some people will automatically take advantage of the premium package if it's available. It doesn't have to be huge; if your main product costs $99, you might add a paragraph of copy that says something along the lines of, "For a limited time, we also have this package available for $37 more." And *bam*, all of a sudden your $99 sale has jumped to $136. Even a small incremental increase can make a big difference over time.

We've seen people do this where they're selling a premium upgrade for several hundred dollars instead of a few dozen. So if $99 is the base fee, you can also have a super premium package available for $495. Even if you plan on offering them that upgrade later, don't be afraid to try it on your order form, because that does a couple of things. Not only will it get your average ticket price up (because some people will take that option right away), it notified everyone that you're going to make another offer available to them soon. When you do go back to them, they're already familiar with it.

Even if you've never thought about using direct mail

before, it's time to do so. Find ways to incorporate these strategies into your business, because they can help you make some serious money. There are very few businesses out there that can't benefit from direct mail strategies. And don't just try it once and give up; continue to try it until it works for you. One of the nicest things about direct mail is that you can test small but aggressively. Your direct mail package can be expensive, which lets you do a complete job of selling. But even if it *is* expensive, you won't lose your shirt if you test it to small numbers of prospects first. If that works, you can roll it out and make a fortune.

Since you *can* test small, I suggest you test everything you can, even if you're not sure it will resonate with people. Test different offers, different formats, different mailing lists. Here at M.O.R.E., we're starting a new business where we're testing three different direct mail pieces. Two are postcards; one is a more complete package. We'll see how that works for us, and then we'll take the results in the direction the response indicates—because direct mail is a never-ending process of testing new things.

And again, it's all about salesmanship. A good direct mail package replaces some or all of the things a salesperson would do to clinch a sale. It present the benefits in the greatest light, answers the prospect's biggest objections, wears down their sales resistance, and makes them want to know more or even want to buy.

Direct mail is exciting and fun, so don't look at it as work. Consider it a labor of love. It's so exciting to pour your heart and soul into a good direct mail package, throw it out there, and then wait for the response. That waiting can make you feel like a little kid again, waiting for Christmas Day.

Marketing Secret #65:
The Safe Way to Take Bigger
Risks Without Losing Money

We've all heard the phrase, "The greater the risk, the greater the reward." The opposite of that also holds true: small risks bring small rewards. Well, what if you could take no risk at all and *still* get big rewards? I'll show you how to do that in this Secret. It's a 100% safe method that won't lose you a dime.

That said, it's a truism that you have to spend money to make money. But remember what I discussed a few Secrets ago: What something costs doesn't matter; what matters is how much profit you can make with it. Usually, the flaw in the "risk more and make more" method is that you end up taking uncalculated or poorly calculated risks that turn into failures that end up costing you a bundle. Are there times where you lose money? Yes, that happens to us all; but if you're taking the right kinds of smart, calculated risks, then you can spend, and subsequently make, more money.

Taking baby steps or being timid with your marketing efforts won't give you the kind of results you're looking for. The best way to invest your marketing money is to make irresistible offers to existing customers. You already know they're interested in the kind of items you offer, and have liked your previous offers. Testing with them first lets you determine if the general market will be responsive to the offer. If you get a poor or lukewarm response from your best customers, then drop the idea and move on—because people who don't know you already won't buy it. If your best customers really like it, then you can roll it out big to new prospects.

We recommend two-step marketing for this. First, ask

people to raise their hands and request information from you. Then follow up intensely, doing all kinds of things to remind them they need to do business with you. This is where many businesses fail: they shortcut it and spend little or no money on the follow-up. If you'll do the opposite, you'll start out at the head of the pack and stay there. This is the safest way I know of to take the big risks required to grow your business.

If you always market to your house list first, you'll hardly ever miss. From there, it's just a matter of maximizing your return on investment (ROI) for your advertising dollars. How much can you spend, and how much can you make? Always monitor the numbers, making sure they continue to hold out.

If your best customers don't respond positively to an offer, then it's either the wrong offer for your market, or your approach is wrong. Now, you have to realize that even when you get a very nice response from your best customers, when you make the offer to new prospects there *will* be a falloff in response. That's why if your best customer response is lukewarm, you shouldn't even bother making the offer to a "cold" list. You need a strong, enthusiastic response from your best customers to overcome the dilution you'll experience with a cold list.

Your best people will respond to almost anything you do, so move forward *only* with the most popular offers. Your goal is to attract more people who are just like they are. It's all ROI—money spent versus dollars made. P.T. Barnum, the great marketer, once said, "Most people are trying to catch a whale by using a minnow as bait." They're hoping for results all out of proportion to their efforts. But to really make money, you have to be willing to spend some money—which segues nicely into our next marketing secret.

Marketing Secret #66:
Why You Have to Spend More
Money to Make More Money

Stop fishing with minnows if you want to catch whales; that's just not going to work. You need to spend significantly more money to close your sales and guarantee a greater income, not just in terms of absolute numbers but in terms of percentages as well.

First of all, you have to pitch only to super-qualified prospects. It's all about doing everything you can to pre-qualify your prospects. You have to get people to go through a process that proves, by the actions they're taking, that they really do want what you're offering. Second, you have to sell products and services with good profit margins; the bigger the profit margin, the better. The offer still has to be competitively priced, but if the margins aren't there, forget it.

Thirdly, follow up relentlessly and aggressively. As long as you've done a great job of pre-qualifying the prospect "no" doesn't always mean "no." It may mean, "I don't know enough" or "I don't know why I must buy right now." You can't just take no for an answer with pre-qualified prospects. If they're not taking the steps you want them to take, don't assume they're not interested until you do a whole lot of very aggressive marketing. You have to follow up like crazy. You have to be relentless. You can't let go of them.

Here's an example from one of our current campaigns. We're running a 27-word classified ad in hundreds of newspapers across the country. If it works, we'll roll out in thousands of newspapers across the country. In that ad, there are two calls to action. The first one is in the ad and says, "Call our recorded hotline." That leads to a 14-minute recorded message. I think it's a pretty good message, but if you're not a serious prospect, there's no way you'll sit there and listen to it, no matter how exciting it is.

During this 14 minutes we try to tell them everything they need to know to start. We assure them that what we have for them is legitimate in every way, and explain the basics so we can ease their doubts, fears ,and concerns. Then get them to take the next step, which is to go to our website and fill out a 15-20 minute application.

They don't have to listen to the recording, and they don't have to fill out that application. But if they do, their actions tell us how serious they are. We're doing everything we can to filter out the insincere, uninterested, and lazy, so we should end up with hardcore pre-qualified prospects. Anyone else is useless to us; we're happy we filtered them out. Those willing to jump through these hoops are serious.

From this point forward, they can be worth a lot of money to us. So we're now going to follow up in the most aggressive way possible. We're going to send them daily e-mails. We're going to reach them on social media; we collected their social media URLs and other avenues of communication in the application. We're going to have all kinds of ways to contact them, and of course we'll put stuff in the mail to them.

We're going to do everything possible to build a solid relationship with them, because when you get right down to it, no matter what we sell, all of us are really in the relationship business. It's all about getting people to trust you and to feel they can count on you, because you're distinct from and better than all the other companies they're looking at. Nowadays people have many options available to them. As long as you're pre-qualifying them enough, though, you can follow up in the most aggressive way possible, and it's all money well spent.

We're trying to make our daily e-mails as exciting and stimulating as possible. People are bombarded with e-mails; the first thing most do is look at the headers and start deleting as fast as they can. So we'll make ours compelling. We'll create and send those for the first few hundred days, and then it will go on an auto-responder sequence to all of the new prospects who answer our future ads, assuming we're able to roll out this campaign. We might have written those e-mails 6-8 months before, but they'll be brand-new to the new prospects. They'll follow a sequence designed to slowly but surely win their hearts, to get them to the point where we can do a large amount of business with them. We'll show them that we can benefit them in the greatest way possible too.

If it's not altruistic, if it's not focused on them, then it's not going to work. It's not what *we* want that matters; forget what we want. These people can be worth a huge amount of money to us, but all *they* care about is *them*. So all our messages will reek of altruism, because it's all about giving them more of what we know they want the most, because we pre-qualified them thoroughly.

There's no question that this formula works well; we've proven it hundreds of times, and plenty of our friends and competitors have done the same. Sure, we want their money, but we don't just come out and say it. They know it anyway. What they want to hear is what we have to offer, and that's completely fair. So that's what we stress. There have been times when we haven't followed up enough, and we've suffered the costs. I don't won't you to have to deal with that, so I urge you to beat this into your head: *you have to follow-up as long as it's profitable to do so.* When you do follow-up, you may use very similar versions in the first and second mailings, but you should make changes once you get into the third and fourth follow-ups. What you originally thought was the best approach may not be as far as the prospect is concerned. So mix it up a little.

For example, Russ von Hoelscher is working with a wonderful lady who's offering health and wealth benefits to her customers. Although they originally thought people would be most interested in making more money, they're finding that many customers value health over wealth. Russ is glad they learned that, because it shows you what people *really* care about. And while people *are* interested in making money, there are also many people who are more interested in preserving the money they already have. It's good to know such things, so you can vary your follow-ups accordingly.

There's no reason not to keep following up aggressively if you have a live prospect who got in touch with you, raised his hand, and showed that he was interested in what you had. You didn't force him to respond; in fact, you encouraged him not to by making it difficult to do so. When that's the case, you can follow-up many, many times—as long as it's still profitable to do so. Just change the approach occasionally. Change the headlines or a few of the benefits, or add new benefits, and you'll see great results.

Again, where most marketers go wrong is that they don't spend enough money. When you can afford to, you *must* consistently remind pre-qualified people that they still need to do business with you. If you don't, you 're missing out on sales. If you have a super-qualified prospect and your profit margins are good enough, you're only hurting yourself by not continuing to follow up. The premise here, of course, is based on the assumption that you're really delivering on the benefits you've promised them. If that's true, then it's in your best interest, and theirs, that you don't give up on them.

People often ask us how we know if we've followed up too much. Usually the answer is that you're never going to reach that point—but if you do, it's when it's no longer profitable to follow up; in other words, you're not making enough money to cover your costs and leave you with some leftover earnings. If you're still making a profit every time, then don't stop! Keep reminding them they haven't done business with you. Sometimes people put it off. Sometimes they forget. If you need to, remind them that your offer is still valid but time has almost run out, or sweeten the pot with a bonus.

At some point, response rates may drop so low they no longer pay for the cost of the follow-up and earn you a profit. Stop following up then. But let me reemphasize: Most marketers never make it that far. They give up far too early, and simply miss out on money that could be theirs. You have to continuously remind people that they still need to do business with you, which usually means spending more money to keep your message in front of them, not less. As long as the profits are good, and you're keeping an eye on your numbers, you can keep doing it indefinitely and still make a profit.

Think very carefully about all of this. Pre-qualify heavily, sell products and services with high profit margins, and then follow-up in the most relentless way possible—and you'll be light years ahead of all your competitors.

Marketing Secret #67:
The Things That Sell Best are Often the Most Surprising

Sometimes, the items that sell best for you are the most unusual—and sometimes the most ridiculous. Consider Pet Rocks and Chia Pets. They catch someone's attention, they get reported on, and suddenly everyone has to have one. Like the Kardashians, they get a lot of hype and generate excitement because they *sound* so exciting. Those that continue to do well offer a big, bold promise as well—no matter how unusual, avant-garde or ridiculous they seem at first.

Writer H.L. Mencken once said, "No one ever went broke underestimating the taste of the American public." This was his wry way of pointing out that we fall for some pretty unusual and tasteless things at times. This tidbit of wisdom seems truer today than ever. Russ von Hoelscher has a saying: "What's new in the news can make you the most money." If you're a good entrepreneur, you're always looking for something new, something different, and something to tie yourself to and really get ahead on.

Years ago, 900 numbers came on the scene. This was a way to get people to actually *pay* to call your company. Experienced entrepreneurs knew that this would be hot immediately. You could (and still can) charge people several dollars a minute, or even more depending on the information or service you're offering. Well, Ross got involved right away, and started to write a big manual of how to get rich with 900 numbers. He had a feeling from the beginning that it was going to be good—and it was actually better than he ever imagined. He ran ads for six months in *USA Today* and people called in droves. He offered free info and even a free video on 900 numbers. The course started out with a price of $595. Initially, Russ thought it would take some persuasive literature and that video to get people to buy—but most people just gave him their credit card numbers and bought the course immediately, right there on the phone.

When that happens, you know you have a hot money-maker—because they don't even want the free information, they just want to jump right in. In addition to selling the course, Russ made a deal with another company that offered an infoline, a dateline, a psychic line, and a financial line. He set up customers with these 900 number business lines and then set things up for the operators, and Russ's business got 20% of net. And boy howdy, did he make money from those folks for a while! Then, about two years later, the pornographers took over the business with their phone sex lines, and pretty soon they killed the golden goose for everyone else.

Soon after, the Internet came online...and people like Russ and I said, "Wait a minute here." We'd already been heavily involved in bulletin board services (BBSs), the precursors to the Internet, and we immediately moved to the Internet as one morphed into the other. We took what we'd learned with the BBS business, and soon had courses showing people how to make money on the World Wide Web.

People like Russ and I have spent our careers looking for and taking advantage of what's hot. For example, Russ got started showing people how to get involved in self-publishing their own books. For well over 100 years, you had to go to a major publisher—many of them in places like New York—to publish your book if you wanted to be published. But when new technology allowed insta-printing, Russ saw the opportunity to profit and joined forces with other successful people in the business, offering very successful seminars and courses.

What's hot now? Baby Boomers and the elderly. Americans are becoming older on the average, and they want to live better and longer. Health is a hot trend, especially alternative health items—things not typically accepted as valid by the medical community. Always look for what's hot and new and in the news, because if you can catch that wave and capitalize on it right away, you can make a fortune quickly.

Back when Russ was involved with the 900 numbers, he reluctantly got started in December—reluctantly because Christmas was coming, and he figured people were going to spend their money on Christmas gifts. He wanted to start in January, but he was so excited about his course that he began promoting it December 1—and proceeded to have his most profitable December ever. When you have something hot, it doesn't matter if it's winter, summer, spring, or fall, you can make money hand over fist.

When considering what's hot, think about those infomercials you sometimes see on TV. Generally they're for fad items that are often short-lived before their burnout—but sometimes they make millions of dollars while they *are* hot. And frankly, it's no wonder that some of these things don't last long, because they're so offbeat and ridiculous that you scratch your head and say, "Really? Why in the world is that thing popular? Anybody could have come up with that." Sure—but the point is that someone else did, and now they're making loads of money, because they saw a marketplace for something others viewed as silly. Either that, or they created the marketplace from scratch, then filled it.

These things are often a flash in the pan. Even if they're well-established and useful, they could go away overnight if a new technology replaces them—like BBS services gave way to the Internet, and buggy whips to automobiles. But if you're on top of trends and keep track of the news, you know when it's time to move on to the next hot item. There's a whole culture of infomercial businesses that specifically look for those kinds of items, constantly studying the marketplace and testing items. Some of these companies are excellent at finding those hot items and selling them while they're hot. Consider the Snuggie, which was hot recently. It's basically a blanket with sleeves, but the infomercial businesses built a fad around them and sold millions of the things.

Watch late-night TV and you'll see the current fad items. Heck, they're still selling Chia Pets. Cooking and food preparation gadgets are still popular. Viagra and other male enhancement type products remain popular, though I believe they're more fad than legitimate. Yet the branding and the advertising that industry has done has created a really hot marketplace that might not be there otherwise.

One of the most brilliant things that I think that the latter market has done is that one of their smart marketers took what was just a side effect—and a negative side effect at that—and turned it into one of their biggest selling points (it works for Cialis and most similar products as well). In some instances the stuff can work too well—up to four hours. or longer. If it does, they tell you to seek medical help. Well, if it works *that* well, it must be good stuff, right?

It's surprising and ridiculous, if you ask me. Yet, they've

built an entire multimillion dollar industry around it. And that's just one example. You'll see dozens if you pay attention, especially to late-night TV. All those ludicrous and not-that-great items, but they've built them into fortunes. So keep your eyes and mind open for what might just be the next big thing, no matter how weird it looks at first. There's probably a marketplace that's hungry for exactly those kinds of products—and it might be yours. Even if it isn't, how can you adapt that idea to your business?

Stay open and receptive. If other people are making millions of dollars with something, you can potentially make millions of dollars with it as well. And remember, you've got to believe you can before you see it. Catch the vision, and see that it *is* possible to make a lot of money with such things. We do it every day here at M.O.R.E. Inc. If you'll do that, you can hop on something as it appears.

Marketing Secret #68:
How to Create Money Out of Thin Air

I'll admit that this title is a bit of a tease; you'll never be able to just conjure cash out of thin air, and you're certainly not allowed to print your own! But the reality is, all of the money you want, need, and deserve is out there already, right now, in people's pockets, bank accounts, and credit lines. You just have to learn how to get them to reach out and give it to you. Now, you may be thinking, "Oh, is that *all*?" in a snarky way right about now, but it's not as difficult as you may believe.

What you have to do is take the old alchemy route. Back in the old days, the alchemists—precursors to chemists—were busily searching for two basic things: the secret of long life and a way to turn base metals into gold. Well, we can do the latter now in nuclear reactors, though it costs way more than the gold is worth. But there are other ways to turn things into gold: through marketing. It takes some effort, and it's not magical at all, but it *works*. All you have to do is come up with a great idea and then write a sales letter that generates all of the cash you need.

That's not as difficult as it sounds; and the great part is, you can earn while you learn your craft and hone your marketing edge. The ultimate goal here is to write so well than you convince your prospects that you're exchanging value for value—because you are. Whatever you offer had better have the potential to do exactly what you say it does, so you need to stick with what's proven. This method of generating cash from thin air has been proven so often and for so long that it's obviously real.

Consider this: if you own a fast food restaurant and I'm hungry, I can exchange five or six dollars for a cheeseburger, fries and a Coke. That's a fair exchange of value for value. Well, when you write a sales letter, you're doing the same thing. You're offering a certain group of benefits to prospective customers, hoping they see the value there—that it is, in fact, at least worth the number of dollars you're asking them to exchange for it. That's the only real way to create money from thin air: to provide value to prospects in the hope that they will find value in what you have to offer.

There's no greater way to do *that* than to be able to write a great sales letter and turn it into profits by having people respond. In fact, many of the secrets included in this book have covered important strategies for crafting sales letters. In the general sense, the goal is to work closely with a marketplace that you have identified and come to know very well. You seek through your sales letter to provide them the value *they* seek so they can pay you for whatever it is you're offering them.

100 MARKETING SECRETS

Just to show you a quick example of how this works, recently I've been busy thinking about the kinds of products and services our clients want (as I often do). I had access to an offer written by one of our good friends that I know was successful in the past. So with my friend's permission and blessing, I set about developing a new offer using this powerful, proven strategy and copy. It took only a few days to remake and revise that item into a new offer.

This ended up as a 32-page sales letter for a $700 product. Among other things, we also included an order form, several pages of Q&A where we try to answer our prospects' biggest objections, the reply envelope, and an outer envelope— so it worked out to about 40 pages of paper. But you know, those pages were blank in the beginning. They were the kind of paper you can take pick up at Wal-Mart by the ream for a couple of bucks; so the individual sheets of paper cost almost nothing.

It's only when you put words on the paper that it gains significant value. In this case, we're trying to turn those 40 sheets of paper into an order worth $697. How do you do that? By providing the value people want, and giving it to them in exchange for what they have—money. In essence, we have learned the secret of alchemy. It's not based on turning cheap metals into precious metals; it's even cheaper than that. It's paper into profits. And that's what it's all about: coming up with a great idea, writing a sales letter to convey a message to your prospects, and offering certain benefits in exchange for the money they have. Applied with the right sense and aforethought, it really does create money out of thin air.

This works for just about any business, even standard local businesses. It puts you ahead of the game, too, because most local business people have gone through their entire business lives just putting an "Open for Business" sign in their window and thinking that's enough. They accept the businesses that happens to come to them, rather than seeking new business. That's not good enough. If you want to be a true entrepreneur and maximize your profits, you can't just wait for people to show up at your door. You have to go after them in a focused, aggressive way. This is why you have to learn to write sales letters—or be willing to pay someone to do it for you.

Start by collecting a list of contact information for all your buyers, and market straight to them. When you have something they've responded enthusiastically to, go out to the broader marketplace to bring more people in. Ordinary paper, which has very little value alone, can turn into hundreds of thousands or even millions of dollars through a sales letter, if you market it correctly. That's true alchemy. It creates cash flow—money where none existed before. We like to think of the world as one giant safe. If you can hit on the right combination, you'll open it up and money will just fall out.

Right now we're working on tapping into a brand-new marketplace of 30-50 million small business people. We're selling a tremendous advertising service, and along with it we're giving away—absolutely free—something that other people are selling for as much as $500 a month. Again, it's all about crafting that right offer. If you put things together in the right combination, the money will flow.

Marketing Secret #69:
Customers Go Where They're Invited and Stay Where They're Appreciated.

Like so many other Secrets in this book, #69 sounds so

simple—but it can make you a mint. For some reason, also like so many of these Secrets, your competitors will probably never figure it out unless they read this book. If they do, they won't put it into play aggressively enough. Customers go where they're invited, and they stay where they're appreciated. Period.

When I first heard that on a marketing tape, I pulled the car over to the side of the road, grabbed my legal pad, and wrote it down. I memorized it, and I've thought about it consistently since. It's so damned simple—but here's the problem. First, there's so much competition out there. That's not a negative thing, but you do have to wake up and smell the coffee. There are so many marketing messages bombarding us that we've basically tuned them out. The average person only has so much money to spend, they only have so much time, and they have things in their life that are very important to them. Just because you're all hyped up on whatever you're selling doesn't mean that they are.

Since people are so tuned out, you have to not only invite them in, you've got to continue to re-invite them. You have to craft irresistible offers, put them out there, and get them to bite. Once they've expressed an interest, follow up aggressively.

I've already discussed my wife's pet boutique. One of her strategies is to hold free events for her customers every month. She has an e-mail list of about 600 people, and leverages Facebook and other social media. She brings in local vets and dog trainers to make the events fun and informative. Typically, only a few people come in for each of these free events. But all her customers are constantly invited and re-invited, and that makes a difference. That helps her stand out from all of her competitors.

If I were forced to boil marketing down to just one thing,

that thing would be "differentiation." You must separate yourself from everybody else in the marketplace. That's one of the things Eileen is doing here: she's re-inviting people to do business with her constantly, to separate herself from the crowd. We do this with M.O.R.E. Inc. also. We constantly communicate with our customers.

We're also preparing to launch a new company we're passionately excited about, and we'll do the same there, too. We've already determined that once we get a customer, we'll do everything we can to keep them happy. That's the second part of the equation: showing them they're appreciated. We're going to have free events at least once a month. We're eager to build that long-term relationship. That's what people are looking for.

Once you get people to start come back, the power of habit will kick in. We're all creatures of habit—we buy from the same people repeatedly, once we're comfortable with them (as long as they don't screw it up totally). So get them to keep coming in by re-inviting them, and then let the power of habit take over. They'll form an emotional bond with you that strengthens as you're able to do things that show you appreciate them.

Most customers don't feel they get enough appreciation. They love to have businesses reach out and say kind things to them. Most businesses today, whether international, national, or local, seem to spend most of their time, effort, and money trying to attract new customers. While there's nothing wrong with that, you're a fool if you neglect the customers you already have. These are the people who've made it possible for you to support yourself and your family. So in your haste and desire to acquire new customers, don't overlook the people who have kept you in business.

I know marketers who have become millionaires by working

with small customer lists of 200 or less, because they've constantly taken care of their clients by being there for them, by showing them their appreciation, by offering them great deals on new product and services they knew their clients wanted. Never neglect your existing customers! Invite them to come and invite them to stay. Otherwise, your business will suffer and ultimately fail.

Some marketers think, "Well, they just bought something from me. I don't want to offer them something too quickly. I don't want them to be upset that I'm trying to push something else already." But in my experience the reality is that if you're providing value to them, and they chose to do business with you the first time, then you really are doing them a disservice if you withdraw at that point. They're interested in hearing from you again because you're helping them. No one has to do business with anybody for any reason, so you can't force them to be your customer; but you can encourage them to stay with you and buy a second, third, fourth, or fifth time, once they've chosen you in the first place. All you have to do is offer them something of value.

Make them feel appreciated. It's always easier to get a happy existing customer to buy from you again than to convince a new customer to buy for the first time. But never, ever forget that you do have to make an effort to invite them in in the first place.

Russ von Hoelscher worked briefly with a printer in San Diego who did a wonderful job. He found out about him through a referral, and then started sending him a lot of his business because he did such excellent work. The man was a perfectionist. He wouldn't turn anything out that had a smudge on it. Russ was impressed with the guy, but he was located out of the way in the very last store of a little strip mall. Even though Russ was doing quite a bit of business with him, he was hurting, always complaining that business wasn't good. So Russ told, "Well, you're kind of buried in the back of the strip mall." The printer pointed out, "But there's a sign out front," and Russ responded, "Yes, but it's got about 14 businesses on it and you're toward the bottom—and cars are shooting by here at 50 miles an hour, and they don't see it. What you need to do is round up some college kids and have them pass out flyers within a five-mile radius. There are hundreds of businesses in that area, all potential customers of yours."

Russ could tell his advice wasn't sinking in. The guy just gave him a weird look and said, "Look, I'm a printer. I've got a sign out front there that says I'm a printer. If people want printing, they'll know where I am. They'll have to come to me— I'm not going to them." It was a ridiculous response, and Russ could see the writing on the wall. Sure enough, the printer was able to hang on for another year or so, but he finally went out of business because he had such a bad attitude.

It doesn't matter if you're a printer, an insurance agent, a shoestore owner, or a real estate agent, you'd better go out and get some business. You can't just sit back and wait for someone to come to you, or the cobwebs are going to grow. Customers only go where they're invited—and just putting your sign up doesn't cut it. It reminds me of that Kevin Costner movie, *Field of Dreams,* where the message was "If you build it, they will come." That's the way many people think about their businesses. They put their signs up, get a Yellow Page ad, and think, "Hey, I'm open for business now, baby, bring it on!" They fail to realize how competitive and over-saturated the marketplace is, and how the average consumer is just so wiped out and overwhelmed by all the ads and messages. Sadly, that printer's attitude is pretty much the prevailing attitude of small businesses.

Marketing Secret #70: Black Magic Persuasion Skills

The world's most notorious con artists use what some of us in the business call "black magic persuasion skills." They can talk anyone into anything. Consider the biggest con man in history, Bernie Madoff, who took in billions of dollars simply by telling people, "I'll guaranteed a 12% or better return on your money each and every year." Apparently, in the early days, he actually *did* earn people a lot of money on their investments. But he wasn't content to run a small shop; he decided to bring in some of the richest people in America, based on his reputation. He got everyone from Steven Spielberg to some of the richest people in New York to give him billions of dollars—for what was basically a Ponzi scheme.

These cons know how to paint their offers. They do such a beautiful job of getting people excited and ready to spend their money that we as marketers can learn from them: that is, we can use their persuasive methods to legally and ethically make a boatload of money. Just expose yourself to such people from a safe distance, and study what they do. Watch some of the programs on CNBC about crooks, con artists and suckers. These people know how to get people to spend money without threatening them. They just make everything sound so irresistible people can't help but get involved.

The key to *legal* black magic persuasion skills is also to create irresistible offers, but to do so in an ethical, moral way, making sure that the things you're selling are genuine. Back them up all the way down the line, and offer a great money-back guarantee to further benefit the buyer. If you can do that, this strategy is very useful. But do be absolutely sure you're legit all the way around. Don't become a con artist yourself. Just find ways you can bend over backward to promise people the world—and then deliver. Market aggressively. Be appealing. Be absolutely above reproach.

When you can deliver, you should do everything possible to get people in your marketplace to respond, because you're providing them with a benefit they're not going to get anywhere else—one they desperately need. Armed with that assumption, it's in your prospect's best interest that you do everything possible to make the sale. If you give up on them too early, you're doing them a disservice.

I'm a big fan of the HBO show "The Sopranos." In fact, I've watched the entire 88-episode run, many a dozen times or more. While the characters can be vicious, I admire that mob tendency to make their own rules. It's essential to the entrepreneurial spirit. Entrepreneurs look around and say, "No matter what comes at me, I'll figure out a way to go around it, under it, over it or through it. I'm not going to let this stuff bother me. If there's a way through, that's great. If there's not, I'm going to make one."

One of the world's most successful mobsters once pointed out. "You have to have the heart of the lion and the mind of the fox if you want to succeed in the biggest way." So I went out and found a little glass lion and a little glass fox that I keep as symbols to remind me of that. The heart of the lion is bold and aggressive. The mind of the fox is cunning; you rarely see them in action. In business, you need both to do well.

CHAPTER EIGHT

SECRETS 71-80

Marketing Secret #71:
How to Avoid Legal Nightmares

This is a simple idea that will help you stay 100% legal—but it also happens to be a Secret that no lawyer will ever tell you. A lawyers' job is argue the gray area. In the legal world, there is very little black-and-white—quite possibly because lawyers themselves write the laws, and all levels of government are overrun with lawyers. They think they're the only ones smart and qualified enough to tell the rest of us what to do. It would be very difficult to write a law that would be universally black-and-white in any case; generally, laws are full of loopholes, so arguments can be made on any side.

Look at how many times the Constitution has been amended and re-interpreted. Here we have a very strict, limited document that says how our federal government is supposed to run. Yet over the couple of hundred years of existence since it was enacted, lawyers and legislatures have interpreted it and reinterpreted it, especially in federal courts. Very seldom do those arguing about constitutional law go back to the original document. It's a lot more likely that they'll actually argue case law, which means they'll argue about prior arguments instead of the document itself. That's how you end up with this gray area that most businesses operate under.

So when I talk about avoiding legal nightmares and staying 100% legal, I think that the key here is to spend less time focused on the black-and-whites and the dos and don'ts of business, because those are very hard to interpret, and more time focusing on this defensibility of your argument. In particular, I'm thinking of some businesses that might be heavily regulated by the Environmental Protection Agency. There's a long list of things that they can and can't do based on EPA codes and regulations. Very few are black and white. Most are written so they can be argued; and sometimes, when a company is questioned about a certain regulation, the lawyers will spend time on both sides making cases and arguing for why they are or aren't in violation. They go back and forth, the EPA makes a ruling for one side or another, and then the business gets back to work.

Some businesses have teams of lawyers that exist for no other reason than to tell the business how they can or can't operate within the law. But again, in many cases they're arguing not over fact and figures or rights and wrongs, but over gray-level interpretations of the regulations that govern their industry. Most marketplaces are heavily regulated, so there are times when you risk violating some rule or other unintentionally. If you want to utterly avoid those risks, then stay out of business altogether— because all business is risk, especially in today's litigious society.

Just do your best to conduct your business as ethically and morally as possible, while also making sure that you have defensibility. If you feel comfortable checking with a lawyer, then check with a lawyer. They'll tell you what I've already told you about defensibility, and the gray area we work within— which was set up that way purposely.

Understand: Lawyers don't get paid to argue black-and-white. They get paid to argue that middle ground no one really understands and few people find comforting.

Do your best to stay out of the webs of attorneys. I've known some who were wonderful people, but the grayness they work in rubs off on most. They thrive on conflict, so they don't want anything to be resolved simply. They want to do battle. It's a game they manipulate to make the most money possible, even if that sometimes involves urging their clients to do things that aren't kosher.

And besides, you can't keep track of all the laws out there. Many are placed on the books, and few are removed. As I heard one attorney say years ago, "The average person breaks about 21 laws every day, just going about his business." There are so many laws today that you're bound to break some just by existing. Just try not to break the big ones.

My father worked for the government for 30 years. I loved the man dearly, but he was a typical government bureaucrat. He was a lawyer first, and then he became a judge. I used to meet with him once a week for lunch, and I would say to him, "Hey Dad, what are you doing after this?" And he'd say, " I have a meeting." And I'd say, "Tell me more about it." He would say, "We're going to talk about what we're going to talk about at the next meeting." In other words, they just drag it out. Attorneys get paid by the hour—and I guarantee they're trying to do as little as they can for the highest pay they can. They have a vested interest in dragging out every issue as long as possible.

Here's what I tell my lawyer all the time: "I've heard all the lawyer jokes. Even Shakespeare said, 'First, kill all the lawyers.' But whenever someone is in serious legal trouble, all the jokes go right out the window. All of a sudden that lawyer becomes the most important person in your life." My lawyer told me this, and I like the quote: "If the law were black-and-white, there would be no need for me." So let me reiterate: build lots of defensibility into everything you do, to protect yourself and maintain your freedom.

Marketing Secret #72:
Three Skills That Can Make You Financially Set for Life

There are only three skills you really have to master to achieve the essence of all good marketing. Skill #1 is the ability to generate large numbers of the very best prospects for whatever you're selling. That takes considerable skill, though there are plenty of ways you can learn to do that and hone your skills, earning while you learn. Do your best to get them to pre-qualify themselves. Every decent marketplace has a vast audience who could potentially be giving you their money. So get them to identify themselves and come to you.

Skill #2 is your ability to convert those prospects into first-time buyers and customers, earning as much money as you can as quickly as you can. You usually have to do that through a series of follow-ups; this process doesn't just happen overnight. Skill #3 is your ability to extract the most profit possible from each customer over the longest possible period of time. That may sound a little ruthless to you, since, as I'm pointing out, you're extracting profits from customers. Sounds like pulling teeth, doesn't it? But you're doing it with their permission, offering tremendous value in exchange for their money. I've tried to make that clear throughout this program. You're not taking advantage of anybody without also having them take advantage of you. It's an even trade.

Earlier I referenced a project we're working on now to get an infusion of cash into our business. We have an irresistible offer we're preparing to make to our customers. We know it's irresistible, because it is based on a sales letter that generated over a million dollars very quickly 12 years ago, and the creator of that letter has given us permission to rewrite it to our needs. I spent a weekend rewriting it; then Chris Lakey and I worked on polishing it up, and we'll keep doing it until it's just right.

Next we'll present this offer to our very best customers to create that infusion of cash. That's just one example of Skill #3—continuing to go back to your customers with new offers they salivate over. They'll get so excited about giving you their money they can't even stand it. The last time we mailed this offer, we had people FedExing and even wiring their money to us. I have every reason to believe it's going to be hot again.

It's all about creating value: that's the only thing that gets people to come back repeatedly. They have so many choices these days, and they can go anywhere for what they want. They don't need you, they don't need your company, they don't need your product or services. Therefore, you do have to go overboard and bend over backwards to attract them, which is what this skill set is all about.

If I had to break marketing down into just three important skills, these would be the ones. Just like the primary colors—red, yellow, and blue—you can use these skills in various combinations to create an endless number of "hues." You can spend your entire life learning everything there is to learn about different aspects of marketing, but it really does boil down to these three things, and It's easy to see the importance of each individual part of this three-step process.

But let me clarify one point. Some people think that just

because someone has bought once or even twice, that makes them a customer. I don't agree. Before you can consider them a customer, they have to do business with you on a regular or semi-regular basis. Your ultimate goal is turn as many buyers as you can into loyal customers. Then you can get into the mathematics of what a customer is worth.

Let's say you own a restaurant and someone eats there once a week, every week. If that customer has been with you for five years, that means they've visited your restaurant at least 250 times. In 10 years it would be 500 times, possibly more. Multiply that by their average purchase, and you'll get some idea of the value of that customer. Depending on what they buy and how often, the value can be much higher than you ever thought possible—which should make you realize that your ultimate goal must be to turn your leads into long-time, highly appreciated, and very active buyers.

These three skills really are the foundation of a successful business, and you have to learn how to master them all. The big payoff is the third skill. Skill #2 helps you recover your initial marketing costs, but the real profits come from reselling to your existing customers. Your business will grow based on your ability to do more business with people who already have a relationship with you—people who know and like you.

Think of your existing customer base as a big bucket. There's a funnel coming into it that all your new prospects are pouring into. Unfortunately, the funnel lets only a few people through—and your bucket has a hole in it, caused by customers leaving the market, moving, dying, or just having less money to spend. Whatever the case, your bucket is leaking, so you want to continuously use your front-end marketing methods to attract new customers to fill the funnel, which dribbles in new customers—all the while continuing to do more business with the customers already in the bucket. You need to be sure that the bucket is constantly full of customers.

If you don't keep doing new customer acquisition, you'll stop having new people drop into your bucket. If that happens, the bucket will eventually run dry just from attrition. If you don't continue doing business with your existing customers, you'll lose them because they'll leave. It's important to do all three of those things effectively. Learn them and practice them often, because they'll be the lifeblood of your business

Does that sound simple? Good, because it is. But that doesn't mean it's *easy*. No, it takes some serious work. Burn this process into your memory. Start practicing the principles I've shared with you in this chapter, and you'll never lack for money.

Marketing Secret #73:
How to Use Deadlines to
Force Yourself to Become Wealthy

Two of entrepreneurship's worst enemies are procrastination and indecision. We human beings often spend too much time just dragging our heels. Many of us also have trouble with making up our minds and sticking to our decisions. In a previous chapter, I mentioned the indecisive business owners who let their employees and spouses make business decisions for them—a huge mistake. You have to do your own marketing, and control every aspect of it as tightly as possible. Advice is one thing; control is another.

Marketers must learn how to make decisions with

authority, and stop procrastinating so much. One great way to do that is to force yourself to make decisions and get things done. When I'm working on a project, I'm always aware of that deadline or timeline—even when I'm working on other things. Those deadlines help me commit to doing the things that most people won't or can't do—and that's to make the decision to get to work. We should make promises to our customers, especially our best and regular customers, that we're going to do this or that for them by a specific date, so we can force ourselves to do it— to plan how much to do each day, and to stick to it. *Never* underestimate the lack of progress suffered by a person who isn't making decisions—or who's just procrastinating their life away.

As a deadline draws near, we feel forced to do something, because we've made a commitment that we *would* do it. We should always make it to ourselves first, but we can (and should) also make it to our clients. That keeps our feet to the fire—and the answers will often come as the deadline comes closer, because when you really, really have to get something done, it's amazing how those ideas will develop for you, arising full-blown from your subconscious mind. It works like a miracle sometimes—but it's really not a miracle at all. That it occurs at all means you've finally concentrated fully on the topic.

No one likes deadlines, but it's very much to your detriment to avoid them, because they really do force you to get stuff done. Setting deadlines is a powerful incentive, especially for someone who's not used to getting things done on time. You make the commitment that you *will* get it done on time or earlier, first to yourself and then to everyone else related to the deadline. When you do that, positive, profitable things will start to happen in your business.

I think that the negatives surrounding deadlines make

many people avoid them. We're afraid of the commitment a deadline requires, so we do everything we can to avoid the pressure that comes with setting one. You always can lie to yourself and set a fake deadline in your own mind; it's easy to break, because there's no commitment level there. For example, you might say, "I want to lose 20 pounds by this date," or "I would like to make this much money by this day," or "I would like to save this much or pay off this bill by November 1." You can make your own commitments in your mind, but they're like those New Year's resolution you make annually. If no one else knows you've made it, how hard is it to break? Not very, because no one's going to be there saying, "I thought you wanted or needed to do this by now."

One the other hand, a deadline made to a client is chiseled in stone. You have commitments that must be fulfilled. Sometimes you can get away with extending a deadline or telling a client a project won't be finished on time; those things can and do happen. But a deadline that you make to a client via a promise of delivery will push you towards fulfilling that promise, because you have the pressure of an order that's unfulfilled until you can deliver on it.

One of the deadline incentive strategies we've used many times is the prepublication sale, where you write a sales letter in which you tell your customers that you're making this offer to them now at a special price because the project isn't done yet. Maybe it's a book you're writing, or an audio program you're producing. We deal a lot in the information publishing world, so we do a lot with paper and audio both. If you sell it before you've produced it, you make a commitment to the client that forces you to finish it. You describe it in detail, tell them what it's going to be and do, and the solutions they'll receive when they buy, so they'll look forward to it. From that point on, you have orders coming in. People pay for the product, expecting delivery by a specific date—and that sets the process in motion.

As you approach that deadline, the pressure mounts, forcing you into action. This is a good thing. Some people think that pressure and deadlines are all negatives; and admittedly, no one really likes the pressure of a tight deadline. But it drives action, forcing you to act. So don't view deadlines as negative things. Look at them as opportunities to spur yourself on, to get projects done in a timely way. That, in turn, translates into more profits.

I have a problem with procrastination. I've got all these projects I'm working on, and I get behind on all of them—and that creates a tremendous inner turmoil. A lot of it is work that I don't enjoy doing, which is why I put it off. So I practice an absurdly simple technique to overcome my procrastination: I promise myself to devote a few minutes to each project. If, after a few minutes, I want to stop, then I stop. But most of the time, I've gotten into the project by then, and I'm able to keep going for half an hour or longer. It all starts when I tell myself that all I need to do is stick with it for just a few minutes.

Getting started is the hardest part. If I can commit to just a few minutes, then in nearly every case I end up spending at least 10-20 minutes on it instead of the 3-5 minutes I committed to. It chips away at the stone, breaking off a little piece at a time—and ultimately I end up with a sculpture. I try to follow this plan every single day, seven days a week. Eventually, I complete the project—even if my dedicated time is working on an order form on my laptop, while half-watching TV with my wife.

It feels wonderful to get something done. I want to avoid

that terrible feeling of not accomplishing anything, so I keep chipping away at that stone every day.

Marketing Secret #74:
Writing Sales Copy That Earns Millions of Dollars, Fast!

Writing sales copy tends to be under-appreciated and undervalued in the marketing world. All the ad agencies have their secret ways of advertising products and promoting your business, and forget about learning the art of DRM! Well, blowing off DRM sales copy is a huge mistake, so in this Secret I'll introduce a simple five-point formula that will help you write better sales copy.

What will this formula do for you? That depends on your offer, the marketplace you're selling to, and a 101 other factors that contribute to the success or failure of a specific promotion. But: we've brought in millions of dollars with these strategies, and there's no reason at all why they can't work for any offer that reaches the right audience.

Step #1 is to start with a basic idea that you think your marketplace will respond to. We've talked before about the importance of selling to the right marketplace and knowing that marketplace thoroughly. Armed with that knowledge, consider who you want as your best customers. Think about who your best customers are already, if you have an existing customer base. What do they want the most? What kind of offers will they respond to best? *That's* the kind of offer you want to make to them. You want to make them a killer offer that they can't refuse.

Step #2 is to kill some trees. Get it all down on paper; or if you'd prefer to stay fully digital, on the computer screen. It's basically the same. Go crazy with your copy. Dream and imagine what the offer could be or what you would *like* it to be, by writing down all kinds of ideas. This may include some actual copywriting, but you're not really writing a sales letter at this point.

Something you should know (if you don't already) is that writing a sales letter rarely happens according to a particular format. You don't just sit down at your computer and bang it out in perfect order, from the headline on through to the P.S. It never happens that way. Usually you start with a brain-dump, capturing lots of notes and ideas about what you want your offer to be, including the benefits you know the prospect wants. Then you organize and reorganize until it's in the order you like best.

Now, be careful here, because sometimes your brain starts throwing out negative comments about your ideas even as you're writing them. Avoid the temptation to listen; just let the ideas flow. Don't worry about whether they're feasible or not; don't worry about implementation. Just imagine a best-case scenario in which you can get everything you want, with no concern for how you'll pull it off or how much it costs. Right now you're just putting your ideas on paper. Get all your ideas out, as many ideas as possible. This may take several days, or even weeks. I suggest you set a deadline, so you don't just keep going and going; but do spend some time letting the ideas flow, and don't throw away anything just yet. When you're done, sit on it for a while before coming back to it.

Step #3 is where you boil it down. Separate the best ideas and copy from the rest. Start looking for things that would make good headlines for the offer. Look for the strongest benefits. Pore over your notes and weed out the unusable material in favor of the best of what you've written. Once you've massaged it a while and started separating, sifting, and sorting, you'll start to see the rough outline of what will be your sales letter.

Step #4 is to identify 3-5 of your strongest benefits—or even as many as 10, if your project is especially large or far-reaching. Start rewriting, looking for effective ways to incorporate those benefits into your sales copy. This is where you start to really refine your brain dump. The quantity isn't important; just start with the strongest benefits. Then you can decide if you have room for others. You may find that the biggest benefit should be your headline—the biggest, boldest, promise you can make to your prospect. The other good benefits might become into bullets that describe what the buyer will get when they buy your product or service. Remember to keep your copy benefit oriented, *not* feature oriented. People don't care about features *per se*; they care about the benefits you can provide. Then pull together your sending, writing a call to action, a close, and maybe a P.S. before polishing it up and adding the finishing touches.

The fifth and final step is to test the sales letter, so you can determine whether or not this baby has legs and whether it's going to be what you thought it would be back in the daydreaming phase. Get the letter in the mail to your best customers and see how they respond. Be sure to analyze the numbers carefully. Code your letters so you know where the orders came from when they do come in. That's critical. Test, analyze, revise, and retest; and with a bit of luck, success, and skill, you can have yourself a hit offer. Then you can start testing it to people who don't know you. As I've outlined before, you start with your best customers and then you move on to new prospects.

Those are the five core strategies for writing sales copy

that can produce millions of dollars in the right setting.

One advantage we have in the information-selling business is that we can actually dream up the ideal product. If we're interested in real estate, we can start thinking about unusual ways for people to make money with real estate, then start writing copy for something that doesn't exist yet. Now, if you're a merchant who has a certain type of product you're trying to sell, you can't just start dreaming about things that don't exist yet, because you're in business to sell that particular product. What you need to do is start thinking about writing copy for offers that bundle your various products and make them more attractive. You might tell them that if they'll buy this product for X dollars, you'll throw in another product for half-price. If it's a cheap product, you might even throw it in for free. So you still have the ability to create copy for something that isn't offered by your store or business yet, and make it work that way.

The key is to start thinking about innovative ways you can market things, and get them down on paper. Write down everything you think of, and don't judge anything until you're finished brainstorming. Only after you've killed a lot of trees do you run it all through the filter and decide whether what you've written is worthwhile. You'll discover that some ideas are unworkable, while others may simply seem silly. Sometimes they're even kind of crazy—but some of those crazy ideas will also be great ideas, once you've modified them to reality. Just look for things that best fit your offer.

One of the best things about creating information products is that they have no set intrinsic value; you can charge whatever you think they're worth. You always have the leeway to dream up new things, even if you're tied down to specific products; you can always bundle them with compatible products, services, or bonuses. In doing so, you distinguish yourself from competitors who do business the same old vanilla way, day after day. Just be aware that this is a process with a learning curve, and that the best way to get good ideas is to get a *lot* of ideas. Sometimes it takes months or years to get good at this; in fact, your best ideas often come after you've been in the market for a while. Don't be discouraged by that, because in the meantime you can make plenty of money.

Marketing Secret #75:
How to Double Your Sales, Starting Right Now

If you implement this simple strategy, your sales and profits will soar. It's amazingly simple: all you have to do is double the time you spend in front of the people in the best position to say Yes to what you're offering. Needless to say, these are the best qualified prospects, those who prove by their actions that they're interested in and willing to buy what you have to offer.

As I've already outlined, it's all about generating the highest possible number of the most qualified prospects for whatever you're offering, converting as many of those people as you can to sales, and then continuing to do more business with them. That's marketing in a nutshell. With DRM, it's easy to spend more time in the follow-up process that generates more business from these highly qualified people.

You have to follow up like mad, because that's where the *real* money is. It's what you do with those high-quality prospects that will determine your income. You have to stay on top of them, repeatedly reminding them to order. Just because someone doesn't buy from you right away doesn't mean they never will;

they may ultimately become one of your best customers. People are busy, they're looking at all kinds of options, and they only have so much disposable income. There are many reasons why someone you thought was a good prospect may not make a purchase immediately. Those who follow up most aggressively with qualified leads will always make the most money.

And consider this: a qualified lead is really *pre*-qualified, and there are simple techniques you can use to pre-qualify people. The easiest way is to get them to spend some money initially, because usually they're your most serious prospects. As long as you have a pre-qualified prospect you're convinced is serious about your offer, and your profit margins are large enough that you can make good money even with bad conversions, then you *must* follow up aggressively.

Sometimes all it takes is a little follow-up to generate more work. A while back, Russ von Hoelscher was talking to a publisher friend in Oregon, who told Russ that business was terrible. He said, "I have to do something to generate some money, because we're going backwards." What did he do? He looked up the phone numbers of his customers, many of whom hadn't dealt with him for several months, and he called them up. After an hour and a half of phone calls, he had more business than he could handle.

Imagine that—the business was right there in his customer files. All he had to do was pick up the phone and contact his people, and he was flooded with business. They were happy to hear from him, and when he told them about some of the new services he was offering, they said, "Hey, I could use you right now!" So once again, you can see the value of going after existing customers.

And let me repeat—because I feel the need to pound this idea into everyone's head—the three ways you make money in business are: One, you generate as many of the best and most qualified leads you possibly can; Two, you convert as many of those leads as possible into buyers; and Three, you turn as many of those buyers as possible into long-term customers, people who give you repeat business month after month and year after year. Learn to do those three things, and you'll never hurt for business.

If you're a car salesman, that means spending more time in front of people who want to buy a car. Don't hang around the showroom sipping coffee; go out and talk to customers. The more you talk to them, the more likely you are to make more money and sales. If you do all your business by direct mail, it means you'll have to get more mail out there, especially mail that has been proven to make a profit.

I've talked quite a bit about direct mail follow-ups , but this strategy works no matter how you get in front of your customers and prospects. The worst thing you can do is to *not* be in front of them. If you have a business and nobody knows you're there, then you won't do well at getting new customers. If you never tell existing customers about your offers, they'll forget about you.

If you're constantly in front of your customers, they won't forget you. They *can't* forget you, because you're constantly reminding them that you're still there, ready to do business with them. Doubling your sales is as easy as spending more time reminding your customers that you exist and you're ready to help them. More contact with customers produces more sales, assuming it's the right kind of meaningful, sales-driven contact where you're specifically asking for their business.

100 MARKETING SECRETS

Marketing Secret #76: In DRM, Knowledge is Power

When you learn direct response marketing, you'll have a huge advantage over all of your competition. I'd estimate that 98% of your competitors don't know beans about direct response marketing. They use Open For Business signs and ads in the Yellow Pages, PennySavers, and newspapers to try to acquire their business. It works to some degree, but nowhere can they compete with the power of DRM. When you learn how to use this power, you will make greater profits than any of them—I promise you that.

Needless to say, you need to read all the good books, from the classics to the contemporaries in DRM right now, written by experienced people who have the information that can help you become super-successful. It's an exciting process, because when you really learn this field you'll have so much business power that you'll inevitably have the upper hand over the competition—and you'll own a piece of the heart and minds of your customers, too. That's the most important thing here, because you'll know how to make irresistible offers to them. You'll know how to treat them the way they want to be treated. You'll learn exactly what your customers love, what they hate, what they want, and what they fear. When you know those things, you can start pushing the right buttons to make them respond to your offers like never before.

There is no question that DRM can double, triple or quadruple your business, and give you the edge over any competition. When I say that 98% of your competition doesn't know anything about DRM, I'm sure that's true. You may have one or two competitors in a large marketplace that *do* know DRM and are successful at it, but if you learn it, you'll join them at the top. If you have no competitors that know DRM, then you'll be at the top of the heap from the word go. DRM is simply the most powerful form of marketing on Earth if used correctly, and the best part is that anyone can learn how to do it. All it takes is some time and study. So get busy, and start learning DRM ASAP.

You may be familiar with the phrase, "Knowledge is power." You might even realize that only *applied* knowledge is power. You see, it doesn't matter what you know; it only matters what you *do* with what you know. When I think about DRM, I think of the power of words. The spoken word is a powerful force, but the written word works just as well. If you can't directly speak to someone, the only way to build a relationship with them is to write to them, using the same words you'd use if you were face-to-face.

Books can have such a emotional impact on people, so much that some people have a hard time putting a book down once they pick it up and get into the storyline. That's a good example of the power of the written word, which can be even greater than the power of a good movie. You don't just get the experience the producer wants you to have; you get a totally different experience based on your perception of what you're reading. Let's say you're reading a novel. As you read that story, your mind puts the characters and setting in a visual format in your head. You live out the story as your mind sees it—and there's a lot of power in that, because of how your mind processes what you're reading. I think that that happens with good sales copy as well.

One of the benefits of selling by direct mail, as opposed to doing broadcast commercials on TV like some of your competitors may be doing, is that it's a stealth method. Your competitors won't know what hit them. If they're paying attention, they'll see that you're doing well in your business, that you're getting more customers, and that they seem to have a bond with you—but they won't understand why. They won't understand how to compete against that. They'll keep running their "image ads" in the same old way, never making that personal connection, while you're out there writing to your customers...and they can't see it because it goes through the mail or email. That's another reason why DRM is a great sales method.

Take the time to study DRM in depth: the psychology that goes into it, the strategy behind it. I've discussed and will continue to discuss many different facets of advertising and marketing throughout this book, but frankly, learning and implementing DRM is the most valuable asset you can apply to your sales efforts. It will set you up for success, and there are very few businesses it doesn't work for.

One point I want to re-emphasize before I move on is that the more you know about DRM, the more you'll *want* to know about it. It becomes addictive. It's exciting. But be careful here: don't get so stuck on the knowing and learning that you don't implement. Only massive action will make you money, not theory and thought.

And one other thing: DRM is not advertising as such. In fact, I don't think about it as advertising at all. If someone wanted me to define it in as few words as possible, I'd say it's simply salesmanship. When you have a good direct mail piece out there making money for you, it incorporates all the best elements you get from a live salesperson—and a damned good one at that. Everything in the selling process can be done through DRM. As Aristotle Onassis once said, "The secret to

business is to know something your competitors don't know."
DRM is that something.

Marketing Secret #77:
A Multi-Million Dollar Secret from a 2000 Year Old Book

Nope, it isn't the Bible. This particular book is called *The Art of War* by an ancient Chinese strategist named Sun-Tzu. Most of us in the English-speaking world had no idea the book existed until 1905, when the first partially translated version appeared. The first complete English version wasn't released until 1910.

In this Secret, I'll discuss how you can use a basic strategy in *The Art of War* to destroy your competition. Here's that strategy: "Every battle is won before you go to war." Think about that. While Sun-Tzu intended his book for military use, it also works in business, marketing, and advertising as well. The principle here is that if you're going to do something, spend a lot of time preparing for it first. Similarly, Abe Lincoln once said that if he had to cut down a tree in six hours, he'd spend four hours sharpening the ax.

This is a similar strategy, which you can approach from several different angles. If you want to be a good direct response marketer, for instance, you should spend a lot of your time learning DRM. You should also practice writing sales letters. You don't just write your first sales letter and throw it out there; you first prepare by becoming a good copywriter. If you intend to dominate a certain marketplace, it would be best to prepare in advance by learning not only what it takes to dominate that marketplace, but also everything possible about its constituents. Success requires deep, intimate understanding of the marketplace. You leave yourself exposed to a much higher risk of failure if you don't prepare.

Another part of *The Art of War* discusses a Chinese saying that's still common today: "If you know your enemies and know yourself, you can win 100 battles without a single loss. If you only know yourself, but not your opponent, you may win or lose. If you know neither yourself nor your opponent, you will always endanger yourself." For me, this brings to mind Sam Walton, the founder of Wal-Mart, who said he spent a lot of time at Kmart, his biggest competitor. You'd think that he would avoid his competitors; but he wanted to know everything he could about them, to the point that he probably visited Kmart stores more often than any Kmart executives. It got to the point where they would escort him out as soon as they recognized him.

If you know yourself and your competitor, then you can win 100 marketing battles without a single loss.

You not only need to know what you're trying to do and how to successfully promote your business, you have to study the marketplace itself, as well as your competitors in that marketplace. Doing your research will greatly increase your odds of success. Will you succeed all of the time? Probably not. We all have our successes and failures, and not always because of factors we can control. Business is cyclical; there will be ups and downs no matter what. But there are ways to position yourself so that you're much more likely to succeed than fail.

I like to think of marketing as war without all the death and mayhem. But studying war, and the people who fight it, can teach you a lot. Years ago I read an autobiography of General Dwight Eisenhower, the man who commanded the U.S. forces during the invasion of Normandy and the subsequent campaign that brought down Nazi Germany. That campaign required a great deal of planning; he and his people had to work with other Allied troops, learn the lay of the land, and study the cultures of the countries his troops passed through, whether Allied or Axis. But he said the thing that he worked on the hardest was his profiles of the German generals and field marshals.

He learned the tactics each had used in previous battles, especially during the early part of the war when they were fighting the French and British. He learned their tendencies and strategies. By studying these men, he learned how they would react to specific attacks and counterattacks, which was very important to his campaign.

This is even easier in the marketing arena. To learn who your competition is, just acquire their sales material, catalogs, sales letters and ads—online, TV, or radio—and study closely what they're doing. Then you can see what they're doing right as well as what they're doing wrong. You can determine how to overcome their flaws and take advantage of what you've learned in your own marketing efforts.

Of course, DRM isn't war in the true sense of the word. You're not going to be facing enemies who are trying to kill you, but you *are* facing competition. When your direct competitors capture business you don't, they're hurting you, because they're taking money that could be yours. So follow the Boy Scout motto and be prepared. The best way to do that is to study the competition so you can learn how to beat them.

A few months back, I was in a meeting with my lawyer, and he said something so interesting that I wrote it down immediately. He learned this quote from his mentor: "Proper preparation prevents piss-poor performance!" I like the alliteration, and I've printed it out to hang on my wall. I paid $195 an hour for that quote, and it's yours now. This comes from one of the best attorneys that I've ever met in my life.

Proper preparation is the secret to success. Proper preparation is doing everything you can to learn about your market and competitors. It's thinking everything through. From a marketing standpoint, it's having several great answers to every objection your best prospects will have. It's never being caught off guard; no matter what, you can handle it. When you know that you can overcome any objection to purchasing your product or service, that creates confidence in you. Confidence itself sells products.

Marketing Secret #78:
Six Words That Determine How Much Money You Make

No matter what you do or try to make money, a small phrase containing just six words will ultimately determine your income. That may sound unbelievable at first, but bear with me and I'll prove it to you. The six words are: "What are you willing to do?"

Earlier, I brought up one of the greatest entrepreneurs ever, Sam Walton. He was willing to do whatever it took to succeed, at least within his personal moral and ethical constraints. No matter the price, he was willing to pay it. He wrote an autobiography, *Made In America*, just a few years before he died. It's a great book, and you can see this principle in the background all the way through. In fact, when you study the great entrepreneurs, you'll see that it's a common denominator they all have.

Back in the early 1990's, my wife bought me a gift that means more to me than anything else she's given me. It's just a little keychain with three words on it: "Whatever it takes." That's what I'm willing to do to succeed. I think about that all the time. I've failed plenty of times in the past, and I can look at all my failures and see that I failed because I *wasn't* willing to do whatever it took. People who are willing to do whatever it takes, no matter how many times they get beaten down, keep getting right back up until the succeed. They won't be stopped.

Think about those six words: "What are you willing to do?" Think about the three words on my keychain: "Whatever it takes." Elvis Presley had a saying he immortalized on the big TCB chain he wore around his neck; it stood for "Taking Care of Business." That was his version of the same thing.

What *are* you willing to do? At the moment, we're starting a new business. We keep having setbacks, but it's proceeding. It's an exciting business. We've done income projections that show we can bring in millions of dollars per month in pure profit if we play our cards right; no doubt about it. We know the potential is there; but we also know that this is a hard road we're getting ready to travel down. We're not fooling ourselves about that. It will take long months, possibly even a few years, to crack the code and figure it all out. That's why no one's done it already.

But we're practicing the gospel I'm preaching right now. We're starting locally with a service that can be sold all over the world. One of the reasons we're starting locally is so we can meet with our prospects in person. Before we take it national, we've decided to bloom where we're planted. We're going to do free lunches and consulting sessions with our prospects. We're going to spend quality time with them, trying to figure out their biggest problems and challenges, what they want the most, and what they definitely *don't* want. We're trying to develop that ultimate service here, because if we can develop it for local clients, there are 30-50 million other people in this country alone who are prime prospects for what we're selling.

We're willing to do whatever it takes. We're not going to make the mistakes I've made in the past, where we suffered a few setbacks and then gave up and went on to the next shiny object. That's the way entrepreneurs tend to be. It's one of the reasons they fail. They don't have it in them to stick to difficult projects; I can say this with authority because I've been guilty of this myself.

So don't give up. You really do have to be willing to do whatever it takes to see your project through, assuming it's worth the effort. Sure, sometimes that's no fun, because you'd prefer an easier road. But successful people are willing to pay the price. Once you do so and achieve success, you'll look back and say, "Boy, I wish I'd done that sooner and made those commitments earlier. I could've reached this plateau a year, two years, five years or even 10 years ago."

It really does comes down to doing whatever it takes. If they knock you down 10 times, you've got to get up 11 times. Now, you can't be so stubborn that you try and try and try to sell the same thing when it's obviously never going to sell. There's a limit to this principle; you just have to recognize it. Sometimes even wonderful copy won't sell a product people don't like or aren't ready for. But you can often transfer some or all of that copy to another product or service you know that people *will* buy. You're going to find the silver lining in there, some way to make it work, and you're going to be successful.

My dear friend and mentor Russ von Hoelscher tells me

that I'm a good example of this, and I like to think he's right in paying me that compliment. If nothing else, I'm stubborn. I've failed many times in business, but I have never, ever given up. I'm willing to persevere, spending enormous amounts of time to perfect the business opportunities I promote. I may procrastinate sometimes, like we all do, but I keep moving forward. If you want to be successful, you have to do the same. Look ahead, beyond your normal range of vision. Know that if you can believe it first and see it in your mind's eye, eventually it will manifest itself in the real world, right in front of you.

Where do you want to go? What are you willing to do to make that happen? The world is full of people who will take the easier path, so take the road less travelled. Dream big, and ascend to that place on high that the most successful of us have made their own. There's plenty of room at the top—mostly because only a few people are willing to work and dream hard enough to get there.

When you get right down to it, this is a life lesson as well as a business lesson, because no big goal—whether it's to shoot under par at the golf course, or to lose 50 pounds—happens overnight. You have to be willing to make the day-to-day commitment to make it happen. That's the hard part. You can look back and see what eventually transpired, but you usually can't see it in the day-to-day, especially early on. You think, "That goal's so far out there I'm never going to reach it." Well, what are willing to do to make sure that you *do* reach it?

Chris Lakey's family recently got a new puppy, and they worked for quite a while to potty train her and get her to use the bathroom outside. It didn't happen overnight. You can't kick a puppy out of the house the first time it piddles; it takes a while to reach each milepost in the training. You have to start with the long view, knowing that a year from now, you'll see the fruits of your labor. Chris's dog is a small Yorkie, and it can take up to seven months to fully train them—so he was in it for the long haul.

You could, on the other hand, just say it's not worth it, and end up cleaning up after the dog all its life...but that's not a worthwhile outcome. If you stick to it and are willing to go through the trouble, you'll get the reward of having a well-trained and well-behaved dog in several short months.

There are all kinds of other life applications this applies to as well. It's a good thing to ask yourself, "What do I want? What am I willing to do?" for all these. What are your goals in life, business, relationships? Most importantly, what are you willing to do to make them happen? Don't rely on other people. Don't play the blame game when something doesn't work out for you. What are *you* willing to do to make *your* goals a reality?

If you focus on those goals and make achieving them a daily commitment, you'll see success. Not every time, because success is sometimes elusive; but you'll experience a lot more successes than you might otherwise. Don't give up. Consistently be willing to do what other people are not, and someday, you'll achieve your dreams.

Marketing Secret #79:
Why Many Businesses Fail—and How You Can Avoid It

You've heard the stats. You know that most businesses cease to exist within 3-5 years after they're founded. Some sell out; some just disappear suddenly; but most experience a slow decline before they fall apart. We've all seen it; some of us have experienced it. It often occurs because the owners become overwhelmed, working so deep *in* the business that they have no time or inclination to work *on* the business. Sometimes, they just lose interest in maintaining, and down the slippery slope they go.

Even the best, most successful of us will take a foot off the accelerator when business is going well and the money's just pouring in. But heed my advice: don't do it. Even when you're slamming the competition, keep it up. If you deliberately drop back, for whatever reason—satisfaction, complacency, personal reasons, anything—a competitor or circumstances will eventually overtake you. In business, if you're not moving forward, you're moving backward. Take it from someone who learned this the hard way. No matter how good things are now, you have to keep the pedal to the metal.

There are simple ways to avoid this problem, but you have to practice them constantly to make them work.

First of all, keep honing your edge. Sure, make time to rest, and get plenty of it; but if you're not out there regularly, being as creative as you can be and working passionately to build your business, then have someone you trust doing it for you. Business success requires unremitting attention to detail. It's too easy to slack off a little when things are going well—or at least, well enough. But if you lose that edge, you lose your focus, and focus is critical. Clearly visualize the goals you want to achieve in your mind's eye; then work toward achieving exactly what you see.

Next, never lose your hunger. Once you've achieved a measure of success and collected all the toys that signify success for you, you may find you don't want more. If so, find a way to whet your appetite. Use some of your money in a creative way, perhaps to help others. Find reasons to make more so you can *give* more. Some of the richest people in our society are also the biggest philanthropists. So give some back—not to the freeloaders in our society, but to the people and other causes that really need your help.

When you stop doing bold, creative things, you lose your edge. You no longer have your original passion to build the business. You become complacent, and things go downhill fast. Guard against the natural human tendency to lose track of this reality. Some of you reading this are still striving to be successful, which probably means that you *do* have an edge and a hunger to achieve, that your focus remains tight and sharp. Stay that way. Some of you to have already experienced some measure of success, but you have to realize that once you *have* the success, it won't necessarily stay with you. It's not something you earn and then kick back and enjoy for the rest of your life. Events may conspire to take it away. No matter how successful you are, no matter how much money you make, keep your edge and focus. Visualize the prize and go for it constantly; there's no standing still. You're either moving forward or backing up; there's no in-between.

All of us suffer from this problem to some degree when things go well. We get complacent, and start to slip a little. But that downhill slide is hard to stop once it starts. Oh, there are hills and valleys in business, a cycle that depends partly on the economy; and if you're down for now, hopefully that's temporary, and you'll end up back on top again. But it's not something you can really count on, so don't slack off. Keep pushing. Fight against that tendency to slip by maintaining your competitive edge. Even when things are good, don't take your foot off the pedal. Keep fighting for breakthroughs, setting new goals that stretch you farther. Complacency will do your business in.

As Victor Hugo, the famous French revolutionist, pointed out: "Those who live are those who fight!" In business, there's always competition—and these days, the marketplace is saturated. There's only so much disposable income to go around, so your back is against the wall and every day is a battle. Those businesses that make it are those that fight. I know this from experience. But I've also experienced the clarity that comes from fighting my way to the top.

Every day is a new day for a wise man—another of my favorite quotes. Every day we can start fresh. So keep your goals as high as you can. If you reach a goal, set a new one. If your business bores you or things just aren't working out right, it's up to you to look for newer directions that are more lucrative, more profitable, and more exciting. Keep feeding the fire of your desire—because a fire that never wants for fuel never goes out. Your fuel should be newer, bigger, fresher goals—potentially lucrative things that excite you greatly. This helps you recover your passion if you ever lose it.

Some of my worst performances have occurred when business has been so good it lulls me to sleep. We all go through those moments—but don't let them stop you. Start fresh every day and keep your goals in front of you. Keep setting bigger, more exciting goals, keep looking for lucrative areas to explore, and you won't make those common mistakes that cause businesses to decline and fall.

Marketing Secret #80:
12 Brilliant, Profitable Secrets from David Ogilvy

Just about everyone in advertising circles has heard of David Ogilvy; he's a legend in his field. Back in 1962, *Time Magazine* called him the most sought-after wizard in the advertising industry. Many people still view him as a wizard long after his death. Now, when I think of a wizard, I think of someone who can do magical things. Ogilvy could do that, because he was a master at direct response advertising, our old friend DRM.

The 12 quotes I'll discuss here derive from a speech Ogilvy gave at an advertising meeting in Paris. These quotes are funny, insightful, and will help you as you think about DRM itself and how to be a better direct response marketer. Ogilvy created a new kind of advertising that turned the advertising world on its head; it really made people rethink what successful advertising was all about. When he gave this speech, he was talking to people who were used to traditional forms of advertising, whom he called "generalists," whereas he referred to direct response people as "directs." You'll note a distinct disdain for traditional advertising, as opposed to his optimistic attitude about DRM.

Here's that first quote: "There is a yawning chasm between you generalists and we directs. We directs belong to a different world. Your gods are not our gods." Right off the bat, Ogilvy's saying, "Those of you who believe in traditional advertising aren't like us. We're as different as night and day." He's drawing a line in the sand, and I can just imagine the looks on people's faces as he threw down that gauntlet.

The second quote is: "You generalists pride yourself on being creative, whatever that awful word means. You cultivate the mystique of creativity. Some of you are pretentious posers. You are the glamour boys and girls of the advertising community. You regard advertising as an art form, and expect your clients to finance expressions of your genius." That's an awesome statement. I'm sure it offended people; in fact, when he said that, people probably walked out of the room. Here, he's contrasting the creative nature of traditional advertising with DRM, which is "ugly advertising." It's not meant to be artsy, unlike some of the traditional advertising you see.

Number Three: "We directs do not regard advertising as an art form. Our clients don't give a damn whether we win awards at the Cannes Film Festival. They pay us to sell their products and nothing else." Again, he's contrasting "advertising art" and DRM.

Number Four: "You must be the most seductive salesman in the world if you can persuade hardheaded clients to pay for your kind of advertising. When sales go up, you claim credit for it. When sales go down, you blame the product." He's slamming the traditionalists and their advertising, especially their refusal to accept responsibility when their "art" doesn't produce sales—even though they demand huge prices for it.

Quote Number Five: "We in direct response know exactly to the penny how many products we sell with each of our advertisements." In traditional advertising, you throw a lot of money out in all directions. You can gauge overall whether your ads are working or not, but you have no genuine accountability for them. You don't know *exactly* what's working and what isn't. That's expensive and wasteful, because even if sales are good, you don't know where they're coming from. With DRM, we can track our advertising precisely. It's accountable and easy to track, so we can monitor the results.

Number Six: "You generalists use short copy. We use long copy. Experience has taught us that short copy doesn't sell." In DRM, we take the time to go into detail, so our copy is usually longer—and it usually works better. There are exceptions, and today's reader isn't as willing to read as much as people once were. Traditional advertising wastes space. You might see a full-page ad with just a few words, and an attention-grabbing graphic. A direct response ad uses the whole page, with few if any images. It contains all the words needed to sell the product, often in fine print.

Number Seven is: "In our headlines, we promise the consumer a benefit. You generalists don't think it is creative." Direct response ads have wordier headlines than classic ads—up to 20-30 words long. A traditionalist would have problems with that, because it doesn't look pretty. But our headlines are meant to deliver a promise.

Number Eight: "You've never ever had to live with the discipline of knowing the results of your advertising." If you're charging people to create fancy ads and you have no accountability for the results, the customers have no way of knowing whether your ads are working or not, except in the most general sense. They're a lot less likely to fire you for poor performance, unless the entire company is doing poorly. DRM is accountable. You know whether it works or not. If someone doesn't produce the results you want, you can fire them. Again, he's poking fun at the traditionalists and their artsy pretentions.

Number Nine: "We pack our advertisements and letters with information about the product. We have found that we have to if we want to sell anything." Your goal as a marketer is to produce sales, which requires information about the products and benefits.

Number 10 is, "Develop your eccentricities while you are young. That way when you get old, people won't think you are going ga-ga."

Number 11: "Unless your advertising contains a big idea, it will pass like a ship in the night." No one notices little ideas!

And finally, Number 12: "Remove advertising, disable a

person or a firm from proclaiming its wares and their merits, and the whole of society and of the economy is transformed. The enemies of advertising are the enemies of freedom." Many marketers think our country is headed in the wrong direction lately—that many of the restrictions and regulations on doing business are in direct competition with free enterprise. Think about how the economy works. *Nobody* makes any money unless things are bought or sold. Some things are sold to consumers, some things to businesses; but stuff *has* to be sold, which means that advertising has to be out there working.

With this speech, even this quote, Ogilvy was splitting the advertising world into the traditional and the revolutionary. He was urging us to see that DRM is the way to go. You offer specific benefits to consumers, and add accountability to the selling process, because you can track results. If you remove the ability of businesses to advertise—especially using DRM—then you're removing freedom.

This speech was brilliant, and so was Ogilvy—no doubt about it. I'm especially struck by his argument that the enemies of advertising are the enemies of freedom—especially now that there are so many restrictions in advertising. For example, there are all kinds of creative new products that have come on the market for healthcare. But the big pharmaceutical companies don't want the competition, so they go to the government and say, "We want you to close these people down, or at least put a damper on them." This happens in so many ways in direct response that the government is the enemy of freedom, because they often work hand-in-hand with the competition.

One of Ogilvy's most brilliant points is, "We have to establish our results. There is no hiding from the results we're getting when we do DRM." You can erect billboard ads that say,

100 MARKETING SECRETS

"Buy Miller Beer" or "Enjoy Coca-Cola." You can put them in magazines and on TV—and in fact, that may be the way you *have* to promote advertising for Coca-Cola and Miller. Sometimes industrial advertising really is the way to go...but it's still hard to tell exactly whether it will work or not. In most cases, with most products, it doesn't. Even with those big exceptions, it's hard for the people to tell where the results are coming from: NBC, CBS or Fox News? The *New York Times*? Billboards? There's no way to know. But you *need* a way to tell which ads are working and which aren't.

For most of us, most of the time, direct response will *always* beat this industrial type of image advertising. We know exactly when we're successful and when we're not. That gives us power. You don't have to limit your marketing to the PennySaver or the Yellow Pages. You can quantify your marketing if you'll follow the techniques I'm teaching you here, finding more creative ways to get paid richly for the money you spend on advertising. Forget image advertising. Don't try to be cute and clever. Cute and clever doesn't work well in a small business arena. Go for the throat—like Ogilvy did with his speech. He came down hard on the traditionalists, trying to shake them free of their delusions. It's all about making sales and profits, and *that* needs to be your entire focus.

Most of the advertising executives who create those cute, clever and worthless ads have never sold anything in their life. Maybe they've won awards, but so what? Business is about sales. How can someone who's never sold anything go out there and make an impact? It's foolish to think that way. Don't fall for it. DRM is the *only* way to go for a small business person.

CHAPTER NINE

SECRETS 81-90

You'll find as many recipes for success as you'll find commentators—whether those commentators are the armchair kind or experienced entrepreneurs. Some of their formulas will work for you, while others may not; but I recommend that you focus on the secrets from people who've actually been there, who know what they're doing based on their own experience. Beyond that, success boils down to a hardnosed willingness to push hard, keep trying, and always stay hungry. Don't let the everyday bog you down.

In this chapter, I'll offer a mix of both real-life inspiration, from people who've been there and fought the good fight, and proven methods to help you stay pointed toward the stars. Let's start with one of the former.

Marketing Secret #81:
P.T. Barnum's Greatest Secret

P.T. Barnum was a very successful marketer who's probably most famous today for something he never really said: "There's a sucker born every minute." He did know how to separate people from their money, though, and one thing he *did* say in one of his books was, "You can't catch a whale using a minnow as bait." I've mentioned this before.

Most business people just don't get it. They're so deluded in their expectations that they don't comprehend the market forces working against them. Those forces include increased competition, lower profit margins, demanding consumers, the growing skepticism of the marketplace, and their customer's apathy towards marketing messages. People have built up an immunity against marketing and advertising. They're overloaded with information, subjected to so many competing sales pitches that very little gets through their shields anymore. The average consumer is more educated and cynical than ever. Add it all up and here's what it means: they don't believe a single word you say. They're certainly not in love with your company, products, or services the way you are.

Most business people have never bothered to think this through. They convince themselves they can run a few TV or radio commercials or throw some postcards into the mail, and people will flood their business. Sorry—that's just insane. They'll barely be noticed in the crowd. When you think it through, you can't possibly believe that such a small amount of advertising is going to produce big results—and yet, most marketers do. They want big results for minimal work, and they should know better.

To succeed in this oversaturated, apathetic market, you have to be willing to do *more* than everyone else, not less. If you want to make more money, you have to bait your hook with something huge. You have to sell like crazy, and you have to use DRM.

Why do we keep talking about DRM over and over and over? Because, as David Ogilvy pointed out more than 50 years ago in Paris, "We in DRM know exactly to the penny how many products we sell with each of our advertisements." I'll admit that using DRM does take some time and work to master; everything worthwhile does. You have to work with competent, capable people to learn the process in the first place, and there's a steep learning curve involved. But once you do that, you can spend money safely on your advertising, knowing what's working and what isn't.

Think of it this way. You're not just spending money—you're investing. You spend money, but you make money in return. DRM offers, give you quantifiable results that are easy to track, so you can spend more on what works, abandoning what doesn't. Most of your competitors won't use DRM, so they'll never figure out what you're doing. As I pointed out in a previous chapter, DRM is stealth marketing. They may see some of your advertising, and notice that your business is growing by leaps and bounds—but they'll have no clue why, because they'll never bother to learn about DRM.

People were making the mistake of fishing for whales with minnows back in P.T. Barnum's day. They're making it now. Don't fall prey to that. This is your chance to make more money, *if* you're willing to spend more and do more. You can learn a lot from Barnum; he was a hard worker, a great showman and marketer who did things in a big way. When his shows traveled, he had a huge tent designed for the towns he visited, whether large or small. One of his people asked him, "We're not going to have that many people, Boss. Why are you making these tents bigger and bigger?"

Barnum replied, "When we're on the outskirts of the town setting up our tent, and people are passing back and forth going about their business, I want them to see this gigantic tent and start thinking, 'Wow! This is really special. I'd better get the wife and kids and take them to see the show." Basically, he was a big thinker who encouraged others—including his prospects—to think bigger, which resulted in greater success.

Always make an effort to outthink your competition. If

you're just getting started, you can't outgun them and you can't outspend them. Eventually you might be able to match them in those areas, but right now, work on outthinking them. What can you do that will have the greatest impact on the people likely to buy your service or product? When you start thinking along those lines, you'll rise to the top, because most people in business are just open for business. They're not thinking about *increasing* their business.

The best news is that so many of them are using that traditional advertising David Ogilvy destroyed in the speech I discussed in the previous Secret. The generalists aren't focused on results-oriented advertising at all; they've been taught not to be. Even when they even know about direct response, they don't understand it very well, so you're already heads and shoulders above them just based on what you've read in this book.

It's as simple as this: if you're using the wrong bait, you're going to attract the wrong customers—at best. More likely, you won't have any customers. It's crucial to attract the right kind of customer from the very beginning. You only do that by using the right bait and presenting it well. Study your market. You'll see many of your competitors making these mistakes. Bait your hooks with large, meaty offers, and you'll land the big fish. If your competitors survive, they'll have to take the crumbs that fall off your table.

Marketing Secret #82:
It's About Creative Money-Making Breakthroughs

It's a good idea to always have a handful of projects going at the same time, so you can bounce back and forth between them. This helps keep you interested, which is crucial when you're working on your business. You don't want to get bored; you want to stay *excited*. Some of your projects should be difficult: big, high-potential moneymakers. Some should be simple things that are fun and easy to work on. A technique that works for many of us is to focus on a major project until you hit a brick wall, then set it aside and turn to the fun project. After you've done that for a while, go back to the difficult project. Often, it will be easier to get moving with it. While you've taken your conscious mind off it for a while, your subconscious mind never gave up on it.

Your subconscious mind is so powerful that it can actually work on things when you're not even aware you're thinking about them. When you get back to your big project, things may well come to you much easier—solutions you just didn't see before. You'll find answers to problems that you want to improve upon, answers that can be rewarding both intellectual and financially. This is a technique that can work for many people—but few ever use it. Those who do profit a great deal from it.

Consider trying this the next time you get stuck. Rather than let a roadblock on an important project derail you completely; shift to something secondary. Of course, the secondary project should be important in itself, so working on it pushes you toward a new profit center. This strategy helps keep you on task, even if it's on a different task than the one you were working on. Personally, at any given time, I have several different things available to work on. Using this strategy helps me be more productive.

I may spend a few hours working on a specific project, until I get to the point where my brain hurts and my creative juices are running dry. Well, there's an old saying: a change is as good as a rest. So I'll switch to something completely different. Now I can be creative on a new front for a while—and then maybe I'll switch to a third project, or return to the first. You may have to switch several times a day or just a few times a week.

It can take several weeks to put together a good sales letter. You write and write and write, getting all of your ideas down before you stop—and then you set that project aside for a few days. You think about it subconsciously, and sometimes even consciously, though you're not actively working on it. A few days later you go back to it reenergized and attack it from a new perspective, because you've had a chance to let the ideas develop in your mind. Occasionally, I'll return to a project that's several months old. For whatever reason it didn't work, or the timing was wasn't right before; but when I go back, I may find a new perspective on it. It may hit me in a new way, or the timing is better.

So always have multiple things to work on, to help you stay fresh and productive. If you only have one thing going and you're burned out on it, what are you going to do? Go to the gym for a while? Go to the freezer and eat some ice cream, or whatever else you can think of to distract yourself? That's not necessarily a bad idea, but having multiple things to work on is a better one, because it helps you keep your productivity high. Make that commitment, and your best will keep getting better.

Marketing Secret #83:
The Most Powerful Leverage Secret in the World

One of the Secrets to becoming super-rich is properly using leverage. You need to be able to leverage your own skill-sets, assets, and relationships as well as those of other people. Some of the world's most successful people used this Secret more than any other to get where they are today, and it can be superbly useful for you, too. Just study the situation, and determine how it can gain you more power and wealth.

Leverage is what allows you to decouple your earning power from the per-hour trade-off that most people base their careers on. Often, it works so subtly that it seems like you really don't do anything to get ahead—but you're still moving forward, leveraging existing resources (including your money) to earn more money. You no longer have to work as hard for every dollar.

The core of this Secret is simple: surround yourself with people who are smarter, better, or more talented than you are. Then do everything you can to help them get what they want, while you help yourself get what *you* want. That's really what this Secret is all about. The most successful people in the world do *not* work alone. Most aren't as smart, skilled, or talented as you think they are. Their real talent lies in finding the right backup.

Sometimes that means they have a staff that takes care of specific aspects of their businesses. In other cases, they may have teamed up with other experts in a joint venture arrangement. These may even be people they've hired to consult with or coach them, or to specifically help them learn what they need to. Whatever the case, surrounding yourself with people who can help you get what you want is crucial to success.

"No man is an island," as John Donne pointed out centuries ago. Few people become successful working completely alone. In almost every case, they have a team helping them. If you want to be one of the most successful in your circle, city, state, the entire U.S. or even the world, just know that it takes more than you can provide to get there. You *must* surround yourself with people who are smarter, better, more talented, even better looking than you are. Let them lead the way on each specific front—sales, accounting, product development, marketing, etc. Then you can all reap the rewards. If you're working with a consultant, let them be your tutor, and absorb their methods so you can use them as your own in the future.

Everywhere I look in business, I see people who don't seem all that bright making enormous sums of money. That's when I tell myself, "Aha. They know to surround themselves with the best people. They may not seem smart to me, but they have a talent for picking the best and brightest to help them succeed." Here's an example: a while back, my friend and mentor Russ Von Hoelscher owed a movie theater in downtown San Diego that played cheap double and triple features, charging only a few bucks total. A lot of people came to see these films, especially when the Navy fleet was in.

The man Russ was dealing with in Los Angeles had hundreds of these types of movies. Russ picked some of the films himself; he knew John Wayne westerns and Bruce Lee films would be winners, but he wanted the advice of the film library owner, whose name was Milton. Several times he asked Milton which films would make for good double or triple features—but he and finally stopped asking, because all Milton would say was, "I don't know. People like westerns, mysteries, horror movies. What the hell's the difference? Just throw it up there." Russ knew this wasn't the best answer, so he was on his own.

That is, until he met Milton's general manager, Bobby, who was sharp as a tack. He sat down with Russ and told him what worked in other theaters and what didn't. Russ could see within half an hour that Bobby was the person who made Milton successful. Milton had inherited a bunch of money and gotten into the movie distribution business. Bobby had the brains to keep him in his millions.

I see this sort of thing surprisingly often. The person in charge may not seem to have much on the ball, but they're savvy enough make sure the people around them do. Those people make them richer by the day. In fact, this is my personal secret: I've always surrounded myself with the very best people, starting with my wife Eileen. I went through two different business partners before I met my wife; she became my third and last business partner. My other partners left a lot to be desired, and those were very short partnerships. I hit gold with Eileen. She put together a great staff that I might have run off on my own, and ran the company's day-to-day business for 12 years before stepping down. I wised up a little, kept most of her staff, and added some new people later on.

I always try to hire people who are much smarter and more talented than I'll ever be, and then look to them for direction and advice. You have to make it a win-win situation for those people; you can't keep the best people unless they also benefit. That doesn't just mean money, either. You have to do everything possible to make things exciting, fun and interesting for them. Then maybe they'll reciprocate.

Marketing Secret #84:
Four Reasons Why Knowing *Less* Can Make You More

This Secret is counterintuitive. Everywhere you look in the marketing world, people are telling you that you have to know everything about your product or service so that you can sell it better, more effectively, with more enthusiasm. And while that's important, it doesn't hold a candle to *prospect* knowledge. I believe it's more important to understand the people you're selling to and what they want than it is to understand the features of what you're selling. I have four reasons for this.

Reason #1: So you won't get so bogged down in all the boring details.

Reason #2: So you can stay excited about the main advantages of whatever you're selling, directing your focus towards the end results achieved by using it.

Reason #3: You can take care of the prospect's potential objections with a strong risk-reversal guarantee that makes it easy for them to back out if they're not happy. If you're with a prospect and they have a lot of questions, you can always just say, "Don't worry about this." Then go back to repeating the main benefits and assuring them that if they're not 100% satisfied, then you don't want their money. They'll get it back instantly.

Reason #4: It allows you to stay positive. Believe it or not, there's amazing power in not knowing all the details behind every product or service you sell. Your only focus is on the big promises and the big picture. This makes things seem simpler and easier for the prospect. Any of the difficult objections they bring up can be addressed after the sale by customer service. Your job is to bring in the sales; customer service's is to make them stick. Features tell, benefits sell.

Now: what *is* a benefit? It's the emotional end result the prospect can get when they give you their money. So what's in it for them? What are they *really* searching for? What will they get when they give you their money? You have to know what they want more than anything else, and how your product or service can give it to them. The emotional end results are all that people really want.

Back in the 1980s, before I started my first business, I sold roof and parking lot coatings. You put the material over the parking lot and it made the asphalt or concrete last longer; you put it on the roof, and you could save yourself from having to do a roofing job. It was a kind of preventive insurance. All kinds of scientific material came with this stuff I sold; there were all kinds of studies and statistics I was supposed to learn, but didn't. Yet I was able to sell a lot of it just from an amazing idea I got from the company I was working for. It was a brilliant idea. I made thousands from it.

All I did was take an Alka-Seltzer from a two-pack and, right in front of that prospective buyer, I'd use a tweezers to put one tablet into a little cup that was filled with this sealer I selling for maybe 10 seconds. When I pulled the tablet out, it was coated with the sealer. Then I threw it into a glass of water—and it just sat there. It didn't fizz at all. Then I took the other Alka-Seltzer tablet, tossed it in the water, and it bubbled like crazy.

I made so much money on that simple trick. *That* was what sold people, not all the scientific facts and figures about the product. The fact that it could make an Alka-Seltzer impervious to water was a huge selling point. They loved it, especially when I let them seal the Alka-Seltzer themselves. I was selling the benefits, and was letting them see the benefits directly by using that little demonstration.

Everybody is looking for things to make their life simpler, easier, and more fulfilling. They want answers to questions like, "Will it make me money? Will it take my pain away? Will it make me happy and safe?" So it's important to focus on the benefits before the features. My simple sealant experiment was a brilliant way of illustrating this, and it shows that people can be influenced by the simplest things, as long as those things reach out and touch them in a way they can relate to it. If you have simple solutions to anything major that plagues people, as well as many of the minor things, you're going to make a lot of money. Just tell people you can make their life better—and then prove it.

That's all they care about. They don't care about you or anything that went into developing the product, or even the years of study you had to endure to become a professional. They just want to know if you can make them money, if you'll make their life easier and happier, or if you'll make the pain go away. If so, you'll make money.

Think about the pharmaceutical ads you see all over nowadays, especially the ones in print. The front page has big bold promises and all the things it's going to do for you. On the back are all the disclaimers in tiny print that tell you about the potential side effects. We sell benefits. That's what people want to buy. Fortunately for most of us, we're *not* selling things that have adverse side effects; but even if they exist, we want to downplay them. Everything has a positive and negative side, which most people realize. That's the reality of just about every product that we use. When you're focused on the benefits, you do a much better job of selling.

Again, this is especially true when you couple those benefits with a strong guarantee, because it's your job as a marketer to put your customer or prospect at ease. Too many marketers are too shy when it comes to guarantees. If you can make one, you're telling your prospect, "There's no risk here. If you're unhappy, you get your money back. If you don't like the results, we'll buy the product back from you."

Decide what kind of refund policy to use, and then put it in play. Just about every product should have a guarantee. That guarantee should be reasonable and thorough, allowing you to focus on the benefits of your product, guaranteeing the delivery of certain promises—or their money back, period. In many cases, if you have a compelling enough offer, people will respond quickly and confidently, knowing they're assured a refund if they're not happy. It will make them feel more comfortable, even before they have all the facts. Even if they still have some concerns at the end, they may order anyway because they know they can do their due diligence after the fact. They don't want to miss out, and they don't want to lose the discount or the free bonuses you offer. It all comes down to them knowing that if they decide to buy and something doesn't check out, they know they can get their money back.

Let me re-emphasize: the more you focus on the benefits and the positives, the more you can sell. People want benefits, but most don't need to know the details of how the benefits work. They just want to know that they do. That being the case, trying to tell them too much becomes a hindrance, because it gets in the way of that positive focus. Telling them too much can also reveal some of the negatives, which may hinder your ability to sell a product. I'm not encouraging you to sell products that don't deliver your promises, or that have no real benefits; just don't focus on the negatives. All products have pluses and minuses, and too much focus on the negatives will result in a lack of enthusiasm that will hinder your ability to do whatever it takes to make a sale.

You do need to know your material, because sometimes

prospects will ask some tough questions. What they want to know, though, is not necessarily the answer to all those questions; they want reassurance more than anything else. They want to see that you know your stuff, and that you really *are* going to deliver. Often, they're also trying to control the conversation and the entire sales process too. Just be sure you have an answer for every objection; and whenever possible, work it into your pitch, so you answer the question before they even ask. Stay relentlessly upbeat, and always accentuate the positive.

Marketing Secret #85:
Your Creative Breakthrough

A creative breakthrough occurs when you push through a barrier of comprehension, and suddenly understand a point you didn't grasp before. It can happen in a flash—but it doesn't necessarily happen the first time you think about it. It takes a lot of preparation and practice, beginning with a thorough knowledge of your marketplace based on constant, in-depth study. The more you put your mind to work, the more likely you'll experience that flash. Until that happens, you'll get frustrated sometimes, because you don't feel like you're getting the answers you want. But if you stay in tune to it and keep your mind's eye on the prize, you can accomplish great things.

I'm a firm believer in the adage "If you can believe it, then you can achieve it." It just takes time and effort; as the old cliché puts it, Rome wasn't built in a day. Getting to the point where you're making tons of money doesn't happen overnight. Despite what certain celebrities would have us believe, success doesn't result only from positive thoughts; it happens when you combine positive thought with positive action. Success isn't magic. It's a reward for working hard, for working creatively, and for deeply understanding what people in your marketplace want—and for fulfilling those needs.

God really does helps those who help themselves, so don't listen to false prophets who tell you otherwise. When it comes to making money, this is especially important. Don't let someone fool you into thinking something that logically can't be true.

Unleash your creativity as you think about your business, and give yourself plenty of time to do so. I've already introduced you to my 5 AM Club concept, in which I get up very early every morning and brainstorm. It's a simple but powerful concept. Although the results may not jump off the page at you at first, eventually you'll be amazed at the ideas you get for making more money. So find time for your business. No one can do it for you. You might have employees who can help, but *you're* going to have to think.

The more you think, and the more you record your thoughts, the more you'll see yourself achieving what you want to achieve, in exactly the way you want to achieve it. Don't just say to yourself, "Hey, I want to be a millionaire!" Tell yourself, "I want to increase my income to a million dollars a year. To do so, I'm going to have to do A,B,C, and D." When you start thinking along those lines, you'll see some amazing results—and you won't have to listen to false prophets or phony gurus to make it happen.

There are both physical and mental aspects to marketing. Both are a part of who we are as human beings; and yes, there can be some metaphysics involved. Some people spend too much time in the metaphysical world, just thinking about their business; so they never get around to the *doing*. Folks, the thinking and the doing go hand-in-hand. While you may not implement everything you think about, nothing you think about will become reality unless you deliberately set out to make it happen. Anyone who thinks otherwise is suffering from magical thinking—the equivalent of believing in the Easter Bunny and Santa Claus. Look: the best way to succeed in all aspects of your life is to be of sound mind and body both. You must be healthy mentally, spiritually and physically.

Don't just *assume* good things will happen. Make them happen. Do things that produce sales and profits for your company and business. The mental side of the job is very real, and yes, you'll have to spend some time there; but don't forget to also spend time in the real world of actually doing. A lot of people struggle with this, because thinking about your business—or dreaming about the way things should be—is so much easier than actually making it happen.

On the other side of the coin, if you get out there and put your ideas to practice without carefully considering the possibilities, you risk failure. Most businesses encounter this problem at some point, because no matter what, we're perfect in our minds. No matter our age, ability, or experience, we tend to misjudge how well we'll do if put into a situation where we have to perform. This is an actual phenomenon recognized by psychologists; it's called the Planning Fallacy. We overestimate how well we can do something, and underestimate how well others can do the same thing.

You can think all day about success in business, and it *is* important to do that; but unless you start putting your ideas into action, you'll never achieve any success. I'm not saying you'll always succeed if you try, but if you never try, you'll never succeed. You'll just be a thinker who will never know whether or not your ideas are any good.

Chris Lakey and I have been working on a new business for months now, and by the time you read this book, it should be coming to fruition. It's exciting. A part of me has been itching to move forward with this for a long time, and sometimes I feel it's never going to happen—yet we're on the precipice of actually getting it started. At the same time, a part of me loves to keep it in the dream world, because I'm afraid it's going to take a lot of hard work once we launch. There will be some failure involved. Some things won't work no matter what we do. We'll have to tweak others to get them to work the way we want. The numbers look good on paper, but we *know* some things won't work perfectly. That's always true. Hopefully we'll be able to adjust on the fly.

You have to consistently make that leap from ideas into the physical world, and into the actual doing, if you want to have any success with marketing. Thinking is important, but it doesn't pay the bills, it doesn't send you on vacation and it definitely doesn't build your business. Admittedly, it all *starts* with the idea, the dream. It's great when it's all on paper and you can play with the numbers and spreadsheets and get it to work out as you've planned. It's ecstasy—but you do have come down to the real world.

Remember Napoleon Hill's book *Think and Grow Rich*? It should have been called, *Think, Work Your Ass Off, and Grow Rich*. But that wouldn't have been a pithy title. Too bad, because it causes some people to miss the point. Similarly, people have misinterpreted Rhonda Byrne's *The Secret* in such a way that they seem to think that money is just going to rain down like manna from heaven if they think positively.

That's New Age thinking, and it's unrealistic. I've known

a lot of New Age thinkers; I've been sucked into it myself. But you know what? Most New Age thinkers in the business field are dead broke. They sit around dreaming in their little fantasy world, which is a great place to be. I love it too...but they're not making any money, because they don't connect action with thought.

Marketing Secret #86:
10 Words That Can Earn You Big Money

Throughout this book, I've offered you occasional short phrases that can be enormously profitable to you, if you'll just remember them and reflect on them occasionally as you go about building your financial dreams. Here's another: just 10 brief words that will encourage thousands of people to gladly give you money.

You must entertain people first in order to educate them.

This little gem comes to us from our good friend Eric Bechtold, who has certainly made plenty of money himself. And it works everywhere. Consider how this statement applies to the news industry, specifically the cable news industry—CNN, MSNBC, Fox News and the like. These networks have to have stories to discuss, or else they have dead air—and nobody's going to tune into that. So they fill their time with shows featuring pundits and pedants; and because the ratings services are keeping an eye on the number of people watching, they're very careful about what they broadcast. They need to sell ads viewed by large numbers of people, so they can make the money they need to operate.

As of this writing, Fox News consistently sits at the top of the ratings in most prime-time categories. It's simply the most entertaining news network. They've done the best job of not only providing content that people are interested in, they've done a better job of entertaining people. That allows them to distribute the information they want to distribute in the way they prefer to distribute it. On the other end of the dial is NPR. Many people knock National Public Radio because they think it's dull. The pace is deliberate, unexcited—and boring. One of the reasons that's true is because it's publicly funded. They get their funds from a source that *requires* them to be unexciting—and they don't have to fight for ratings. So while they can be very educational, most of the time their hosts are tiresome to listen to. To them, education comes before entertainment.

The business lesson here is that if you want to get people to give you money, they have to pay attention to you first. You don't want your message to be boring or come across as monotonous. In the direct-mail world, if your copy isn't entertaining or interesting to read, people won't make time for it. They're too busy to be bored by you. You don't offer anything to shake them out of the daze they're in as they go about their mundane lives. To get their attention, you have to entertain them. Once you've captured their attention, *then* you can sell them on your offer.

A word of caution here: be careful not to be a comedian. That's not to say you can't tell jokes, but trying to be funny doesn't necessarily help your sales message. You don't have to make your prospects laugh; just capture their imaginations and keep their attention. Find a way to get them to step out of their busy world and listen to your message. To do that, your copy has to be exciting. You have to grab them by the throat and pull them in. Keep them reading, especially when the copy goes on for multiple pages. The only reason a person will continue to read is if they're excited. Remember: people buy for just two main reasons. First, they crave or desire a certain benefit. It can be related to money, health, romance, or whatever; the benefit depends on the person.

The other reason people buy is to make the pain go away. In this sense, pain can be not having enough money; a sickness; or the fearing that as they get older, they'll be abandoned. We fear or crave so many things. You, as a marketer, need to understand that people will gladly give you lots of money if you can give them either the benefits they want, make the pain go away, or both.

Nowadays, most people feel apathetic toward sales messages. They're busy, they're overwhelmed, and they've built up an immunity towards them. That means that to get to them, you really have to go over the top. You have to wake them up and shake them up. Part of doing that is entertaining them. Don't be afraid to do so. Don't hold back. People want to be entertained, and we're in the business of giving them what they want. Some of the highest paid people on the planet are entertainers. Think about that.

In addition to giving them what they want or need, our job is to educate people on all the reasons why they should give their money to us instead of our competitors. To educate people, you first have to entertain them enough to get them to pay attention to you. Don't dare put them to sleep. Be the Fox News of your marketplace, not the NPR.

Marketing Secret #87:
Don't Hold Back At All

In this Secret, I'm going to tell you why playing it safe might be the most dangerous thing you'll ever do. *The conservative approach is almost always wrong*. If you're playing it safe, you're inevitably going to hold back. Your ideas won't be as good as they otherwise might be. You won't be as excited and enthusiastic as you should be. Salesmanship is infectious enthusiasm, a process of transferring your enthusiasm to the prospective buyer so they'll also become enthusiastic, more ready and willing to buy.

If you hold back, your work will always suffer, because your ideas just won't be as powerful as they could be. You're not going to make as much money as you should. Your entire project may be doomed to failure. As I've outlined before, there are market forces working against you constantly that you must struggle to overcome, especially all that competition. You have both direct and indirect competitors to deal with, some of whom are super-aggressive and razor-sharp. They're not holding back.

Today, the average consumer has too many choices, but not enough time and money to spend on them. This is true whether you're selling directly to consumers or business-to-business. As I've pointed out before, the old adage that the customer is king no longer holds true; today's customer is an extremely demanding child dictator with a short attention span. Also, modern people suffer from a terrible disease called information overload. We're overwhelmed with data, coming at us from all sides.

This immunity towards marketing messages is a survival skill. Add up all these the market forces arrayed against you, and you'll see that it takes more today than it did 20 years ago to make any kind of an impact on people. You have to be super aggressive. You have to go over the top, at least by your definition of the term. Realize that just because *you* think you're going over the top, that doesn't mean you are, given the general apathy in the marketplace. You have to get really excited to break through.

Earlier, I told you about a new business we've been working for a while now. It's changed and grown during that time; and about six months ago, we got very clear about what we're going to do. We've been frantically working at it since, and we're thinking big. We have something that every town of over 5,000 people needs. All we're setting out to do is to make a measly $725 per city. If we get 25 advertisers to give us $29 a month, that's $725 per town. Multiply that by 5,000 towns, and that's $3,625,000 a month.

If we can do it in 10,000 cities, then it's $7,250,000 a month, which is $87 million a year. Now, that's thinking big! Is there any guarantee we're going to make $43.5 million or $87 million a year? No. But when you shoot for the stars, at the very least you end up in the treetops. If you just aim for the treetops, you're likely to wind up in the lower branches...if you make it that far. You've got to think big and stay very excited. You have to act with great haste. You have to get out of the dream world, stop working the spreadsheets, quite living in your head. You have to get out there and work your ass off.

As I've pointed out before, you can take even the wildest, craziest, most aggressive and expensive ideas and risk very little as long as you test them on a small scale. Sometimes it takes that kind of craziness to penetrate and overcome the market forces working against you. You have to do things that make the biggest impact. Just do so carefully, and when one of your ideas pan out, you can be on the road to millions.

I'm one of those people who doesn't hold back; and I

think the late, great marketer and copywriter, Gary Halbert, was that way too. He wrote fiery copy—stuff that would jump off the page. If he didn't like someone, he'd say flat out, "This guy's an asshole!" Some of us were shocked. We'd wonder how people were going to take some of the words he used in his copy. But as time went on, we realized that those words weren't for all of *us*, but for the people who got excited about his work. They would say, "Gary Halbert tells it the way it is." He made a ton of money.

Now, did he lose some of the people his copy reached? Sure. People had trouble with some of his language at times. But some got over that, because they were aided by his brilliance. Lots of people just loved the frank, direct way he talked and wrote. So it just goes to show you that you *don't* have to hold anything back, and that you shouldn't.

One thing I like about Donald Trump, even though he has an ego bigger than New York City, is that he just says anything he wants to say. You don't have to believe or like everything he says, but by God, he's going to tell you exactly how he feels. Contrast that with a politician, Democrat or Republican; they won't tell what they really believe. They'll tell you what they think you want to hear. Well, I think the American public likes people who don't hold back, people who are spunky and are willing to shock people with what they write, say, and promote.

Take this lesson to heart. You don't have to use language that would make a sailor blush, but it won't hurt your business to take aggressive positions on the things that relate to your customers. Get to know who your customers are: their dreams, their hopes, their fears, their passions. Once you do, you can make some very strong statements that you're pretty sure they'll be in sync with—as long as you believe them yourself. When you take a strong position—religious, political, or otherwise—you'll be amazed at how many people will gravitate to your business. Some business owners make their religious values clear. That may turn off some people, but it also attracts a lot of people to their business.

Some people are known for their strong political stands on certain issues. People gravitate towards that, too. You lose some people who may not like your position, but they're not your target market anyway. If you fully understand the type of people you're dealing with, you can avoid many problems, because you know what you can say. People will respect you for it.

And here's the thing: even when most people go all out, they're *still not going that far.* No matter how far over the top you think you're going, many of your prospects won't view you as over the top at all. So if you're holding back, reconsider that strategy. You're probably not going as far as you could safely go. And don't worry about killing your company because you take an extreme risk; just test small. You never know how something will work until you try it. Keeping yourself from looking ridiculous may actually cost you sales. If you do it on a small scale, there's really no crazy thing that you can't try. The worst that happens is that you find out it didn't work like you'd hoped it would, and you lose a little money. Then you re-tool and try again.

If you're wondering why things aren't working well, or thinking about how you can do more or make more money, pull out the extreme card and give it some serious consideration. At first, just think about off-the-wall advertising you might do. Then write it down, shaping it into a coherent message. Once you've finished it to your satisfaction, give it a few days to rest and clear your mind—then look at it and ask yourself if it's as crazy as you thought it was. If it really is, tone it down; if not, you might amp it up a bit.

When you're initially writing an offer, don't worry about all the things that might not work. During the creative process, don't try to talk yourself out of anything. Just get all your crazy ideas out of your system—then later, go back and flesh them out as necessary. But again, let it rest before you start killing off ideas. For now, be as wild as you think you can. Even if it still seems wild but possible later, test it on a small scale to see how people respond. You can expand or retract from there.

The thing about moving ahead with the unconventional is that you'll make a bigger impact, completely and totally separating yourself from everyone else. Almost all modern marketing messages are homogenized, as if they were planned by a committee of fearful people afraid to upset anyone. They're watered down and make little or no impression. If you can take the opposite tack, you'll interest people, attracting them when they ignore everyone else's vanilla marketing.

Marketing Secret #88:
How to Think on Paper

I've talked about this method in passing on and off throughout the book, but it's time to take it a step farther and reveal the full Secret. I'm a very strong believer in this technique, and so is my mentor, Russ Von Hoelscher (in fact, I learned it from him). I've repeatedly described my Five AM Club method. I start most mornings with a pot of coffee, sitting down with pen and paper at hand. When it comes to drinks, you can use water or soda, whatever works for you; the point is that you're comfortable and have something to sip. Start at the top of a blank page with a problem to solve or inspiration you're looking for. You might write something like, "I need to know…" and then fill in the blank. When I do that, it triggers my thinking process, and I just start writing.

A lot of what I write is crazy, but that's okay, because those ideas will evaporate as I push through my first crowd of thoughts and start setting down better ideas. As I mentioned earlier, this isn't the time to decide whether your ideas are crazy, far-out, or good. Just write. Fill several pages before you stop. You can go back later and cross out the ideas you don't want, while highlighting those you know are relevant.

Training your brain to do this is the key. Learn to just sit there, think, and write. Keep doing this until you have it down. Don't worry about whether your ideas are crazy or not. In this state, you have absolutely no way to know if those ideas are impossible or unusable. Worry about that later, because you may produce some gems right from the beginning…although frankly, I often go from crazy to not so crazy to good. Just start writing after you do your thinking—and train yourself to *enjoy* the process of thinking.

Most people hate to think. I've noticed that even many successful people don't like to think, even when they could be much more successful if they did. We just don't want to put in the hard work, and most of us don't really like change, because it pushes us out of our comfort zones. We do the same things over and over, and get the same results. That's fine if that's all you want, but it's a deal-breaker if you want to truly succeed.

So train yourself to think and write. Do it as often as you can—several times a week at least, even if it's only for a half-hour at a time. You don't have to figure out what you're doing until later; in fact, don't try. This isn't the time to analyze. Just keep writing. Fill as many pages as you can, then at some later time, pick up the pages and make the decision as to whether or not there are things on those pages you can implement. Each time you do this, it'll become easier, you'll enjoy it more, and you'll learn more. Soon answers will start to appear.

You see, everything we need to know to make our lives better, to make more money, or to have better relationships—almost any aspect of our lives—lies in our subconscious mind. The secret is to get it out and down on paper. But again, the answer is not simply to think, and it's not just to create; it's to take action. Once you've invented solutions you believe can improve your life and business, implement them. If you can do this, you'll find yourself on a creative journey that will yield satisfying answers to many of the problems that plague you, whether they deal with money or any other aspects of your life. You'll be amazed how much better your life will become.

Think of it as creative, directed doodling, if you like. Often doodling is unproductive, but it doesn't have to be. You don't even have to do it on paper; I've always been able to write longhand for long periods, which is why I use legal pads, but some people find that difficult. Chris Lakey prefers typing on a laptop, because his hand starts to cramp after writing longhand for a while. I suppose it's largely due to what you're used to and how you learned to think. Chris grew up with a computer in front of him from middle school on, so he'd rather type than write out ideas longhand. But he still keeps a note pad on hand for visual doodling, which can also lead to new ideas, as well as jotting the occasional quick note when the computer isn't handy.

It's one thing to just let your thoughts freewheel, but you

really have to pin those ideas down; otherwise they'll get away. A pen or pencil's good for that. We've all woken up from a vivid dream, only to forget it within hours because we didn't jot down the details. Your brain runs so fast and so constantly that ideas and dreams flood through, coming and going faster than you can process them. If you don't write them down, they're gone.

If you're adverse to paper and ink, try Mind Mapping software. It allows you to start with a central theme on your computer screen, and do the same kind of brainstorming you can do in print. You can enter ideas and join them into a graphic or flowchart, creating a visual image of all the things you come up with. You can revise them as needed. When you're done you can share them online, or you can print them out.

Whenever you do it, however you do it, just take some free time to think about your business. The details of the process aren't necessarily important, as long as you get those ideas out and start mapping them out. As you get them out of your head, they'll start piecing themselves together. It might turn into an offer you can make to your customers, or a new product or service—maybe even a new line of products you can introduce to your marketplace. You might invent a new way to makeover your retail store. All these possibilities can arise just from thinking about your marketplace and about how to better serve it. So hook those slippery fish with a pen or its electronic equivalent.

Realize that refining this strategy may take a while; it's an ongoing phenomenon, not a one-time process. Your best ideas will improve as you gain more practice. And let me pound in this nail again: don't expect these ideas to pop up full-blown. Just get the concept down on paper. We used to have a seminar center where we hung giant banners with positive sayings like,

"Concepts first, details last." That's one of my favorites. You're not really trying to think things through too much at first—just letting your mind run free.

The way to get good at coming up with great ideas is to get good at coming up with a *lot* of ideas. Quantity has a quality of its own. It's simple, it's productive, and it's inexpensive. Even though I prefer using a note pad, I learned to use mind mapping software in about 15 minutes. If I can do that, so can anyone else—and there are free versions out there on the 'Net. Try them.

Marketing Secret #89:
The Mailing Lists That Can Make You a Fortune

In direct mail, we depend on mailing lists to present our offers to a targeted market we know is pre-qualified, because they've already purchased similar items. For businesses like ours, mailing lists are among the most important business items. As the title suggests, they can make you a fortune—and there are only three that matter. In this Secret, I'll tell you what they are and how to get the most out of them.

You business has many parts—its infrastructure, your staff, your physical assets, products and services you can sell. But when you depend on direct mail, you cannot function without a mailing list. It's the lifeblood of your business. You can take a mediocre product and turn it into a best seller if you have the right list. On the flip side, you can have the best product in the world, but if you're trying to sell it to the wrong people, you're not going to have much success. What do you do? Where do you come up with the list? What *is* the right list?

The very first list I'll discuss is the best of the three: the list of your current group of best customers. These are the people who have done the most business with you, or have spent the most money with you, or have done business with you the most recently; what makes them the best customers is up to you to determine. They've probably spent a lot of money with you over a long time. Our best-customer list consists of people who have bought from us within the last year. Someone has to have spent at least $100 over the last year to be on that list. In many cases, they've spent considerably more than that.

These are people you have relationships with. You don't have to build trust. They know you, like you, and trust you already. There's no barrier to them doing business with you, except to convince them of the value of the offer you're making now.

Your second best list is previous customers who haven't bought anything for a while, or who didn't spend much money. There's less commitment there, but they still know who you are. With some effort, you can bump some of those middle-of-the-road customers up to your best customers list, making it profitable to mail to them. They have *some* relationship with you, but you might have to do some rapport-building.

The third list is still important, but it's at the bottom of the list of lists. These are new prospects. They could belong to a list you rented, or a joint-venture list you received from someone else, or a list you traded for. They've never been customers and don't know you. This list is the hardest to use is because there's no relationship there.

These people have to learn that you're legit before they buy. You have to build enough trust for them to respond to your offer. That may be done quickly, through reading a bio about you or otherwise learning your story. Maybe you have some YouTube videos they can watch. Build a connection through web copy or two-step marketing, or maintain a sales staff that spends time on the phone getting to know them and building rapport. Before they can feel comfortable doing business with you, they have to feel like they *know* you.

The more expensive your offer is, the more rapport you need to build. If you have a local widget store and sell widgets that only cost five bucks, most people don't need that rapport. If you have a restaurant selling expensive food, people will try it once without having built rapport, often on the recommendation of a friend. Those sorts of businesses can benefit from the Internet sites where people rate and review businesses. There's always some rapport building happening there.

When you have a new offer, it's always best to start with the best list, the one you feel is most likely to work. That's always List #1. If you have a hit working there and you're ready to roll out to more people, then you can send it to List #2. If it still works there, then and only then do you send it to List #3. I recommend you use your lists in that order. However, if you don't have your own lists already, you have to start somewhere. Any list is better than none; just make sure it's a *good* list, packed with people who have bought something similar to what you have to offer. We'd done entire programs, reports, and books on mailing list selection, so if you're interested in learning more, check our product list or contact us directly.

I find that businesses often don't treat the people on List #1 with the respect they should. They're so interested in generating new customers they neglect their existing ones. Don't do that! Your existing customers are the ones who will make you rich. They're the ones who do business with you on a regular or semi-regular basis. They're the ones who should be treated like fine china, polished up and attended to regularly.

Some businesses are so thoughtless in this regard that they give discounts to new customers but not to existing ones. A lady told Russ Von Hoelscher a while back that she went to a mattress store that was running a promotion. She'd bought from that company several times over the years, and was told she couldn't have the discount because she wasn't a new customer. I can guarantee you one thing; she's no longer an old customer, because she's no longer a customer at all. How many times do you think they pulled that trick? It's the utmost in business stupidity. *Never* make such a blatant mistake. *Always* remember to take good care of your best customers, and they'll take good care of you.

Your mailing list is the single most important factor in your direct mail equation. You can have the best offer in the world, but if it's not going out to the right people, then forget it. Your numbers are going to suffer. Conversely, you can have a mediocre offer that goes out to exactly the right kind of people and makes a bundle. The more you know about your best customers—what they want the most, what their biggest problems are, and how you can help them the most—the better you'll be able to attract new customers.

Chris Lakey and I are just starting a brand-new business. Our first task is to turn leads into sales—and then our most important job is to get to know those people. We're going to do that by getting face-to-face with them, rubbing elbows with them, doing all kinds of things to get in front of them and pick their brains. The more we know about them, the more we'll be able to attract other people just like them.

Marketing Secret #90:
The Simplest, Fastest Marketing Technique Guaranteed to Make You a Fortune

The above title may sound like a wild claim, but the Secret probably won't surprise you after what you've already read. It's direct mail marketing, which is quite simply the fastest and simplest way I know of that's virtually guaranteed to make you a fortune. You can make millions of dollars with the right campaign.

Direct-mail is the most powerful advertising medium that there is. You're in total control of the entire selling process. When it's done correctly, having a million direct mail packages in the marketplace is like having a sales force of a million of the best salesmen money can buy—only you don't have to pay them or put up with their problems and idiosyncrasies. The key is to spend 20% of your time, money, and effort to attract new customers, and the remaining 80% to resell the maximum amount of additional products and services to your established ones.

Many people know this Secret, but very few practice it. When you ask them, "What are you doing in a systematic way to attract the largest possible number of new customers, and then to resell to those people as often as possible?" they'll look at you like you're speaking a foreign language. But it's not like they don't know better. That's the key here. Use direct mail to attract the best people, and then to resell to them again and again.

There's more to it than that, but this is the basis of the formula. All the money you want is out there right now; all you have to do is sell enough stuff to enough people often enough at a high enough margin per transaction, with the greatest efficiency, and you can make all the money you'll ever need. Eileen and I learned that from Russ Von Hoelscher early on, when he taught us to boost our income by 25 times in just nine months, from $16,000 a month to $400,000. I've mentioned this story several times in this book alone. That's why I busted my hump for eight years to learn how to write good, profitable sales copy that drew in new customers as well as served older ones.

It does cost more to use direct mail, but it's worth the effort, especially when you use the two-step method I've outlined elsewhere to get people to qualify themselves, and then follow up with repeated sequential mailings. If you turn to direct mail, you can't do it on the cheap; it doesn't work. You need all those little salespeople out there doing a good, effective job of selling—because good direct-mail is salesmanship in an envelope.

These little salesmen are answering all the prospect's objections and overcoming their resistance. They're making these people a great offer they can't refuse. You can do all that in a direct-mail package. There are a lot of strategies you can use in conjunction with direct mail, but direct mail marketing is king. It's all about return on investment, ROI, and you won't get a better ROI than with direct mail. It doesn't matter how much you spend, but how much you make in the end. So spend more money and do a more effective job by using direct mail in the first place. The only thing that works better is actual face-to-face selling.

Recently, Dan Kennedy and Chip Kessler released a book called *No BS Marketing to Boomers and Seniors*, in which they included some mind-boggling statistics from a research study they conducted. Here's one thing to keep in mind: while many of us are marketing to people younger than 35 years of age, often using the Internet to do so, this isn't a demographic group that has a lot of money. Plus, folks younger than 35 perceive direct mail as coming on very strong. Well over 50% of people 50 years or older prefer direct mail to anything on the Internet—so they're the ones you should market to. They see direct mail as more honest and trustworthy than online marketing.

One of the things that's important to know when you're advertising is where your marketplace is looking for information. So who's your customer? If you have really young clients or customers in their teens and 20s, you should use the Internet and use it often. But if your customer is anywhere near middle age, you'd better do business by direct mail. People 50 and over control well over half of all the wealth in America. Older Americans still want to receive direct mail. They still even read newspapers, which some people think is archaic. They prefer the things that they grew up with.

A lot of people think they know direct mail when they actually don't. Many business owners have tried a little direct mail. They might have written a postcard and mailed it out to a few clients, but that was about it. They've just dabbled; they haven't done it correctly. They haven't learned the strategies. One of the things that we always teach our clients is the proper way to do direct mail. We describe all the things that go into making a direct mail campaign successful and effective.

Direct mail is the most effective way to sell just about anything to your target market. It's one of the simplest and easiest ways to make a lot of money— but you have do it right, because if you don't, it may go wrong and sour you on the process for good. Then you'll be one of those people who says, "I tried that once, and it really doesn't work." Well, it might not have worked for you, but it *does* work for a lot of people; you just have to know what you're doing. So I encourage you to study more about direct mail, to learn the tips, secrets, and strategies that make up successful direct-mail campaigns.

I said this on the previous Secret, and I'll say it again here. We've developed entire programs, books, and reports about direct mail marketing, and we're happy to tell you how to acquire those if direct mail interests you. There's a lot to know, including some basics you need to understand to get started. From there you can just do it, learn as you go, adjust on the fly, do plenty of testing, and grow your business. No matter what you sell, there are very few things that don't or can't work by direct-mail. It's a great marketing method when you understand it.

My best advice is to pay very close attention to what other people are doing. Keep a swipe file, and become a student of good direct mail marketing. Stop calling it junk mail: that's an excellent first step right there. It's not junk mail if it's making people money.

CHAPTER TEN

SECRETS 91-100

One point about business that many people somehow miss is that you have to make every effort to ensure your business survives in the face of all the market forces arrayed against you. You have to deal with competition—some of it pretty harsh—as well regulatory changes, market corrections, high unemployment, and any number of other things you have no control over. So in addition to ruthlessly competing in the market yourself, you must implement strategies designed to make you attractive and useful enough to keep around. In this chapter, I'll reveal a few secrets about how to do this.

Marketing Secret #91:
Marketing Must Always Be About the Customer

I've discussed this before, but it's so important that it deserves to be repeated. I freely admit that I repeat important points sometimes, because they *are* so important. And there is *nothing* more important in business than realizing the importance of your customers. Everything you do should be directed at them. To succeed, you have to know exactly what they love, what they hate, what drives them crazy, what makes them happy, what gets them excited. Marketing is all about the customer.

Often, the ads you see in newspapers, print journals, and the Yellow Pages mention how the company had been in business for so many years, and say things like "We offer quality and service to our customers." Neither is significant. Being in business many years gives you some credibility, but when you talk about quality and service, you may as well be speaking

Martian. *Everybody* claims high quality and excellent service, so the claim has no impact anymore. You can overcome that fact by really getting into your customers. Step into their shoes. Get to know them the best you can. Learn exactly what they want and what their buying habits are. Spend many hours thinking about what you can do for them that your competition isn't doing. How can you make their lives easier and better? Those long hours of thinking and planning will be richly rewarded, because your customers will love you when you give them things tailor-made to their needs.

That's what it's all about: filling unfulfilled desires. It's understanding all the emotional and physical forces that cause them to keep spending their money for the things that are important in their lives. Spend some time getting to know your customers. Talk with them. Don't just expect them to come in, spend money, and leave. Get a feeling for who they are and what's important to them. You'll discover things you never realized they'd want, and realize that though you thought you knew why they were buying something, you really didn't.

An analogy I've used before involves the car business. Some people just think of cars as transportation, and sure, that's what they are at a fundamental level. But people don't buy cars just for transportation. Transportation gives them the *idea* to buy a car, but they usually buy a specific car because it makes a statement about them. They buy it because they think it will make them look sexier or smarter, or any of 101 other reasons. If we all just needed transportation, we'd buy something cheap and reliable. But we often buy for psychological and physical comfort, and are willing to pay a lot for it.

This is also true for many other products and services we

buy. If someone's buying clothing, they're not buying it just to cover themselves up or to protect themselves from the sun and the cold. They're usually aiming for a specific look or fashion. People spend money with hidden agendas in every section of business—even though they may not be entirely conscious of that agenda. They might not even know what their own unfulfilled needs are, which is why it's so important for you to get into their psyches. Doing so separates the average businesses from those at the top. You must consider the customer the king and treat them accordingly. It's our job as marketers to find out what they want to buy and why. It helps us create new services and products.

Advertising has something of a bad rap, a misperception of aggressive marketers. Sometimes there's a stigma in the marketplace, and society in general, towards anything that's considered salesmanship. Some people may even perceive you as pushing yourself on people—coercing them into buying, somehow stealing the money they wouldn't otherwise spend. These feelings are actually pretty commonplace.

But even if it *is* ruthless or aggressive, good advertising, marketing and salesmanship must always be about the customer. If you're doing an effective job of advertising, and of matching your products and services to the marketplace, you aren't doing anything that would make someone buy something that weren't already predisposed to purchase. If I have a weight-loss product and offer it to skinny people, they probably aren't going to buy it. But if I offer it to someone already thinking about losing weight, I just might make a sale.

It's not about coercing anyone into buying something they're not interested in. It's about identifying a group of people already interested in the kinds of things you sell, and then making them an offer that makes them want to do business with you. If they see the value in what you have, then they may be willing to part with their cash in exchange for your offer. That's a mutually agreeable transaction, and everyone's happy.

That's what the business relationship always has to be about in today's market: serving the customers and giving them exactly what they want. If you prefer to struggle in business, try selling something to people who don't want to buy it. That's a pretty foolish existence. It's better to find something they want to buy and then spend your time finding creative ways to get them to say yes to your offer.

Again, it's all about the customer and your relationship with them. It's one of the reasons I talk about direct mail so much—because it's one of the best ways to build relationships with your customer base. It gives you the ability to write to them as if you were writing to a friend. It lets you get your message to them in a friendly way. Direct mail is an ideal way to make it all about your customer, to focus on them and for them to read your invitation or letter in a personal way. It should feel like a letter from a friend. Make it about them; the more you make it about you, the more you lose.

I love reading about entrepreneurs who have done amazing things. One of my favorite stories is about Henry Ford, who changed the world with his Model As and Model Ts. But after he sold a few million, the market suddenly changed. Now people wanted more than just inexpensive cars; they wanted some differentiation, so they started crying out for more colors. As much as a world-changing genius as he was, Ford stubbornly resisted the changes in his marketplace. When his advisers kept bugging him about offering more colors, he was famously quoted as saying, "They can have whatever color they want, as long as it's black."

In letting his disdain get the best of him, Ford opened the door for General Motors and other companies to enter the market—companies that listened to what the customers now wanted. Who knows how many hundreds of millions of dollars Ford lost because he refused to stay ahead of the market changes? He was so focused on his one vision of keeping the cost of a new car as low as possible that he didn't realize that wasn't all people wanted anymore...and he paid for that. You have to really keep abreast of all your market's changes, or suffer the consequences.

Marketing Secret #92:
The #1 Secret of Business Survival

In the course of day-to-day business operations, you're dealing with things like keeping the cash flow coming in, keeping your employees and customers happy, running ads to bring in new customers and new business from your existing customers—things you do daily and in the moment. But your ultimate goal is survival; you want your business to last. And the odds are against you.

The percentage of businesses that fail within a short time is ridiculously high. Many don't even make it through their first year, and if a business makes it to five years, that's really something. It's got a good chance of continuing indefinitely at that point. And a five-year business venture really isn't that long, considering how time flies.

All the things you do, including good advertising, should

work toward business survival. The #1 secret of achieving this is flexibility. Inflexibility—brittleness, if you will—is often our undoing. So while focusing on survival as your ultimate goal, be willing to adopt a flexible strategy and use tactics that come to hand. Try things out of the ordinary to avoid being shot out of the water by market forces. Adaptability to any environment will save you when things are looking bleak.

Businesses that can't adapt die. You could be outplayed in your marketplace by those who are hungrier or who adjust to marketplace changes better than you do. Maybe you're using old methods, or you react to change like Henry Ford, who wasn't willing to adjust to the fact that people wanted cars in other colors than black. (Obviously, he eventually changed his mind about that). You have to be flexible in your business, and you have to be willing to do things that move your business forward. That means being able to change, grow and adapt as you focus on your customers, as I outlined in the last Secret. When you focus on your customers, you're able to more accurately give them what they want and provide better service.

That, in turn, helps you grow your business. When you get right down to it, flexibility is about finding out what the customers want and then figuring out creative ways to give it to them. Rigidity will kill you in the end. You have to give them what they want, not what *you* want—and you have constantly keep yourself visible to them.

Here's an example of how rigidity can kill a business— one I've used before, but repeat because it fits so well here. As you may recall from an earlier chapter, Russ Von Hoelscher tried to help an excellent printer attract more business, because he was moaning about not making enough money. When Russ gave him the solution—to market himself widely and effectively using some simple, cheap tactics—he looked at Russ and said, "I've got a sign out front. They know where I am. If they want printing, they can find me." Russ argued that his sign was barely visible and his shop was tucked in the back of a strip mall, but the printer was too inflexible to change and soon went under.

I've met people all over the country with similar attitudes. What it really comes down to is this: are you willing to do what you need to do to get more business? Are you willing to do the *one* thing that many people in business don't want to do? That one thing is thinking about their customers first. Not what *they* want, but what the *customers* want.

Many people get so entwined in operating their businesses that they never work *on* their business; they work *in* it. You have to be flexible. You can't decide that people will come to you. Some people have been foolishly led to believe this by that old saying, "Build a better mousetrap and people will beat a path to your door." Well, folks, people have to *know* about the mousetrap before they can beat that path to your door.

I believe Benjamin Franklin said that, and admittedly, he was a brilliant man. But he was living in small world where the word got out quickly about anything, and maybe people *would* beat a path to your door if you had a new product they wanted. But that doesn't work anymore in today's complex business world. We can't expect people just to come to us; we have to go to them with our message.

One of my business mentors once told me something that I believe in fully, and would now like to share with you: he said that you have to work on *yourself* harder than you work on your business. Running a business is a tough road, much more challenging than just punching a time clock, putting in your 40 or 50 hours, and going home. You have the weight of the world on your shoulders. There are great benefits to being in business, don't get me wrong; I love it, and I'm willing to bet that you do too. But you do have all kinds of tremendous pressures, obligations, responsibilities, commitments, setbacks and adversities to deal with. Whenever you solve one problem, a new one pops up. It just never ends.

But it helps to constantly work on yourself at least as hard as you work on your business. Keep your attitude strong. Continue to face all the things that you have to face head-on, and keep grappling with them. Don't let things wear you down; bend rather than break. That's what flexibility is all about.

In the building where I do all my creative work, I have a big, thick piece of leather hanging on my wall. I keep that leather there to remind myself that you can take a sledgehammer to the hardest rock you can find, and it doesn't take much to smash that rock into a million pieces. Even a diamond will break if treated that way. But you can take that piece of leather and beat the crap out of it with a sledgehammer, and barely even do any damage to it. You have to be more like the leather than the rock; flexible and pliable, willing to take a licking and keep on moving forward.

Marketing Secret #93:
The Instant Cash Flow Secret

Considering the nature of this Secret, let's get right to it. It's *urgency*. Creating a sense of urgency creates instant cash flow. The small business person who can give the prospect the strongest reason to buy right now is always going to make the most money. So it's up to you to create that sense of urgency if it doesn't already exist. Give people a strong reason to take action.

Now, there are some problems with this principle. First of all, the average prospect has far too many choices, as I've pointed out multiple times. Often there's not enough time to make a good decision, and their money is limited, so they procrastinate. They're confused and frustrated. That's compounded by the fact that most products and services aren't really unique; while there are many choices, there's not enough difference between one item and the next, at least in their eyes. They're overwhelmed, skeptical, cautious, leery, and sometimes downright jaded. They simply don't believe anything you say. They're very closed off, so it takes so much more to get them to buy from you.

Think about all those problems and how to defeat them. You have to do something that gives those people the strongest reason why they have to take action *now*. When you do, it shifts the balance of power. It puts them under pressure. Normally, the prospect has all the power, given all the salespeople chasing after them. It makes them feel like they're in control. By creating a sense of urgency, you're shifting the power to your side of the balance.

Let's look at a few ways to accomplish this. First of all, we like to hold events of all kinds—seminars, workshops, tele-seminars, and webinars. As we prepare to start our new company, we're going to host a variety of workshops for new customers, some where they have to RSVP and there's a specific date attached to them. Events like those are great for creating a sense of urgency. People know that if they miss the date, they'll miss out on the opportunity. So find ways to use dates to make things more real.

We also use exclusivity to create a sense of urgency. If

everybody can have something, nobody wants it; that's a good rule of thumb. But we're deliberately limiting some of our offerings. We're selling a local advertising service that, in bigger cities, is limited to three businesses in each specific category. In smaller cities, it's limited to one or two. Once the categories are filled, we'll put you on a waiting list...and good luck, because the cost of our service is so low that once people get in, they're going to stay in. We put people under tremendous pressure to join ASAP, which creates the instant cash flow. It makes people realize if they don't act now, they'll miss out on something special.

Limited supply and exclusivity almost always work well, and they're adaptable to most products and services. Just flatly tell your customers, in your advertising or direct mail, "This is limited. If you don't act now, it's gone forever." Then follow up on that, because exclusivity loses its power if you lie about it.

Back before Tax Day I heard a plumber advertising: "It's getting to be close to tax time again. We like to file early, so we're offer a special deal on drain-cleaning and other basic maintenance, because we need some cash to pay our taxes." On the one hand, he's probably revealing too much information. On the other, people can relate to that.

In El Cajon, California, where Russ Von Hoelscher lives, there's a jeweler who holds private sales at night. Once a month or so they host a cheese and wine event from 7:30 to 9:30 PM for their best customers, to reveal the new necklaces, rings, earrings, and other jewelry that's just come out. Some of these are one-of-a-kind pieces they want to make available to their best customers, and they emphasize that those are available in very limited supply. All businesses should consider events like these. What can you do to make an exclusive offer to your customers that makes them feel special?

I think people intuitively understand supply and demand. Consider diamonds; they're not really as rare as most people think they are, but they're certainly more valuable than glass or cubic zirconium, which they closely resemble. We can even make beautiful artificial ones these days that are hard to tell from the real thing. Gold is more valuable than dollar bills. We know instinctively that things in limited supply are more valuable than things in unlimited supply—yet those of us in business often forget this, and go about business in a way that indicates we have plenty of whatever we're selling. We end up hurting ourselves because people feel no urgent need to do business with us.

Let's say your business sells widgets, and you've got plenty in stock. Your doors are open 24/7, so anyone can get a widget any time they want one. If they want five, they can have five—at five AM. As a result, there's very little incentive for them to come in and make a purchase, because they know your widgets will be available at any time. On the flip side, if your widget store is open only once a week for two hours, your widgets are in high demand, especially if there are only 10 available. If someone wants one, they'd better come in early, because they'll probably sell out within the hour. In that situation, the price of the widgets goes up.

You can use that law of supply and demand to your advantage in any business; you just have to be creative sometimes. We occasionally hold events where we offer a limited number of seats. When they're gone, they're gone—and we make sure to tell people that. Those kinds of offers increase urgency. The worst thing for your business is an apathetic marketplace. If they don't perceive the need to act now, they won't.

I can get water out of my tap anytime I want something to drink. I may choose to drink bottled or filtered water, but I can get it easily. There's no urgency for me to buy water, so it's not worth much to me. But suppose there was a natural disaster that cuts my water lines. Now that the only way to get water is at my local convenience or grocery store, my urgency to acquire it is heightened. If that's true, the price I'm willing to pay increases. That's why in a natural disaster or emergency, you often see runs on staples like bottled water. If I go to the store and there's no more water left, where will I get it from? I need it to live, which demands an even greater increase in price and urgency.

When you're on the other side of the cash register, you need to keep in mind that urgency occurs only when there's some kind limit to the product and to people's access to you. It's one of the reasons we coach our consulting customers to limit their availability. If someone can contact you at any time for any reason, you're not really in demand; they assume your schedule must not be that full. When a consultant is in high demand, their schedule is at a premium. You have to leave a message. They're only making appointments for a month down the road. All of a sudden, their time is more valuable, their schedule is booked, and they can charge higher prices.

Even if your schedule isn't really busy, you still want to give the perception of busyness, because it helps you charge a premium price and helps your customers feel better about doing business with you. Scarcity allows you to charge more and builds better relationships with your clients. It's a simple concept, given that everybody knows about supply and demand already...and yet we often lose sight of that. Don't. You'll find yourself making more money, and you'll probably have happier customers in the end.

Marketing Secret #94:
How to Make People Want to Buy *Now*

You're best served if you can get people not just interested in buying what you're selling, but *passionate* about doing so. Generate a compelling desire to own it. The extent to which you can do this is the extent to which you'll get rich. Great salespeople always build a case for their products. If you've ever been to a state fair or anywhere a pitch man is selling a kitchen appliance or similar item, you've been exposed to some of the best marketing out there. I always stop and watch these folks, because I can learn from them; they really know how to get people excited about what they have. They keep the chatter going, telling the audience how important it is for them to own the item, how it will make their life so much simpler and easier.

This is what we all should do. We're not selling the same products, but we want to build that passion like they do, so people feel compelled to buy from us. It all boils down to a transfer of emotions. As excited as we get about our products, we want them to get even *more* excited. We want to pump that passion into everything we offer.

One way to distinguish yourself from everyone else is with your unique selling position, or USP, which I discussed in detail in an earlier chapter. There are many businesses selling the same products and services, and prospects have a wide choice, especially in cities: hundreds of dentists, dozens of plumbers, and all kinds of businesses in multiple numbers. It's vitally important that you separate yourself from the competition. What can you offer that your other competitors can't? "Me too" marketing doesn't work.

100 MARKETING SECRETS

Your business must stand out from all the rest in the area.

Whenever we help the businesses in those areas, they're forever grateful—because while there may be 100 dentists or chiropractors out there, only a few are making real money. The same goes whether you're selling jewelry, shoes, or any other type of commodity or service. There's always going to be a lot of competition. You separate yourself from the competition with a USP, something you do better than anyone else and can promote in all your advertising. It can be as simple as the fact that you just take better care of people. You make it known that you're not just interested in making the sale, but that you also follow-up vigorously after the sale.

There's a pest control company in San Diego that advertises, "We'll come out and get rid of all of your termites. If any show up within the next nine months, we'll come back and do it again for free." That resonates with people. They're guaranteeing their service, proving it's safe to do business with them because if they don't get it right, they'll come back. You should do the same, though I'd recommend a longer guarantee period.

Think about what a USP can mean for your business. 95% of all businesses have nothing unique or special about them. If you'll think about and implement special things, coupled with a sense of urgency, you can see your business double, triple or quadruple.

Making people want to buy right now, right this minute, goes back to the whole point of urgency from Secret #93. (All these Secrets tie together in some way, don't they?). If you don't stimulate a sense of urgency in people, a desire to buy now, then they're not going to buy at all. Like any salesman, you must become a master of getting people to buy what you have to sell.

Give them a *reason* to buy.

Let's consider a normal social situation, with me talking to you about an overwhelmingly positive experience I've had. If I'm truly passionate, I can convey that emotion to you and get you to see that you should pay attention to what I'm saying—whether it's a great restaurant I went to, a movie I saw, or a business I dealt with. Ideally, through my emotional reaction, I get *you* excited about it and make you want to engage in whatever it is. On the other hand, if the experience stunk, I can be equally critical, and convey my emotion that way—and maybe you'd avoid that movie or restaurant.

The principle works the same way with businesses. Whether you're advertising or selling face-to-face or on the phone, you have to transfer your excitement to the customer in order to close the sale. Making people want to buy now means getting them all excited about why they should be doing business with you. Set the tone for them, because people won't see it on their own; with rare exceptions, they're not inclined to sell themselves.

Marketing Secret #95:
Why You Absolutely Do *Not* Want Happy Customers

Many business owners conclude that the ultimate goal of business is to serve people and have happy, satisfied customers. And in a way, that's quite true...but only to an extent. Because if your customers are completely happy, and they got exactly what they wanted the first time, why should they ever purchase from you again?

There are specific circumstances in which this rule doesn't apply, as with consumables, clothing, and other things that eventually wear out. But think about it this way: If you've just gone out for a fancy meal and you've overloaded on carbs and calories, and then you drive by another restaurant, are you likely to go into that restaurant? Of course not. You're satisfied; you're in no mood or prepared to eat again yet. This applies to other businesses besides restaurants. When the customer has just bought, and they're full and happy with what you sold them, why should they buy again?

They're satisfied in the confines of the marketplace you're in. That satisfaction may wear off, leaving them open to doing business again, but it may not. You have to accept that under normal circumstances, when they've reached a point where they feel they're full or done, then you lose the ability to continue offering more products and services. People buy because they're hungry. They go to restaurants because they want to eat. They buy weight-loss drugs or plans because they want to lose weight— they're hungry for weight loss. If people are into fitness, they buy fitness products because they want to build bigger biceps or have six-packs abs. If they're suffering from hair loss, they're hungry to get their hair back. There's no reason to buy if they aren't hungry.

So you have to keep them hungry, providing products and services that satisfy them only temporarily. Smart marketers spend a lot of time thinking about this strategy. You want to have satisfied customers, yes; you don't want them to be disgruntled or upset with you. But you *do* want them to remain in a state of sufficient hunger to purchase what you're offering. So: How can you keep your customers hungry?

For one thing, you need to keep your customers satisfied with your previous performance. Fulfill your obligations completely; give them everything you promised to deliver and more. But if you want to really guarantee their hunger, you have to find a market that's simple insatiable, a niche market that caters to a specific type of client. Do that, and you'll never have to worry about sales again. The late Gary Halbert used to say that if someone is a collector of certain types of books, they don't just stop buying. Some women love shoes and can't get enough. Russ Von Hoelscher recently told me of a friend who bought 35 pairs of shoes at a Nordstrom's sale. When he asked why, she replied that as nice as they were at the price they were asking, she *had* to do it. I think many people are like that with the things they love. With the right advertising in the right market, you can easily keep them hungry and buying—as long as you can deliver the goods.

A really good restaurant is always a good example. Some people go to their favorite restaurant every week. If it has lunch hours, they may go twice a week. If you're in the pest control business, sell a program where you take care of the problem today, but then do regular follow-up and maintenance. If you serve people well, they're going to come back to you again and again—especially if the market is an insatiable one.

Now, let me add one distinction here. Before leaping into business, you should look for markets where people are generally unhappy—frustrated, confused, not getting the results they want. Those marketplaces can be uniquely profitable if you present the right mix of elements. Look for marketplaces where there are huge needs that are *not* being filled—then fill those needs in a way that keeps people coming back for more.

Marketing Secret #96:
Declare War On Your Competition

General George Patton had one simple rule for warfare:

to crush his enemies. You should follow his lead and try to crush your competitors. You need to strike fear in their hearts and minds. His methodology was to strike fast, strike hard and strike often." In this Secret, I'll discuss a few ways to do this.

First of all, let's talk about striking fast. Hit the prospect with your biggest benefit super-fast. Don't mess around; don't be cute or clever. What's in it for them? That's all they care about. They're getting pitched by everybody. All they want to know is what you can give them right now. You have to get them fast, or you'll lose them forever. Here's an example of how we're doing this with our new business, the one where we offer our local advertising service to small business people in both big cities and small towns. Since we're trying to hit them fast, the first thing they'll see, whether they get our postcard or direct mail piece, is our headline: "How to quickly get dozens of new customers for almost no cost." That's the biggest benefit we're providing.

The second part of Patton's rule is to strike hard—in our case, by trying to create that irresistible offer that draws customers in immediately. Your offer needs to be so good they simply can't say no. You have to use lots of risk reversal achieve this. What can you offer that's so advantageous to them and provides so much value on their side of the table that they can't resist it?

We've tried to do that with our new advertising service. If a prospect takes one year of advertising, we're giving them another year absolutely free in another online membership directory we're developing. They get a year's worth of free advertising if they take a year, and they can back out within 30 days if they decide it's not for them. For your business, what can you do to create an offer that's so good it makes it very, very difficult for them to say no?

The third part of Patton's rule is to strike often. Good follow-up marketing is the key to maximum profitability. I suggest strongly that whenever possible, you use two-step marketing of some kind. You might even combine a little one-step marketing with two-step marketing—but always make it easy for people to respond. If they're not ready to make an instant decision, at least it lets them raise their hand and express an interest. Then you can aggressively follow up with them.

Most marketers don't follow up aggressively enough. They're penny-wise and dollar-foolish. They're not staying after their prospects, and they don't realize that "no" doesn't necessarily mean forever when it comes to purchases. When you send something to a prospect and they don't respond right away, the worst mistake you can make—and people are making it every day of every week—is to think those people aren't interested or that they're not serious. If they express an interest in the first place, then you have to assume they're interested. But remember, they're also looking at all kinds of other deals. They're overwhelmed with daily life and everything else going on, and are being pitched by everybody and their brother. Just because somebody doesn't respond the first, second, or third time doesn't mean they aren't going to respond the fourth or fifth time.

You've got to build follow-up marketing into all your marketing campaigns, and stay after people relentlessly. Do that, and you'll get all kinds of money you wouldn't ordinarily get— money your competitors won't get. Think about Patton and his philosophy. He was right up there with his men; he didn't huddle in the back while they took the brunt of the fighting. They respected him tremendously for that.

His strategy translates well to business. Make your prospects an offer your competition isn't making. For example, the most successful realtor in San Diego advertises, "We'll sell your house in 60 days or less—or we'll buy it." How often have you seen an offer like that? Sometimes he ends up buying a house, but he outsells everyone else. A printer might offer some special deal, like giving people business cards for a dollar, just to get them in the door. Make offers that others can't or won't. It doesn't have to revolve around low price. You can make a special service offer that none of the competition is making, and then ask people in your advertising, "Have you ever seen another company in this field make an offer like this?" Then you could add, "Of course not! Some people think we're crazy to do this, but we feel that if we provide the service you want now, you'll remain a good customer. So maybe we're crazy like a fox."

Use the type of advertising that separates you from the competition. Nobody wants to be just like every other business; because if you are, you may survive, but you're probably just barely getting by. Think of ways to differentiate yourself. Make the offers others are afraid to make; say things in your advertising that are sometimes impolite and controversial. Do things differently, and I think you'll see your results go sky high.

Many businesses don't even think about striking at all, much less doing so hard, fast, and often. Business owners tend to be apathetic toward marketing or advertising, which leaves them lacking in sales and business. You have to be an aggressive marketer to acquire new customers. Go out there and strike hard, fast, and often. Striking fast is just leading with your best offer, the one they want most. Put it all out there.

As for striking hard, promote relentlessly. It's not enough just to say, "I have a business, here's the address, come find me." Aggressively promote your business; keep it in front of your prospects' eyes and in the forefront of their minds. Maybe they've said no before, but they may say yes next time. It might take 10 attempts to get through to them. Keep sending mail asking them to do business with you. Be easily visible.

Once you have them as a customer; continuously offer them more of the kinds of products and services they've already bought from you in an effort to maximize your profits. Pay attention to how other people are doing it, and become a good student of marketing. Whenever you see other people doing something phenomenally well, make a note of that. Ideas are interchangeable. The same ideas that are working for others can work for you too—if you're open, receptive, and creative about it.

Marketing Secret #97: Question Everything and Demand the Best Deal

Business brings us face-to-face with everything: the good, the bad, and the ugly alike. It's like real life on steroids. Each year to us can be like 10 years to the average person, because we're involved so deeply in what we do. But if we play our cards right, the rewards can be tremendous.

In order to achieve that success, you must question *everything*. Realize that the more successful you become, the more you'll become a magnet for headaches and hassles. There are people out there who have their little agendas, and they pick on business people constantly in one way or another. The more you have, the more they want—and the less you can trust people. We *like* to be trusting, but we have to keep our eyes open, because there are all kinds of predators out there.

As entrepreneurs, we're rebels, rocking out to our own beats—and that's as it should be. So to maintain that, be sure to question everything, and demand the best deal for everything— your suppliers, your landlords, your insurance company, even your customers. Too many small business owners aren't paying the best prices for what they get. I've encountered some great negotiators, though, and it's just amazing the deals they achieve. Let your suppliers know that you're not someone they can take advantage of.

Many businesses really go astray when it comes to advertising. They willingly pay the amounts quoted on the ad company's rate card, which mean nothing—except that they're the prices for people who aren't willing to haggle. If you're willing to haggle, you can buy display ads quoted at $6,000 for as little as $2,000. I've seen Russ Von Hoelscher do just that. He'll ask for discounts of 50-60%, and often the ad rep will say, "Hey, we'd love to do it for you, Russ, but we can't." So Russ says, "Then I can't advertise with you. Thanks anyhow." It amazing how often the ad rep will call up an hour later and say something like, "Guess what? We just had someone cancel an ad. You're in luck—we can give you that super price that you wanted."

It doesn't matter whether someone really canceled or not, as long as you can buy your advertising at a discount. And more often than not, you can, especially if you're willing to shop around. So don't let them railroad you. When they show you a rate card, don't just accept the rate as set in stone. That rate is *only* for people who won't negotiate.

When it comes to employees, be a little more lenient. You want the best employees possible, and that means you should pay them a good wage—as much as you can afford. But don't get into the seniority thing. If you have unions running your shop, like a lot of bigger businesses do, you have no choice. The union leaders become your bosses, demand seniority, and all sorts of crazy things. Don't let that happen if you have a small shop with only 5-20 people. Don't worry about seniority. Pay well and keep the best people. That's how you demand and achieve the best deal on the personnel front.

As an entrepreneur, you have a naturally rebellious spirit; you don't always accept the way things are, and you're always trying to do more. This Secret should fit right into your personality. Question the quality of everything, and demand the best deal you can afford. It's not just about being frugal and cutting corners, or trying to do things on the cheap. What profits you the most and has the greatest ROI? Can you negotiate a price down and still maintain quality? Some people fear negotiating. They dread going into a car dealership, and never want to ask for a discount anywhere, because they think it's somehow inconvenient to the supplier and they don't want to engage in that kind of behavior (whatever that means). As a business owner, you can't afford that approach.

There's a show called *Pawn Stars* that features these characters who run a pawn shop. They're in the business of buying and selling just about anything that comes through the door. Most of the show deals with them buying rare or interesting things they think their customers would be interested in. It's interesting to watch from a business perspective, even as you get to see people bring in some weird stuff—sometimes artifacts hundreds of years old. Naturally, they want to get the most out of their items. But on the other side you have the business owner or one of his employees, who is interested in purchasing the item and looks at it entirely from a business perspective. Many times you see the customer coming in looking for a ridiculously high payoff, and they're hit with the reality that the market isn't there to pay what they're asking. So, the brokers will tell them what they can get out of it, and sometimes you see them negotiate back and forth.

In some cases, they have to part ways because they can't make a deal. The pawn broker will tell the seller, "I can't make a profit at that price. In order to make money, I've got to get the price at this level instead of the level you're wanting. You might be asking for $1,000 for this item, but I'm only willing to pay you $600 because I think I can only sell it for $1,000. I've got overhead, I have to pay my employees, and this thing might sit on the shelf for a year before I sell it."

It comes down to a struggle between two parties trying to get the best deal for that moment in time. Many times they do make a deal, and both sides are happy. In some cases, they make a deal even though one side isn't really as happy as the other. It's interesting to watch from both perspectives as you witness the struggle of trying to acquire these items and pay fair market value. Now, sometimes the owner tells people they're asking too little; I've seen him actually pay people more than what they were asking, because they didn't have their items valued correctly, and he educates them on why the value is there. *Question the price of everything.*

We have a client whom we've been face-to-face with on many different occasions. He's come to a lot of our events and he's known for asking, "Is that the best you can do? Is that the best offer you can give me?" He does that all the time, and it's kind of a running joke now. But he's doing the right thing in asking.

If you want to pay retail for everything—if you want to pay rate card—just accept what they tell you and take it at face value. If they say this ad is going to cost this much, you can just get out your checkbook and write the check. But do that, and who knows? Maybe over the lifetime of your business you'll pay $100,000, half a million, or even a million dollars too much for everything you buy. It adds up. So remember this principle. It's not always about being a cheapskate or getting one over on people; it's just about making sure you get the best deal and you're able to put yourself in a position to make the most money. That's what your business should be all about.

I keep the statement "Question everything" on the wall in several places, including on the mirror in my bathroom where I brush my teeth every night. Your doubts make you wise. I agree with all those positive thinkers running around talking about the value of being optimistic, but I also know that it's our doubts and the things that we question that make us wise. Question everything—even what I'm teaching you here. I don't question things enough myself, because I tend to be blinded by my optimism.

In every business negotiation, you should always assume that the other party is not telling you everything—that in some cases they're holding back a lot. Even if that's not true, you should *assume* it is. Nothing will ever be as good as you think it is or as good as the person pitching you says it is—except for our offers, of course!

Here's something really good to ask yourself: "How do

you know if the people around you are really being honest with you?" or a related question, "Who can you really trust?" I've asked myself that question many times. The answer is that you can trust someone who doesn't want anything from you. The more someone wants from you, the more you should question. You should question often, because people are always pitching; they're showing you what they want you to see, so you never know if they're being 100% truthful with you, especially when they're trying to get money out of you.

One of my favorite songs is by a Canadian band called Rush: "Something For Nothing." Some of the lyrics of that song are, "You won't get wise with the sleep still in your eyes." That quote keeps coming back to me, because it's so appropriate. You have to open your eyes wide, and question everything.

Marketing Secret #98:
The Only Consultant You Should Pay Close Attention to

Many consultants are simply dangerous to your wealth and, though they're trying to help you, you should ignore them. Then again, there are a few you should definitely listen to. So how do you tell them apart? It's important to understand which is which.

Most consultants are good at giving advice—but they're not so good at following their own. There's a reason why they're consultants or teachers instead of doers. There's a saying that says, "Those that can, do; those that can't, teach." And while it's fine to be a teacher, that doesn't mean a consultant always has practical experience. Now, that's not universally true; there are some good "doers" who are also good teachers. But it's easy for other people to tell you what to do, and there are a lot of people out there giving advice.

So how do you know who to listen to and who not to listen to? Consultants are really good at spending other people's money, and that's one of the reasons they take on consultant roles. It's not as easy to spend your own money wisely, turning it into a growing, thriving business. People who consult usually have no personal risk. About the worst that can happen is that you can fire them and not use them again...but often, consultants can make even those kinds of problems go away just by being good soothsayers, telling you what you want to hear. They will encourage you in directions that *sound* good, even though the results might be contrary to that. They have very little accountability for whether their suggestions work or not. The can run your business into the ground if you allow it.

On the other hand, consultants *can* be extremely valuable to your business, providing profitable ideas and suggestions. How do you balance that? How do you tell a good consultant from a bad one? Who can you trust? Who should you avoid? Again, the first thing to remember—and to *always* keep in mind—is that a consultant, as good as they may be, will never understand everything there is to know about your business. They're never going to know your business like you do; and unless they're in your industry, they're never going to know your customers or your marketplace like you do.

Who do you look for when you look for people who can help you? One of the important things is to look for people who have done what you're trying to do; people with a proven track record of getting where you want to go in your industry. If you're a fledgling restaurateur, then a good consultant would be a former restaurateur, especially one who's been successful selling the kind of food you want to sell. If you're in the direct mail business or would like to be, trust only experts who have practiced DRM, especially direct mail. In general, you're more likely to get useful results from a consultant who has been in the business you're in, especially if they've made big money at it. Avoid the consultants who have spent more time teaching than doing.

If multiple potential consultants have experience in both teaching and doing, lean towards someone who spends most of their time doing the business you want to do and less time teaching about it. If they dabble in business, but most of their time is spent consulting, that might be a red flag. But be careful here; do your research, especially in the information products field. Some of us do a great deal of both teaching *and* business. For example, I'm always teaching people how to make more money, but that's part of my business. Every book, report, audio program, or DVD I produce is intended to be used as a product or a bonus, and they're all part of my business, which I participate in daily.

Consultants may have some good ideas, but those ideas are often untested—until they try them out on you. So look for people who are out there doing what you want to do and getting the results you want to get. Those are the people to pay attention to—and not always in a formal consultant's role. Sometimes you can learn from them as a partner, friend, or mentor. There are many opportunities to study the people who are achieving the results you want to get in your business.

You don't need some egghead's harebrained ideas leading you on, so be careful out there. And don't assume academic credentials denote a real expert; some of the people teaching the dumbest ideas are college professors. Russ von Hoelscher—a *very* effective consultant and mentor—tells me of two such instances in Southern California.

One professor was from the University of California in San Diego. Russ and his colleague Al Galasso were doing a seminar on mail order marketing and self-publishing. This professor announced himself and where he was from, so Russ asked him to come up to the podium and make a few comments. The first thing he started to say was, "I've been teaching business for 20 years. No offense to Mr. Von Hoelscher or Mr. Galasso, but why do business by mail? If you want books, you go to a bookstore. If you want to buy clothing, go to clothing store or to a sporting goods store." Russ thought, "Holy God! Why did we ask this guy to come up here?" He went on to some other topics before they got him off the stage. He didn't know what he was talking about, but he was in academia.

Another incident occurred during a self-publishing seminar from San Diego State; I mentioned this one briefly in another chapter. The professor told us, "I've been looking through some of your advertising material. Do you realize that it's riddled with incorrect grammar?" Sometimes we use "you-isms" and say things to make a point; we're not necessarily interested in grammar, and Russ pointed that out. He said, "Well, I think the first thing someone should do if they're talking about publishing and writing is to make sure the grammar is correct." *My* advice to anyone is, if you need help from an expert, get someone who is really proficient and successful in the field. Don't go to these professors and teachers, because they don't know jack.

They often major in the minors, as I like to say. They don't know how to prioritize. This professor who was lecturing Russ on his grammar didn't know a thing about salesmanship— and that's one of my biggest pet peeves. My wife and I used to have a nice condo in Kansas City, in the historic Plaza shopping area. Right below it was a bookstore, and we used to hang out there for hours. I went through dozens of business books every weekend looking for good ones—and they were hard to find.

Most such books are written by "experts" who are college professors, or CEOs or former CEOs of giant corporations. They have no clue of how a normal, everyday small to mid-sized business works. I went through well over 1,000 business books in the years Eileen and I had that condominium, and I bought very few. It used to upset me that these books were so complicated and confusing. By that time, I'd already been self-employed for well over a decade—and I felt sorry for anyone contemplating starting a business who got ahold of one of those books. They complicate *everything*.

On my wall right now is a cover of a book that I bought on the Internet—and I shouldn't have, but I didn't have the luxury of actually going through the book and trying to decide whether it was good or not. The title is *The 12 Rules of Success in Business*, and it was written by a well-known expert. Care to guess how many times the words "selling" or "salesmanship" appear in that book? Zero. Not once in all the hundreds of pages of text does he mention selling anything, certainly not in any of the 12 rules. Nor does the word "marketing" ever come up. How can you have a whole book on business success without mentioning marketing or selling? That upsets me, because people who buy that book and actually try to practice those rules are destined to fail. Business is *all* about selling and salesmanship. It's about generating revenue and what you do with that revenue. The money comes first.

When Eileen and I first started our business together, back in 1988, I had just turned 29 and she was 31—and we had so many people giving us free business advice, trying to tell us what we should do. Most of that advice was diametrically opposed to what we were doing, and the fact was, most of those people had never even been in business in their lives. Most had never even *tried* anything business-related. I never said anything about it, but I remember thinking to myself what a joke that was: they had never succeeded in any kind of business, and they were trying to tell *us* how we should do things. Eileen and I just basically looked at each other and rolled our eyes.

Marketing Secret #99:
Why Most of Your Competitors are Like Cheap Whores

So: how's that for controversial? I'll admit that this is a little obscene, but it's the truth, and I think you'll find it valuable. My point here is that most business people will work for anybody and everybody for next to nothing. Now, consider the $1,000 an hour call girl, who has a waiting list of men who practically beg her to find time for them. Barbra Streisand played one in a great movie called *Nuts*. She was selective; you had to call for an appointment and get on her schedule before she would see you, and her clients were very happy. The $25 dollar crack whore, though, is like the woman Charlize Theron portrayed in the movie *Monster,* where she slept with anybody in the scummiest of neighborhoods and just didn't care.

I'm using this shocking comparison because I want you to remember this Secret. I know it's off-color, politically incorrect, and controversial—but you need to remember it, even if it's the only one Secret in this book of 100 that you *do* remember. So here's a joke: What's the difference between a $25 crack whore and a $1,000 an hour call girl? Good marketing! It's as simple as that. It's all about positioning and really good marketing. Most people's marketing is the same: bland,

homogenized, and boring. The ad agencies like it that way.
There's no impact. There's no differentiation; nobody stands out,
because they're afraid to offend anyone. They're trying to attract
everyone, so in the end, they attract no one. It's the blind leading
the blind; everybody's following the follower.

In the end, it doesn't do any kind of selling at all. There's
no offer made, no real salesmanship involved. There's nothing to
compel the right buyers to take action. Since I've already said
something controversial, let me continue along those lines.
There's a Jackson Browne song called "Cocaine," and here's one
line: "You take Sally and I'll take Sue, there's really no
difference between the two." That's how I feel about most
businesses. Their marketing (if any) is flat, tired, worn-out,
boring, and makes no impact.

Good marketing attracts the right people while repelling
the wrong people. It makes specific offers that cause people to do
business with you. It's selective, not boring, and *does* make an
impact. It's doesn't care who it offends, just who it attracts. It
grabs people's attention and differentiates your business from the
hundreds like it.

While I know what I've said here is controversial, that
doesn't make it any less true. Don't be boring with your market.
Don't just throw something out there and take whatever it brings
you. Go for the very best customers, the ones who spend the
most money. Don't get down in the gutter with the cheapies and
waste your potential. When you do that, price is the only thing
that differentiates your business, and that makes it very hard to
succeed—because there's only so much you can do about price.
Sure, it works for Wal-Mart and other large businesses, but for
small businesses it almost *never* works. Go for the gold rather

than flopping around in the muck.

The fact remains that most of your competitors are like a cheap date—they'll take what they can get. Don't be the cheap date. Offer something that sets you apart besides price. Be special and unusual. Be innovative. Specialize; go high-class. Businesses that are willing to continually cut their prices to make people happy continually struggle. Then there are those who play hard to get, charging premium prices, with very little room for you in their appointment books—and yet they have all the business they can handle. This is partly due to the perception that the more something costs and the harder it is to obtain, the more valuable it is. No one wants to work with the consultant who instantly has time for you; they look desperate, which kills their credibility and authority.

On the flip side, suppose you contact an expert and talk with their secretary, who claims the expert is busy, the schedule is full, and the next available appointment is four weeks away— and even then, you'll have just 15 minutes. See the difference? There's the perception that this guy isn't just a cheap date. He feels more like an expert. There's built-in demand due to scarcity. If you make customers long to do business with you, you can drive up your prices and fill your schedule.

I have a friend who's a freelance DRM copywriter. He wanted to know what one of his competitors, who advertised in every issue of *DM News* with a big space ad, was charging. So he asked me to pretend I was a customer and get the prices for a simple direct-mail package including a sales letter, order form, one enclosure, and an outside envelope. So I did, and I had to go through a grueling interview process and speak with the competitor's assistant several times before I ever got to speak with the man. It was a living nightmare, and it turns out this guy wanted *$16,800* for a very simple direct-mail piece.

Now, this is something that Russ von Hoelscher, Chris Lakey, and I could easily write in a couple days of working an hour or two here and there—a total of four or five hours worth of work. This guy wants $16,800 for it. No wonder he has these huge ads—he's getting premium prices. That's a lot of money for a direct mail piece—and he charged at least a grand extra for artwork. It just goes to show that if you want to charge premium prices, you have to reposition yourself properly. You have to be like Barbra Streisand in *Nuts* rather than Charlize Theron in *Monster.*

Marketing Secret #100:
Know Who Has the Money to Buy What You Sell

We've made it to the final Secret, and like all those preceding it, it's simple common sense: know which market can afford to buy what you want to sell. All businesses are different, whether you own a bookstore, a jewelry store, or you're a plumber or barber. You're going to have different clients, and you'll have the find those who fit your niche market perfectly.

One place you can start—which I think most people are overlooking—is with Baby Boomers and seniors. More than 50% of all the wealth in the United States of America is controlled by people who are 55 years of age and older. Collectively, that's trillions of dollars. Also, these people have specific ways they want business to be done. It's good for us to know what they like. For example, they like and trust direct-mail more than they ever will the Internet. Many of them are Internet proficient, don't get me wrong; but in various surveys, they put direct-mail distinctly above the Internet as the way they like to receive offers and correspondence.

These peoples' buying habits include dealing with companies they feel are well-established. As marketers, we often say, "People don't give a damn about you or your company. It's only what you can do for them that matters." I've repeated that more than once in this book. That's basically true with all people, but less so for Boomer and seniors than for most. Being in business 25 years doesn't mean much to some folks, but to them it might. It shows you have a good track record and must be doing something right.

So there are certain aspects about these people—and frankly, I'm a member of this group—that, if we pay attention to them, will help us market to them. Trust is important to them. They like well-established businesses. Now, if you're a new small business and have only been in business for two or three years, you can overcome this by getting some good testimonials. Seniors and Boomers like to know what other people have said about your service or products.

We marketers had better understand how America is aging, and realize that more and more of our business is going to come from Baby Boomers, who are in the process of becoming seniors now. If we're smart, we'll make special offers to senior citizens. We need to do everything we can to show them we want to earn their business and trust. The smartest thing a small business can do is have special prices for their senior citizens. This pays huge dividends. These people *want* two-for-one buffet. They want discounts on other things they buy. They want to do business with people who respect them and will give them a good deal. Sometimes they're even a little overbearing about this.

Understand that this is where their mindset is. If you want their business, offer them special deals. We're working on a deal offering special senior cards they can flash when they come into a place of business, to receive a discount on a product or service. Realize that America is changing and aging. If you want to make lots of money, you have to know who has the money—and that's our Baby Boomers and seniors.

And remember, there's substantial overlap there now. The oldest baby boomers are now hitting retirement age, and there are 73 million of them in our population of just under 314 million in the U.S. They constitute a huge demographic with significant buying power, perhaps the most significant in America at the time. Most advertisers focus on that "core demographic" of 18-35 year olds, historically the most coveted demographic. It isn't anymore—or at least, it shouldn't be.

First of all, people are having fewer children than they had before, which means there are fewer people in the younger demographic groups. Chris Lakey's grandmother was one of 15 children. Chris has six, and that's considered an awful lot these days, because our average is going down. One in five Americans decides not to have children these days. The numbers of people in each demographic group is decreasing, which indicates a major economic shift in the making. The Boomers represent a phenomenally influential buying block, with more income and savings that many other groups.

For that reason, your core demographic has to shift upward if you expect to surf the developing trend and continue to profit. You have to know what sorts of products they need; for example, the Boomers are less likely to purchase baby diapers and sports cars. No matter what you sell, they will almost always be a huge factor.

Let me tell you a little more about the very special

advertising program we're developing called Senior Card. It's a simple concept. We understand that while senior citizens control a lot of money these days, they're careful how they spend it, always on the lookout for bargains. Quite frankly, they want to be treated special, and they like companies that do things for them. They've lived long enough now they deserve the very best that life has to offer. My mother is 80 years old, and with every day that goes by she becomes more important to me—especially now that my Dad and my stepfather have passed on. Our seniors are everything. They are sacred.

We're happy to be developing this advertising program for small business people that reach out to senior citizens and the Baby Boomers—like me and Russ von Hoelscher, who are Baby Boomers. We're proud to be Boomers. We're the children of one of the greatest generations that ever lived...and that's where all the money is now.

It's a growing trend and is only going to continue to grow. If you're not doing something to target seniors and Baby Boomers, you're missing out on a lot of money that could and should be yours.

CONCLUSION

There you have it: 100 of my greatest marketing strategies, all of which my colleagues and I use on a regular basis. I hope you've enjoyed and learned from these Secrets. I'm not sure that I'd be able to pick a favorite, because there are so many of them. They're all important. And the truth is, I could write a book containing a full *thousand* Secrets like these, and still wouldn't cover everything you can learn about marketing, because there's so much to share about business and entrepreneurship, making money, and being successful in business. If you enjoyed this, I encourage you to consider some of the other resources we have available.

And while I know we just finished knocking consultants a few Secrets back, know that my colleagues and I, including Chris Lakey and Russ Von Hoelscher, are all willing and available to help. We're doers who also teach what we love. We would be happy to dig deeper with you, to help you get as much out of this book and the original audio program it's based on as possible, and show you how to enact these strategies. In fact, you'll find our contact information in the back of the book; we'd love to hear from you.

I firmly believe that marketing is *everything* in business. I don't mean to discount all the other jobs people do in a business, but without the money, none of those people would be around. The money is necessary for all of the other jobs to exist; every employee in the world owes their living to those who bring in the money. That's what good marketing does. It's not that we're any better than anybody else, it's just that what we do is more important. It takes all kinds to make a good business—people with multiple skills playing key roles. But the money is so vitally important that everything else falls apart without it; and I hope that I've made that clear.

Here's a quick story that I hope you'll find amusing. My wife Eileen is a beautiful person, but she's a rare individual—and kind of feisty. She was especially that way 25 years ago when we started this company together. She was the president and CEO, and my job was to do the marketing. In the beginning, we fought all of the time, even when we were dating, because we're both very outspoken. There's been some fire in our relationship over the years—not always good, but mostly good. I knew that trying to work with my wife was going to be difficult, and she knew the same.

So 25 years ago I said to her, "Look, I'll do the marketing; you run the business. I'll stay out of your hair; you stay out of mine." The funny part is that as I went about my job, Eileen kept saying, "You're stepping on my toes, T.J. You're supposed to just do the marketing—I'm supposed to do everything else." I'd respond, "This *is* marketing." That was my response to every fight we had for the 12 years we worked together.

So much of what we do in business *is* marketing, even if it seems otherwise. Marketing is everything you do in your company that impacts or potentially impacts your customer, from the way the phones are answered to your correspondence with prospects. Anything that has to do with customer relations or the way the customer perceives the business is marketing, which is why Eileen and I fought about it. I still firmly believe that it's all about the customer and how they perceive the business, and that includes a million different things.

The business would not exist without the customers.

We're here to serve them and perform for them, in such a way that they'll happily pay us. Every day is a performance—and there's a *lot* of competition for each performance. So I hope that you'll go back and read this book repeatedly, studying all 100 of these marketing Secrets repeatedly. Don't just read them; really study them and think about them, as if there will be a test—because there will be. It's called real life. To get the full impact from what I'm teaching, you have to consider these Secrets deeply and put them into action. That takes a lot of thought and some real commitment on your part.

Sales and marketing are the lifeblood of all businesses, and they're especially crucial to small business. In dealing with businesses of all kinds over the years, I've found that the people who put a lot of emphasis on marketing and making sales become the most successful. The businesses that push marketing to the back burner often fail.

Admittedly, there's a lot of minutia to deal with in any business. You have to have people in place who can dot the I's and cross the T's. You have to have people who can do the bookwork, take care of the finances, and deal with customer relations. That's all important. Sometimes, as a small business, you have to do it all yourself. But if you don't put a great deal of emphasis on sales and marketing, you'll lose business at a rapid rate and soon be *out* of business.

Always remember: *sales and marketing are the lifeblood of your business*.